MAJOR AND SERIOUS CRIME INVESTIGATIONS

DEDICATIONS

Thank you to my family, Carole, Dan and Josh, for giving me the time and space to devote to a career in policing and to colleagues who helped shape my practice as an investigator. Thank you also to Critical Publishing for the opportunity to write this book, which is dedicated to future practitioners, those who will take investigative practice forward and under who's leadership I am confident the future of investigation is bright.

Richard Carr

I would like to thank Peter Williams and Moya Ward for their expertise, encouragement and support, and the members of the PCDA Team from the Liverpool Centre for Advanced Policing at LJMU. Thanks also goes to my disclosure teaching partner, Brian McNeill QPM, who has been a friend and professional colleague for over 30 years. Thank you to Kim my partner, without whose support I may not have embarked on a new life in academia, and finally thanks to the apprentices on the PCDA programme who represent the future of policing.

Colin Davies

To order our books please go to our website www.criticalpublishing.com or contact our distributor Ingram Publisher Services, telephone 01752 202301 or email IPSUK.orders@ingramcontent.com. Details of bulk order discounts can be found at www.criticalpublishing.com/delivery-information.

Our titles are also available in electronic format: for individual use via our website and for libraries and other institutions from all the major ebook platforms.

MAJOR AND SERIOUS CRIME INVESTIGATIONS

THE PROFESSIONAL POLICING CURRICULUM IN PRACTICE

RICHARD CARR AND COLIN DAVIES
SERIES EDITOR: TONY BLOCKLEY

CRITICAL
PUBLISHING

First published in 2024 by Critical Publishing Ltd

British Library Cataloguing in Publication Data
A CIP record for this book is available from the British Library

ISBN: 978-1-915713-18-6

This book is also available in the following e-book formats:
EPUB ISBN: 978-1-915713-19-3
Adobe e-book ISBN: 978-1-915713-20-9

Text and cover design by Out of House Limited
Project management by Newgen Publishing UK
Printed and bound in the UK by 4edge Limited

Critical Publishing
3 Connaught Road
St Albans
AL3 5RX

 www.criticalpublishing.com

 Printed on FSC accredited paper

CONTENTS

ABOUT THE SERIES EDITOR

TONY BLOCKLEY

Tony Blockley is the lead for policing at Leeds Trinity University, responsible for co-ordinating policing higher education, including developing programmes and enhancing the current provision in line with the Police Education Qualification Framework (PEQF) and supporting the College of Policing. He served within policing for over 30 years, including a role as chief superintendent and head of crime.

ABOUT THE AUTHORS

RICHARD CARR

Richard Carr is a senior lecturer in policing and investigation at Liverpool John Moores University, with more than 30 years' experience in policing. He has been the senior investigating officer on cases involving homicide, gun and gang criminality, serious sexual offending, human trafficking, modern slavery and police corruption, which has prepared him to lecture on these topics and deliver investigative training within a law enforcement environment.

COLIN DAVIES

Colin Davies OBE is a lecturer in policing at Liverpool John Moores University with more than 25 years' experience working for the Crown Prosecution Service. He has a detailed understanding of the challenges involved in investigating and prosecuting major and serious crimes and has prosecuted many serious crime cases including those involving organised crime groups, homicides and international dimensions.

FOREWORD

Police professionalism has seen significant developments over recent years, including the implementation of Vision 2025 and the establishment of the Police Education Qualification Framework (PEQF). There is no doubt that policing has become complex and that complexity and associated challenges increase daily with greater scrutiny, expectation and accountability. The educational component of police training and development, therefore, allows officers to gain a greater understanding and appreciation of the theories and activities associated with high-quality policing provision.

The educational element of Vision 2025 provides an opportunity to engage in meaningful insight and debate around some of the most sensitive areas of policing while also taking past lessons and utilising them to develop the service for the future. While there are many books and articles on numerous subjects associated with policing, this new series – The Professional Policing Curriculum in Practice – provides an insightful opportunity to start that journey. It distils the key concepts and topics within policing into an accessible format, combining theory and practice to provide you with a secure basis of knowledge and understanding.

Policing is complex; the level of knowledge required and expectations for officers is far greater than ever before. This book series provides an in-depth exploration and is explicitly tailored to the new pre-join routes, and reflect the diversity and complexity of twenty-first-century society. Each book is stand-alone, but they also work together to layer information as you progress through your programme. The pedagogical features of the books have been carefully designed to improve your understanding and critical thinking skills within the context of policing. They include learning objectives, case studies, evidence-based practice examples, critical thinking and reflective activities, and summaries of key concepts. Each chapter also includes a guide to further reading, meaning you don't have to spend hours researching to find the information you are looking for.

This book gives the reader a greater understanding and appreciation of the challenges of investigating major and serious crime. As we are aware, these crime types are often those reported on in the media and have a significant impact on individuals and communities. Understanding their investigation, the challenges and the opportunities engages the reader and provides an insight into the issues officers may encounter.

A real challenge for many such investigations is to ensure the opportunities are identified and followed through at the earliest opportunity. This includes how some crimes and investigations that may seem relatively minor can escalate into major and serious crime. Developing investigative skills with this underpinning knowledge is an informative step forward.

We now regularly see the changing nature of criminality. What was seen years ago as serious has almost become mainstream. Individuals need to understand the investigative process, what is available, and how they can conduct and manage successful investigations. This book provides this knowledge and more.

Professor Tony Blockley
Discipline Head: Policing
Leeds Trinity University

CHAPTER 1
INTRODUCTION TO MAJOR AND SERIOUS CRIME INVESTIGATIONS

LEARNING OBJECTIVES

AFTER READING THIS CHAPTER YOU WILL BE ABLE TO:

- understand the difference between the concepts of major and serious crime;

- critically evaluate the challenges associated with escalation of minor incidents into major and serious crime;

- analyse how lessons learned from miscarriages of justice have shaped investigative practice;

- demonstrate knowledge of organised crime groups and urban street gangs and how they impact on communities;

- describe the different levels of investigative practice, what these levels mean in practice and why it was necessary to professionalise the investigative process.

INTRODUCTION

Major and serious crimes often attract a high degree of public attention, meaning it is critical for the legitimacy of the police service that investigations falling into these categories are efficient and effective. There are many examples of successful investigations, such as the investigation into the criminal activities of Levi Bellfield, a serial killer responsible for the murders of Marsha McDonnell, Amélie Delagrange and Millie Dowler between 2002 and 2004; Eamonn Harrison, Ronan Hughes, Gheorghe Nica and Maurice Robinson who were responsible for the deaths of 39 Vietnamese nationals who suffocated in a lorry trailer in Essex in 2019; and Danyal Hussein who was responsible for the murder of two sisters, Nicole Smallman and Bibaa Henry, in London in 2020. However, in these and many other cases, there were missed opportunities that, if recognised, may have prevented these crimes from being committed in the first place.

Murder is one of the most high-profile offending categories falling within the definition of major and serious crime; however, there are other offences categorised as major and serious crime that are wide and varied. This chapter examines the concept of major and serious crime by exploring the different terms, why they are relevant to policing and investigation and how they influence the criminal justice system (CJS). Furthermore, this chapter considers different types of major and serious crime and how relatively minor crimes or incidents can escalate if not recognised and managed appropriately. A review of lessons learned from failed cases is explored, and how the Criminal Procedure and Investigations Act (1996) brought clarity to the investigative process by mandating investigators pursue all 'reasonable' lines of investigation, whether they point towards or away from a suspect, reinforcing that an investigation is in fact a search for the truth. This chapter develops an understanding of serious and organised crime and how there are differences between organised crime groups and urban street gangs. It outlines the national strategy known as the 4Ps, which is designed to bring all government agencies together with a collective responsibility to *pursue* offenders by prosecuting and disrupting their activity; *prevent* people from engaging in serious crime in the first place; *protect* individuals and communities from the effects of serious crime; and take steps to *prepare* to respond when it takes place. This chapter concludes with a discussion of the changing complexity of major and serious crime and how the introduction of the Professionalising Investigations Programme (PIP) in 2003 was designed to improve the quality and standards of investigation, thereby maintaining the legitimacy of policing.

MAJOR AND SERIOUS CRIME

The concepts of major and serious crimes are synonymous; they arguably have the same meaning, but there are subtle differences to consider. According to Her Majesty's Inspector of Constabulary (HMIC, 2009) (now His Majesty's Inspector of Constabulary, Fire and

Rescue Services, HMICFRS), the term *major crime* relates to any offence for which there is a need for the appointment of a senior investigating officer or the requirement of specialist resources. For example, homicide, manslaughter and infanticide would always be considered major and serious crimes due to the complexity of the offence, the level of public scrutiny and the impact on communities, which means there is a need for investigators with experience, knowledge and specialist skills. More recently, the National Police Chiefs' Council (NPCC, 2021a) broadened the concept further to include any other offence for which there is a greater sense of threat, harm or risk. This links to the notion of critical incidents, where the '*effectiveness of the police response is likely to have a significant impact on the confidence of the victim, their family or the community*' (College of Policing, 2021a, p 1; NPCC, 2021a, p 14).

In reality, this means any offence could be considered as a major crime if there is a significant public concern; for example, gun- and gang-related criminality or serious sexual offences are often classed as major crime because they create fear in local communities. Investigations with national and international connections or other offences which are complex in nature or have strategic implications for policing may also be considered as major crime. A key element in the decision of whether to categorise an offence as a major crime is the requirement for the case to be investigated effectively in order to maintain confidence and satisfaction in the investigative process.

CRITICAL THINKING ACTIVITY 1.1

LEVEL 4

You are the investigating officer in relation to an offence of sexual assault, contrary to section 3 of the Sexual Offences Act (2003). The circumstances are that the victim was walking through a local park one evening when they were attacked and sexually assaulted. As part of your investigation, you become aware that there is significant public concern within the local community, who are worried they may be at risk of being victims of similar incidents.

• Could you classify this as a major crime and, if so, why?

Sample answers are provided at the end of this book.

The concept of major crime does not attract a legal definition; it is a term used within policing to assess the individual characteristics of a homicide or other major crime to allow for decisions to be made with regard to the command structure of an investigation and the resources that are allocated to it. In contrast, the concept of serious crime attracts a range of legal definitions, some of which will be considered later in the chapter. They are important to understand as they underpin a variety of themes associated with the law enforcement response to major and serious crime and the broader CJS.

In a similar way to some offences being categorised as major crime, others will also be considered as serious because of their gravity; for example, offences such as murder, manslaughter, rape, acts of terrorism and offences of a similar stature are recognised by the CJS as being serious. Sentencing powers often reflect their severity and by virtue of the fact they are indictable only offences, which means they can only be dealt with in the Crown Court, illustrates their sense of importance in the eyes of the CJS. Some areas of legislation provide additional guidance on the concept of serious crime. For instance, section 93(4) of the Police Act (1997), which legislates for state interference of private property, defines serious crime as *'any criminal conduct which involves the use of violence, results in substantial financial gain or is conducted by a large number of persons in pursuit of a common purpose'*. Additionally, section 93(4) of the Police Act (1997), together with section 81 of the Regulation of Investigatory Powers Act (2000), which legislates for covert surveillance, outlines how any offence could be construed as a serious crime if the individual responsible is someone who has attained the age of 21, who has no previous convictions and could reasonably be expected to be sentenced to a term of imprisonment of three years or more. Clearly, this broadens the scope regarding what type of offences could be considered serious. Finally, section 47 of the Serious Crime Act (2007), amended 2015, outlines how, for the purposes of serious crime prevention orders, specific offences relating to drug trafficking, firearm trafficking and computer misuse are also categorised as serious crime.

Definitions of serious crime are also important for the broader CJS; for example, the Sentencing Act (2020) allows the courts to impose extended or whole life sentences on individuals who have been convicted of specific violent, sexual or terrorist offences or a 'serious' offence, which is 'specified' under the act and carries a sentence of ten years or more. Similarly, the Police, Crime, Sentencing and Courts Act (2022) mandates that government agencies such as police, local authorities, health, education and others collaborate to reduce serious violence; the Act also allows the courts to impose extended or whole life sentences on individuals over the age of 18 years who have been convicted of child murders, where there is evidence of substantial premeditation or in other cases where there is an exceptional degree of seriousness. In these instances, the courts may impose an extended or whole life sentence if they are of the opinion the individual poses a significant risk to members of the public of serious harm and should therefore be considered dangerous.

POLICING SPOTLIGHT

The use of the Sentencing Act (2020) was illustrated well in the case involving Wayne Couzens, a police officer who was convicted in 2021 of the murder of Sarah Everard. In this case, the courts exercised their powers and determined Couzens posed a significant risk to the public, and they imposed a whole life sentence.

In summary, it is clear that comparisons can be drawn between the concepts of major and serious crime, they are intrinsically linked, but there are some distinct differences. Major crime is a term used within policing and allows for the allocation of resources to ensure effective investigation; in contrast, the concept of serious crime holds a range of legal definitions that are used to support the law enforcement response to these types of crime and are also used by the CJS as a vehicle to prevent or deter future offending.

WHEN MINOR CRIMES ESCALATE INTO MAJOR AND SERIOUS CRIMES

Accepting that all incidents and crimes have a degree of seriousness in the eyes of those who are affected by them, there are many instances when incidents or crimes at the lower end of the spectrum have the potential to escalate into major and serious crimes. These incidents pose a significant risk for policing, and all too often incidents or offences involving anti-social behaviour, harassment or stalking, domestic violence, indecent exposure and many more have the propensity to escalate into murder, serious violence or serious sexual offences. Consequently, all matters referred to the police need to be considered against a backdrop of threat, harm and risk. These terms are now commonplace in policing and investigative vocabulary and are built into the National Decision Model (see Chapter 3 in the book *Criminal Investigation*, which forms part of this series) and the broader concept of investigative decision making (see Chapter 2 in this book) and only adopting an approach that considers the potential for escalation will ensure the prevention of what might be seen as predictable and preventable events.

The concept of escalation is not just restricted to incidents or crimes at the lower end of the spectrum. Other offences involving knives, firearms or intelligence relating to threats to life, particularly when there is a link to gang criminality, must be considered as precursor events, in other words, an occurrence that is perhaps an indicator of a potential escalation in offending. These are important elements for investigators to consider, as a failure to recognise the significance of a precursor event can have serious consequences, resulting in death or serious injury while undermining trust and confidence in policing and investigative practice. For example, a random assault may not necessarily be an indicator of future offending, but when the victim is an individual who is known to be involved in major and serious crime, it is perhaps indicative of a dispute between criminal gangs and, therefore, must be treated as having the potential to escalate into something more serious.

POLICING SPOTLIGHT

A case that demonstrates crime escalation is the murder of Garry Newlove. On 10 August 2007, Garry Newlove was attacked by a group of youths outside his home in Warrington, Cheshire, when he challenged them while they were causing damage to his vehicle. Garry was assaulted and died of his injuries three days later. The subsequent investigation into his death exposed a series of incidents involving anti-social behaviour caused by the same youths that had started several years earlier. There was much public criticism at the time because of a perception that if the anti-social behaviour had been dealt with, the crimes would likely not have escalated in the way they did. Three teenagers were later convicted of murder.

LESSONS LEARNED FROM FAILED CASES

While the majority of cases which are investigated and prosecuted do not involve miscarriages of justice, there have been occasions when miscarriages of justice have occurred, resulting in the wrongful conviction of innocent people, which has impacted on public confidence in the CJS and those failures have led to fundamental change.

Among significant historical miscarriages of justice is the conviction of Adolf Beck in 1896 which was based on mistaken identification evidence and ultimately led to the creation of the Court of Criminal Appeal (now the Court of Appeal Criminal Division) in 1907. More recently, notable convictions against Judith Ward and Stefan Kiszko were quashed due to material irregularities in the evidence and cases against the Guildford Four and Maguire Seven were also overturned, leading to an apology by the then Prime Minister Tony Blair for the 'miscarriages of justice they have suffered'.

An important example of the impact of a case which led to a fundamental change in the CJS was the Maxwell Confait case. Confait was murdered in April 1972, and three youths were convicted of the murder based on false confessions which had been obtained by the police. The then Home Secretary, the Right Honourable Robert Carr, ordered an investigation to be carried out by Sir Henry Fisher, who was tasked to examine the circumstances of the case and in particular, to consider whether there needed to be changes to the Judges' Rules, which were a set of rules or guidelines governing suspect interviews and were set by the judiciary. These were later superseded by the Police and Criminal Evidence Act (1984).

The Confait case was also one of the major reasons why the UK government set up the Royal Commission on Criminal Procedure (RCCP) which reported in 1981 and led to two major pieces of legislation, namely the Police and Criminal Evidence Act (1984), which sets out the powers of the police, and the Prosecution of Offences Act (1985) which implemented the recommendation of the RCCP to separate the investigatory process from the prosecutorial function and established the Crown Prosecution Service (CPS) for England and Wales.

The Criminal Cases Review Commission (CCRC) was established by the Criminal Appeal Act (1995). The CCRC reviews possible miscarriages of justice in the criminal courts in England, Wales and Northern Ireland and can refer a case to the Court of Appeal where there is new evidence or an argument that may cast doubt on the safety of a conviction. To understand the court system and processes refer to another book in the series, *Police Procedure and Evidence in the Criminal Justice System*.

An example of such a referral took place in the Post Office Horizon computer case (*Hamilton v Post Office*, 2021). This case surrounded the introduction of a point-of-sales system which recorded counter transactions within Post Offices. The Post Office claimed that the system was accurate, meaning if there were discrepancies between the manual records kept by Post Office sub-masters and sub-mistresses and the data provided by the Horizon system, this was an indication of dishonest conduct. It was on that basis over 750 people were prosecuted for offences of theft, fraud and deception; however it transpired the Post Office were aware of errors in the accuracy of the Horizon system but failed to provide the information to the defendants.

There is no doubt this information should have been provided to the defence because it clearly met the test for disclosure contained in the Criminal Procedure and Investigations Act (1996) (CPIA) in so much as it might reasonably have been considered capable of undermining the case against the accused, or of assisting the case for the accused (Ministry of Justice Code of Practice, 2020b, 2:10). For more details see *Police Procedure and Evidence in the Criminal Justice System*, another book in the *Professional Policing Curriculum in Practice* series. The Court of Appeal subsequently quashed the convictions for the vast majority of those who had been convicted, and a public inquiry into the circumstances of the cases followed.

The concept of disclosure will be dealt with in more detail in Chapter 5; however, this case demonstrates the significance of fairness in criminal proceedings because when miscarriages of justice on this scale occur, they have the propensity to seriously undermine the legitimacy of investigation and the entire CJS. The law is quite clear in this regard. The CPIA Code of Practice (Ministry of Justice, 2020b, 3.5) sets out the duties placed on investigators when conducting a criminal investigation in that they should '*pursue all reasonable lines of inquiry, whether these point towards or away from the suspect. What is reasonable in each case will depend on the particular circumstances.*'

Furthermore, investigators are expected to demonstrate an '*investigative mindset*', which has been described by the National Centre for Policing Excellence (2005, p 58) as '*an inquiring, open minded approach, capable of sensing what might be material from the defence perspective*'.

Lessons can also be learnt from cases where there have been convictions, but in which the circumstances of the investigation have identified issues in the investigatory process, such as the Yorkshire Ripper convicted of murdering 13 women between 1975 and 1980, which led to significant changes in the running of major investigations, and the Soham murders of Holly Wells and Jessica Chapman in 2002, which led to changes in the way police share intelligence.

Although miscarriages of justice should never have occurred, they are part of our legal history and have helped shape investigative practice.

EVIDENCE-BASED POLICING

An internet search for the 'Bichard Inquiry' will take you to a report which outlines failures by the police to adequately check the background of Ian Huntley, who, on 4 August 2002, killed ten-year-olds Holly Wells and Jessica Chapman. During the investigation, it emerged that Ian Huntley had been the subject of eight previous allegations of sexual misconduct, which had not been detected prior to his appointment as the caretaker at the school in Soham, Cambridgeshire, that Holly and Jessica attended. The Bichard Inquiry that followed made wide-ranging recommendations for change, including better information-sharing agreements, improved vetting processes and investment into the Police National Computer (PNC).

ORGANISED CRIME GROUPS AND URBAN STREET GANGS

The general understanding of serious and organised crime has developed significantly in recent years, but this is by no means a new phenomenon. In fact, major and serious crime carrying a level of organisation and sophistication is firmly placed in history, with notable figures in the United Kingdom such as the Kray twins, who were involved in organised crime in the East End of London in the 1950s and 1960s, and Curtis Warren who developed a criminal network between Liverpool and South America during the 1980s. Further afield, organisations such as the Mafia and Mexican drug cartels controlled by figures such as Pablo Escobar and Joaquín Archivaldo Guzmán Loera, commonly known as 'El Chapo', both popularised by docudramas on Netflix, are well established in the consciousness of the public. These and many others were involved in serious and organised crime for financial gain, and often their criminality was supported by violence and intimidation to control their criminal enterprise.

Generally, there has been difficulty in agreeing on a single definition of serious and organised crime; however, broadly speaking, there is a consensus that serious and organised crime involves:

- structure and hierarchy;

- profit from illegal activities;

- violence or threats of violence;

- a propensity to corrupt officials; and

- a sense of continuity, meaning that criminal activities extended beyond the involvement of one person.
                                      (Hagan, 1983, 2006; Albanese, 2004; Finckenauer, 2005)

These concepts have been developed, and the terms associated with serious and organised crime are now well established in policing and wider law enforcement agencies. The Home Office (2018a, p 11) provides the benchmark for policing in the United Kingdom and defines serious and organised crime as 'individuals planning, coordinating and committing serious offences, whether individually, in groups and/or as part of transnational networks'. While particular offence types on their own may not necessarily be considered as serious and organised crime, offences involving child sexual abuse, illegal drugs, the criminal use of firearms, fraud, money laundering, bribery and corruption, organised immigration crime, human trafficking and modern slavery, organised acquisitive crime and cyber-crime are considered key offending categories associated with serious and organised crime (Home Office, 2018a; National Crime Agency, 2021).

Understanding the scale of the threat posed by those involved in serious and organised crime is an important part of the strategy for tackling this type of criminality. Therefore, policing and wider law enforcement agencies use intelligence, arrest or offending histories and records of criminal convictions to 'map' or 'index' organised crime groups (OCGs). Using the data, assessments are made in terms of the group's level of intent and capability to cause threat, harm and risk across communities. This is a process known as Organised Crime Group Mapping (OCGM). According to the manual on OCGM (2010) the 'map' or 'index' creates a consolidated picture in terms of where organised crime occurs, which individuals or groups are involved, where they operate and where they live. The National Crime Agency publishes annual data in terms of the scale of the problem. They estimate there are currently approximately 5000 OCGs and around 70,000 individuals involved in serious and organised crime across the UK (National Crime Agency, 2020, 2021).

POLICING SPOTLIGHT

In collaboration with Dutch law enforcement officers and the International Liaison Network, the National Crime Agency developed intelligence which indicated an organised crime group from Merseyside was involved in an international drug trafficking conspiracy. In a joint operation, six individuals were arrested, and 111kg of cocaine and heroin with an estimated street value of £9 million was seized. In addition, high-value vehicles and watches were recovered.

This is one example of how intelligence is used to lead investigations into OCGs who are involved in major and serious crime across international boundaries (National Crime Agency, 2021).

With a much clearer picture in terms of who is involved in this type of criminality and an understanding of the hierarchical nature of organised crime, a distinction needs to be drawn between those operating at higher levels of a criminal organisation and those individuals, groups or gangs who are engaged in perhaps less organised street-level drug supply, who often protect their territories with violence and the criminal use of firearms. These groups or gangs, some of whom aspire to become an organised crime group in their own right, are called urban street gangs (USGs) (Home Office, 2017a). This is not to say USGs are any less harmful, on the contrary they are often at the forefront of major and serious crime in urban communities and are frequently much more visible; the only distinction between OCGs and USGs is their level of criminality, organisation and control. It is for these reasons that offending at the lower end of the hierarchy can often lead to an escalation in tensions between gangs, which has the potential to make USGs a much greater threat.

EVIDENCE-BASED POLICING

OCGM aims to apply science to assessing risk posed by those involved in serious and organised crime. However, much of the data used in the assessments are open to some level of interpretation. Furthermore, when police and law enforcement intelligence is used as part of the assessment, there is often a 'gap' in the intelligence picture, which means it can be subjective and gaining a true and accurate assessment of risk is difficult to achieve. Denley and Ariel (2019) make these points in their examination of organised crime groups in the West Midlands region of the United Kingdom. They argue how understanding the totality of organised crime can be challenging and while OCGM may have its flaws, it currently offers the most complete picture of organised crime and those who are involved across the United Kingdom.

THE 4PS APPROACH TO TACKLING MAJOR AND SERIOUS CRIME

Serious and organised crime is determined as a significant national security threat, which undermines communities and compromises the integrity and legitimacy of the UK (Home Office, 2018a; National Crime Agency, 2021). The impact on society in terms of social and economic costs is difficult to quantify; however, it is clear this area of criminality affects all walks of life: individuals, families, small, medium and large businesses and international organisations. As a consequence, there is a need for a national approach to tackle serious and organised crime.

The Home Office (2018a) sets out a need for a whole system approach to tackle serious and organised crime in the Serious and Organised Crime Strategy. The police, wider law enforcement agencies, education, health and social care and other local authority networks are required to pool their resources in order to disrupt and deter this type of criminality. In essence, the Serious and Organised Crime Strategy provides a framework in terms of how serious and organised crime will be dealt with as a whole.

There are four overarching aims in the strategy, which are proposed by the Home Office (2018a) as:

1. employing greater use of legislation, greater use of intelligence analysis and greater capabilities brought about by using technology to proactively target the highest harm groups impacting communities;

2. the protection of vulnerable individuals and communities who are exploited through the cyber environment by preparing them to be more vigilant and take responsibility to protect themselves against the threat of serious and organised crime;

3. using education and other preventative measures to divert or deter young people from engaging in criminality in the first place;

4. operating a one system approach, which combines resources from policing, law enforcement and other partners such as education, health, social care, and wider local authority networks to use their collective powers to disrupt high harm criminal networks.

Derived originally from the Home Office (2011) Contest strategy, which outlines the United Kingdom's approach to countering terrorism, the Serious and Organised Crime Strategy provides direction in the form of what is commonly known as the 4Ps. In other words, policing, law enforcement and partner agencies must:

- **pursue** offenders by prosecuting and disrupting the criminal activity;

- **protect** individuals, organisations and systems from the effects of serious and organised crime;

- **prevent** people from engaging in serious and organised crime in the first place;

- **prepare** for when serious and organised crime takes place and have the resources, skills and equipment available to reduce the impact.

Policing is traditionally linked with enforcing legislation and prosecuting offenders through the CJS. This really forms the basis of the 'pursue' element of the strategy, although in policing circles it is frequently said that enforcement alone is not enough to reduce the threat posed by serious and organised crime. As a consequence, a much more collective response is needed, which sees all government agencies coming together in a synchronised way. Being 'prepared' to use their collective resources, skills and equipment and their respective powers and intelligence not only to 'pursue' offenders but also to intervene at a much earlier stage to 'prevent' offending from occurring in the first place, thereby 'protecting' communities from harm.

CRITICAL THINKING ACTIVITY 1.2

LEVEL 5

Organised crime groups who are often involved in major and serious crime are assessed in accordance with their level of intent and capability to cause threat, harm and risk in communities.

- Describe how the Serious and Organised Crime Strategy (Home Office, 2018a) sets out how policing and other law enforcement agencies should tackle this type of criminality and apply this to a real-world scenario.

Sample answers are provided at the end of this book.

THE PROFESSIONALISING INVESTIGATIONS PROGRAMME (PIP)

In recognition of the increasing complexities of criminal investigation and as part of the professionalisation of policing, in 2003, the National Centre for Policing Excellence, now the College of Policing, introduced the Professionalising Investigations Programme. More commonly known as PIP, this programme is designed to '*deliver a professional, ethical and effective investigation capacity for policing in the 21st century*' (College of Policing, 2018, p 5) and aims to provide a set of nationally benchmarked standards of practice at all levels of investigation. In practical terms, this means standards of investigative practice are assured and managed through workplace assessments and accreditation at basic and advanced levels of investigation.

There are four levels of the PIP, as shown in Figure 1.1.

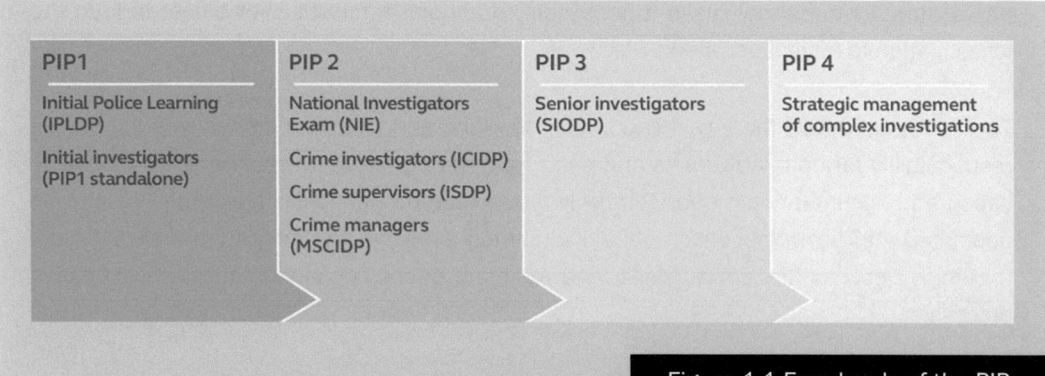

Figure 1.1 Four levels of the PIP
Source: College of Policing (2018, p 5).

- Level one concerns the investigation of priority and volume crime.

- Level two is associated with the investigation of serious and complex crimes.

- Level three is required by senior investigators who are expected to lead investigations into major, serious and organised crime (College of Policing, 2018; NPCC, 2021a).

- Accreditation at PIP level four is required by senior and much more experienced investigators who are tasked with the strategic management of serious and highly complex cases. It is important to note that the person who performs this role is not the senior investigating officer (SIO), who has responsibility for the day-to-day management and progression of the case, but an individual who has the responsibility to act as a strategic adviser or a 'critical friend' to the SIO and provide a link between the investigation and chief officers. The PIP level four role is not required in many cases of major and serious crime, but certainly, in cases where there is a high degree of public concern, media scrutiny or some sort of political implication, they are a key individual in the investigative structure. For example, investigations such as the murders of Rhys Jones, Sarah Everard and, more recently, Olivia Pratt-Korbel, which attracted significant media attention and public concern, will have undoubtedly employed a strategic PIP level four adviser to support the senior investigating officer and, ultimately, the investigative process.

At all levels of the PIP, investigators are expected to demonstrate competency in the role and maintain a level of continued professional development to retain their registration with the College of Policing.

The PIP adds to the understanding of major and serious crime by outlining how this can include offences which have a community impact, for example, crimes with the propensity to develop into serious disorder or where they have escalated from lower-level incidents, or offences that have particular 'offence' or 'offender' characteristics, which mean there are aggravating features that make it necessary to appoint a more senior officer to lead the investigation to mitigate strategic risk.

There is no question the investigation of major and serious crime comes with significant responsibility for both individuals and policing in the broadest sense. The need for qualification and accreditation means that only those with the right skills and expertise can be appointed into key roles, which should ultimately preserve the integrity of investigation, maximize opportunities for success, and maintain public confidence in the investigative process.

CRITICAL THINKING ACTIVITY 1.3

LEVEL 6

Major and serious crimes often attract a high degree of public attention and the police service is rightly held to account when investigations go wrong.

- Critically evaluate the challenges associated with the investigation of major and serious crime and how the police service can mitigate these.

Sample answers are provided at the end of this book.

CONCLUSION

Major and serious crimes are important terms within the policing environment. Major crimes such as murder and manslaughter will always be considered as major crimes because of their gravity but in reality many other crimes may be considered serious if there is a significant impact on the community or if the victim or offender have characteristics that increase the sense of severity. In contrast, serious crime attracts legal status and provides the police and wider CJS with increased powers of enforcement and sentencing.

Clearly, major and serious crime can be spontaneous. It can be disorganised and committed by individuals without premeditation, but equally it can be committed by groups who are sophisticated and well organised. This means investigating this type of criminality can be challenging, and it is therefore essential these investigations are reserved for those who have the experience, knowledge and skill to maximise the opportunities for success.

SUMMARY OF KEY CONCEPTS

This chapter has outlined the concept of major and serious crime and explained how miscarriages of justice have brought about changes to the investigative process in order to preserve public confidence in policing. The content of this chapter enables you to:

 describe the difference between major and serious crime and how these terms influence investigations and the CJS;

$\longrightarrow$

- recognise that relatively low-level crimes have the potential to escalate into major and serious crime if they are not managed appropriately;

- understand how our legal history has shaped investigative practice;

- explain the concept of the Serious and Organised Crime Strategy and how the 4Ps approach applies to a real-world scenario;

- discuss the impact of PIP and what it means for investigation.

CHECK YOUR KNOWLEDGE

1. Why is the concept of 'major crime' important to policing?

2. Under certain circumstances, the courts can use the Police, Crime, Sentencing and Courts Act (2022) and/or the Sentencing Act (2020) to impose whole life sentences. What are the circumstances?

3. Police and wider law enforcement agencies adopt a somewhat scientific approach to assess the threat, risk and harm of those involved in serious and organised crime. What is this called?

4. The Criminal Procedure and Investigations Act, Code of Practice (2020, 3.5) places a duty on investigators when conducting a criminal investigation to do what?

5. What is the purpose of the Professionalising Investigations Programme?

FURTHER READING

National Police Chiefs' Council (NPCC) (2021) Major Crime Investigation Manual (MCIM 2021). [online] Available at: https://library.college.police.uk/docs/NPCC/Major-Crime-Investigation-Manual-Nov-2021.pdf (accessed 22 October 2023).
This text provides comprehensive guidance in relation to all elements of the investigative process in relation to homicide (murder, manslaughter and infanticide) and other large major investigations.

Home Office (2018) Serious and Organised Crime Strategy. [online] Available at: https://assets.publishing.service.gov.uk/government/uploads/system/uploads/attachment_data/file/752850/SOC-2018-web.pdf (accessed 22 October 2023).
This government report provides details of the way in which police and other law enforcement agencies are expected to tackle serious and organised crime.

National Crime Agency (2021) National Strategic Assessment of Serious and Organised Crime. [online] Available at: https://nationalcrimeagency.gov.uk/who-we-are/publications/533-national-strategic-assessment-of-serious-and-organised-crime-2021/file (accessed 22 October 2023).
This is the most recent assessment by the National Crime Agency in terms of the scale of serious and organised crime in the United Kingdom. The report identifies key threats and provides commentary on current challenges.

CHAPTER 2
FUNDAMENTAL PRINCIPLES OF MAJOR AND SERIOUS CRIME INVESTIGATIONS

LEARNING OBJECTIVES

AFTER READING THIS CHAPTER YOU WILL BE ABLE TO:

- understand the principles of investigative practice;

- apply concepts such as the five building blocks, golden hour, ABC and the investigative mindset to the investigative process;

- demonstrate knowledge in the process of investigative decision making and analyse the challenges with a risk-based approach;

- critically evaluate the concept of creating hypotheses to support investigative development.

INTRODUCTION

While crime rates fluctuate over time, analysis of the Crime Survey for England and Wales illustrates how all crime excluding fraud and computer misuse has followed a downward trend since a peak in the mid-1990s (ONS, 2022b). More recently, however, offences associated with major and serious crime have escalated. Between 2013 and 2017, homicide increased by 35 per cent and has continued to follow an upward trajectory; offences associated with the criminal use of firearms have escalated since 2014; and between 2014 and 2019 hospital admissions for assaults with a sharp instrument, which are indicators of serious violence, have risen by 41 per cent (Allen and Harding, 2021; Home Office, 2021; ONS, 2022b).

In contrast, an examination of investigative outcomes illustrates a diminishing trend; homicide investigations resulting in conviction have fallen from 68 per cent in 2016/17 to 44 per cent in 2020/21 (ONS, 2022a); currently, only 5.6 per cent of all crime results in a charge or summons, down from 16 per cent in 2015/2016 (Home Office, 2022a) and significantly only 1.3 per cent of rape investigations result in charge or summons (House of Commons, 2022). Investigations closed because of evidential difficulties are an increasing area of concern, a point drawn out by HMICFRS (2022) in its review of serious acquisitive crime, which highlighted how initial responses to crime set the benchmark for investigative quality; how missed opportunities and failure to secure forensic evidence undermines the potential for positive outcomes; and how excessive demands on resources mean there are failures to gather the most basic information from victims of crime.

There are clear challenges when investigating major and serious crime but victims rightly expect investigators to have the right knowledge, skills and expertise to gather cogent evidence and successfully prosecute those responsible. This means that everyone in the investigative process, including the call handler, first responding officers, crime scene investigators and the senior investigating officer (SIO) must have a thorough understanding of the fundamental principles associated with investigation.

This chapter examines three principal steps in the investigative process; it considers concepts such as the five building blocks of investigation, the golden hour and the principles of 'assume nothing, believe nothing and challenge everything (ABC)', which means investigators should demonstrate professional scepticism and curiosity (ACPO/ Centrex, 2005; Cook, Hibbitt and Hill, 2016; Cook, 2019). The theory behind the investigative mindset is explored with reflection of risks when there is a failure to demonstrate the basic principle of open-mindedness and being receptive to alternative explanations.

The chapter discusses investigative decision making with a focus on the National Decision Model (NDM), which provides a framework to support risk-based decisions. There is consideration of how investigators use their experience, intuition and professional judgement to support effective decision making. The chapter concludes with an examination of how investigators develop hypotheses or reasoned judgements to help fill gaps in knowledge in terms of the nature and circumstances surrounding the crime under investigation.

THEORIES AND CONCEPTS ASSOCIATED WITH INVESTIGATIVE PRACTICE

The process of investigation into offences associated with major and serious crime has the same principles as the investigation into offences at the lower end of the spectrum. Clearly, the severity of the crime, the scale of the investigation and the consequences of failure are much greater but technically, the fundamental principles are the same. According to Newburn, Williamson and Wright (2007), the process of investigation has three key elements.

1. The 'identification and acquisition' of material relevant to the case, such as verbal and written accounts from victims and witnesses, the collection of forensic evidence and suspect explanations in terms of their involvement in crime.

2. The 'interpretation and understanding' of material acquired during the investigation. Specialists in forensic evidence, pathology, digital communication and other fields can help investigators to place material acquired into context.

3. The 'ordering and representation' of evidence into a coherent reliable narrative, which tells the story of motive or reason for the criminal event and any post event actions that may indicate innocence or guilt.

There are many layers to the investigative process, such as the call handler or call taker, who is often the first point of contact for a victim or witness; first responders; crime scene investigators; investigators more generally; and SIOs. All parties associated with the investigative process need to be aware of and apply the fundamental principles of investigation. In support of their actions, there are several key concepts and theories that are critical to the success of an investigation.

THE FIVE BUILDING BLOCKS OF INVESTIGATION

The initial response to any investigation is underpinned by what is known as the five building blocks principle. This principle is outlined in Practice Advice on Core Investigative Doctrine (ACPO/Centrex, 2005, p 51), the Murder Investigation Manual (ACPO/Centrex, 2006, p 35) and the College of Policing's Authorised Professional Practice on Investigation Process (College of Policing, 2021b, p 6). The principle lays the foundation for the investigative process and suggests a staged approach for attending officers to follow, namely to ensure:

- preservation of life;

- preservation of scenes;

- securing evidence;

- identification of victims (and witnesses);

- identification of suspects.

The preservation of life would always take priority for responding officers; however, other elements of the five building blocks principle may be applied at any stage during an investigation. To illustrate the point, routinely a victim or witness may contact the police to report a crime, and their name, address and other details would be established by the call handler. This would be the starting point for the investigation; the identification of a crime scene would be progressed and steps taken to secure and preserve evidence. A successful crime scene examination and witness interviews may identify a suspect, and if the evidence allows, a prosecution would follow. In contrast, an investigation may well commence with the identification and detention of a suspect, and the sequential approach through the five building blocks may operate in reverse order.

REFLECTIVE PRACTICE 2.1

LEVEL 4

Put yourself in the position of a senior investigative officer. You are informed that uniformed officers responded to an anonymous call suggesting a man wearing dark clothing was acting suspiciously in a local park. On their arrival, a man fitting the description ran away; the officers gave chase, and he was detained nearby. When searching provisions of section 1 of the Police and Criminal Evidence Act (1984), the found to have blood-stained clothing and to be in possession of a knife.

- Following the five building blocks principle, describe your sequential approach to the investigation.

Sample answers are provided at the end of this book.

GOLDEN HOUR

The 'golden hour' is discussed within Chapter 2 of the *Criminal Investigation* edition of this series. To refresh, it is a term used to describe the initial stages of an investigation; when victims and witnesses are at their most cooperative, they are more likely to make spontaneous comments that may prove vital, and they are less likely to have been contaminated by outside influences. Equally, this is the period when forensic evidence is at its freshest, meaning there are greater prospects for successful recovery, and suspects are at their most vulnerable because they have been unable to put time and space between them and the crime itself. According to Cook (2019), the first five or ten minutes of any investigation are even more pivotal and may be described as the 'platinum' period, illustrating the importance of time and efficiency during the early stages.

The golden hour is based on the premise that efficient and effective actions during the early stages of an investigation can improve positive outcomes. For example, the very first interactions between a victim or witness and the call hander, which may last seconds, are critical to the acquisition of key information; in the same way, actions and decision making taken by the first responding officer may quickly identify key witnesses or lead to an early arrest of a suspect. It is clear that missed or lost opportunities during the initial stages of an investigation can significantly undermine the investigative process.

Building on this concept, as part of a major and serious crime investigation, the 'golden hour' may extend into prolonged periods; for example, the interview of a key and significant witness may take many hours, the crime scene examination for a homicide or terrorist incident may take days or even weeks, the point is the response to criminal events should be efficient, effective and conducted with diligence to increase the prospects of success.

EVIDENCE-BASED POLICING

A joint thematic inspection of the police and the CPS highlighted the importance of the initial police response to victims of rape (HMICFRS, 2021). This report highlighted how the early stages of the investigative process are critically important, not only in the recovery of evidence but equally they can affect how a victim feels and, in some cases, may influence their decision regarding whether or not to take their case forward.

THE PRINCIPLE OF ABC

Professional curiosity is your friend when investigating all crimes especially major and serious crimes. In other words, it is important for investigators to be inquisitive to challenge the meaning and reliability of all material gathered to ensure understanding of its value to an investigation. This is known as the principle of ABC, which proposes an interlocking concept that investigators should 'assume nothing, believe nothing and challenge everything' (ACPO/Centrex, 2005; Cook, Hibbitt and Hill, 2016; Cook, 2019).

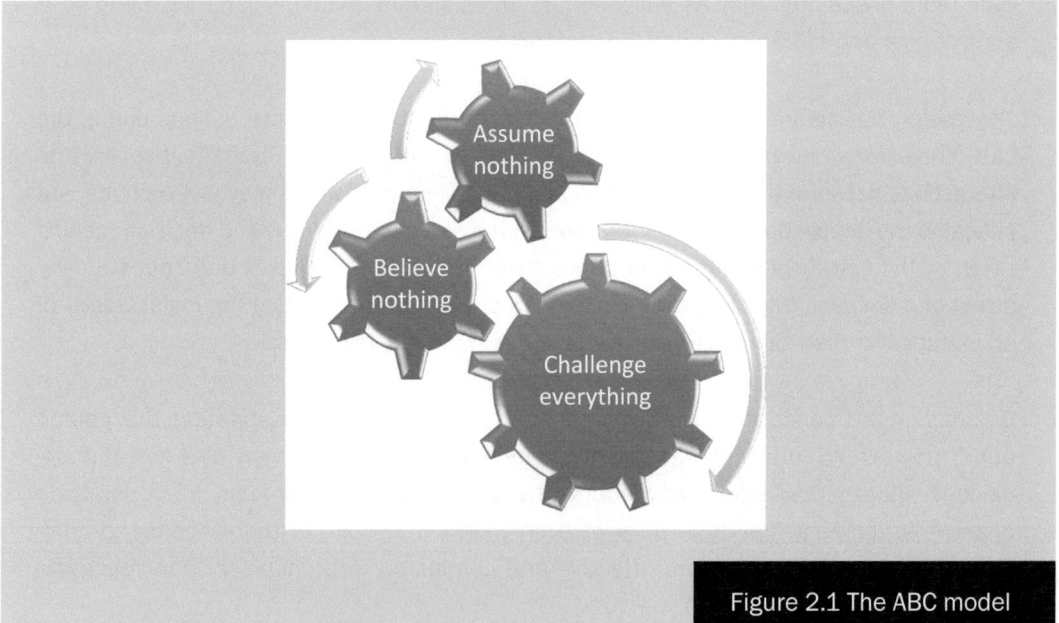

Figure 2.1 The ABC model

It is briefly discussed in Chapter 2 of the *Criminal Investigation* book in this series; however, the principle of ABC applies to all elements of an investigation. For example, accounts provided by victims and witnesses of major and serious crimes must be subjected to scrutiny and be tested against material known to investigators. This is not designed to undermine the importance of ensuring a victim's sense of being 'believed', which is a common area of concern for victims of serious sexual offences (HMICFRS, 2021), but where there are inconsistencies in accounts it is right that clarification should be sought to reduce any misunderstanding or sense of ambiguity. In the same way, forensic evidence, digital or telephone evidence, CCTV and other sources of investigative material should always be carefully examined to reduce the potential for its meaning and reliability to be misunderstood.

CRITICAL THINKING ACTIVITY 2.1

LEVEL 5

Having read the section on the principle of ABC, which means investigators should 'assume nothing, believe nothing and challenge everything', apply this to an investigation into an allegation of grievous bodily harm with intent, contrary to section 18, Offences Against the Person Act (1861). The complainant alleges while they were on a night out with friends, they were subject to an unprovoked attack.

• What investigative actions would you pursue to develop the investigation?

• What would you do in the event you identify evidence that may undermine the account of the complainant?

• Analyse the associated risks when applying the principles of ABC to an investigation.

Sample answers are provided at the end of this book.

INVESTIGATIVE MINDSET

The process of investigation described by Newburn, Williamson and Wright (2007) as the '*identification and acquisition*', the '*interpretation and understanding*' and '*ordering and representation*' of material, together with concepts such as the golden hour and the principle of ABC, requires investigators to be structured, methodical and inquisitive. Developing this, investigators are expected to adopt an investigative mindset, which means being open-minded, being receptive to alternative explanations and being objective by challenging preconceptions or personal bias (ACPO/Centrex, 2005).

Accepting that even the most implausible explanations may be true, the Practice Advice on Core Investigative Doctrine (ACPO/Centrex, 2005) suggests the 'investigative mindset' is comprised of five elements.

1. *'Understanding the source of material'*, which involves questioning where investigative material is from, the strengths and limitations of the source and whether there are any characteristics that would undermine the quality or the credibility of the evidence.

2. *'Planning and preparation'*. For example, prior to a crime scene examination, taking appropriate steps to ensure the right people and the right equipment is available; similarly, prior to an interview with a key and significant witness ensure the time and location are suitable so as to reduce unnecessary distractions.

3. *'Examination'* of evidential material by considering meaning and reliability. In the case of evidence provided by victims and witnesses, only by challenging those accounts and seeking clarification when necessary will investigators reduce ambiguity and ensure true understanding. It is clear how this relates directly to the notion of ABC in terms of accepting nothing, believing nothing and challenging everything.

4. *'Recording and collation'* of specific details associated with the examination of evidence; for example, when, where and how an examination of a particular piece of evidence took place, why the examination was conducted in the first place and what storage facilities were used to preserve the integrity of the evidence.

5. *'Evaluation'* of evidence with a view to seeking corroboration to help support meaning and relevance to the investigation.

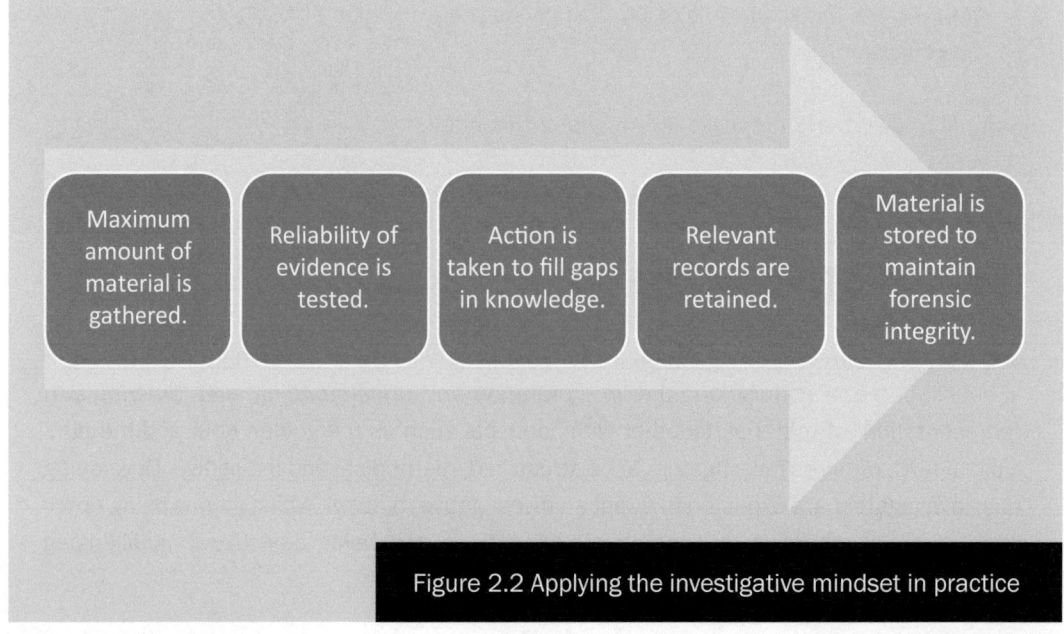

Figure 2.2 Applying the investigative mindset in practice

Figure 2.2 summarises what applying an investigative mindset can achieve. Very often, even the most experienced investigators can become too focused on a particular line of inquiry, which may be at the detriment of other perhaps less visible or less obvious but nonetheless relevant leads. This can be described in terms of confirmation bias, availability bias or anchoring bias. In many ways, investigators of major and serious crimes are fortunate in that they often have the benefit of time, when they can slow things down or 'put their foot on the ball', which allows them to make better, more informed decisions that can be justified and will hold future scrutiny (ACPO/Centrex, 2006, p 42). Adopting the principles of the investigative mindset, where decisions are made with balance and without bias, and when alternative theories or explanations are considered, will support effective decision making.

POLICING SPOTLIGHT

Between 2014 and 2016, Operation Midland was established by the Metropolitan Police Service to investigate allegations of historic serious sexual abuse made by Carl Beech against prominent individuals, including senior politicians, military officers and heads of the security services. For the purposes of anonymity, Carl Beech was given the pseudonym 'Nick'. During the investigation, the names of those involved were released into the media, and senior investigators publicly announced how they 'believed' the allegations without having tested them against other material that may have undermined the credibility of the evidence. As the case developed, the allegations were found to be false, and Carl Beech was later convicted of perverting the course of justice.

In 2016, the investigation was reviewed by former High Court Judge Sir Richard Henriques, who, in his report An Independent Review of the Metropolitan Police Service's Handling of Non-Recent Sexual Offence Investigations Alleged Against Persons of Public Prominence (Henriques, 2016), strongly criticised the police approach, suggesting there was a lack of objectivity and impartiality, which resulted in a failure of being open-minded to alternative explanations. Going further, Henriques commented how a contributing factor was a report by the HMIC (2014, p 52) that encouraged the police service, when recording crime, to 'institutionalise' the presumption that victims should always be believed.

Summarising the issue, Sir Richard Henriques (2016, pp 23–24) suggested:

> The assumption [in this case] is one of guilt until the police have evidence to the contrary. This involves an artificial and imposed suspension of forensic analysis which creates three incremental and unacceptable consequences. Firstly, there is no investigation that challenges the complainant; secondly, therefore, the suspect is disbelieved; and, thirdly, and consequently, the burden of proof is shifted onto the suspect.

> Any process that imposes an artificial state of mind upon an investigator is, necessarily, a flawed process. An investigator, in any reputable system of justice, must be impartial. The imposed 'obligation to believe' removes that impartiality.

INVESTIGATIVE DECISION MAKING

The ability to make considered decisions that are underpinned by reasoned argument is a key element of investigative decision making. Complex and challenging decisions are inherently associated with the investigation of major and serious crime. While professional judgement has its place, poor judgement by investigating officers when making critical decisions is a key area of investigative weakness (Nicol et al, 2004). Flawed judgements relating to parameter setting, lines of enquiry, witness and suspect management, and forensic processing can contribute to poor decision making and result in potentially damaging consequences.

In some situations, there can be an absence of information, and investigators may need to make decisions based on 'intuition', a concept defined by Hogarth (2001) as a decision without reasoned argument or the application of a step-by-step logical process. Sometimes described as a 'gut feeling' or 'sixth sense', more experienced investigators may draw on their knowledge to make inferences about the nature of criminal events to help create hypotheses and generate lines of enquiry. The idea stems from the theory of 'heuristics', which explains how individuals contemplating uncertain decisions draw on their experience or 'learned' behaviour (Bernasco, Van-Gelder and Elffers, 1961). However, heuristics can be influenced by personal biases and lead to errors, which means there are risks associated with this approach. The introduction of a decision-making framework in the form of the National Decision Model (NDM) has helped to mitigate the risk of flawed investigative decisions.

EVIDENCE-BASED POLICING

In a controlled experiment, Wright (2013) examined the intuitive ability of investigators to make detailed inferences relating to homicide crime scenes. A participant group of 40 homicide detectives with an average of 18 years of investigative experience, 70 per cent of whom had experience in the role of SIO, were asked to group a series of crime scene photographs according to their similarities and differences. They were then asked to make inferences in terms of what had happened and how they would progress the investigation.

Results indicated that experience improved the ability to draw inferences from crime scenes. All participants followed a cycle of cognition where, to a greater or lesser degree, they were able to draw out the contextual information and generate hypotheses or plausible explanations regarding homicide type and make inferences about victim/offender relationship, offender behaviour, motive, and whether the offence was spontaneous or planned.

NATIONAL DECISION MODEL

The National Decision Model (NDM) features in many other books in this series, demonstrating its importance in all aspects of policing. Underpinned by a philosophy that risk-based decision making is a core responsibility for police officers, that harm can never be totally prevented, that risk-based decisions require judgement and balance, and that decisions should be judged on the quality of the decision rather than the outcome, in 2011, the Association of Chief Police Officers introduced the NDM, which was intended to help shape professional judgement and decision making in the operational policing environment (College of Policing, 2013a, 2014). With integrity and the notion of protecting the public at the heart of the NDM, there are six key elements:

1. *follow the Code of Ethics;*

2. *gather information and intelligence;*

3. *assess threat and risk and develop a working strategy;*

4. *consider powers and policy;*

5. *identify options and contingencies;*

6. *take action and review what happened.*

(College of Policing, 2013b, p 1)

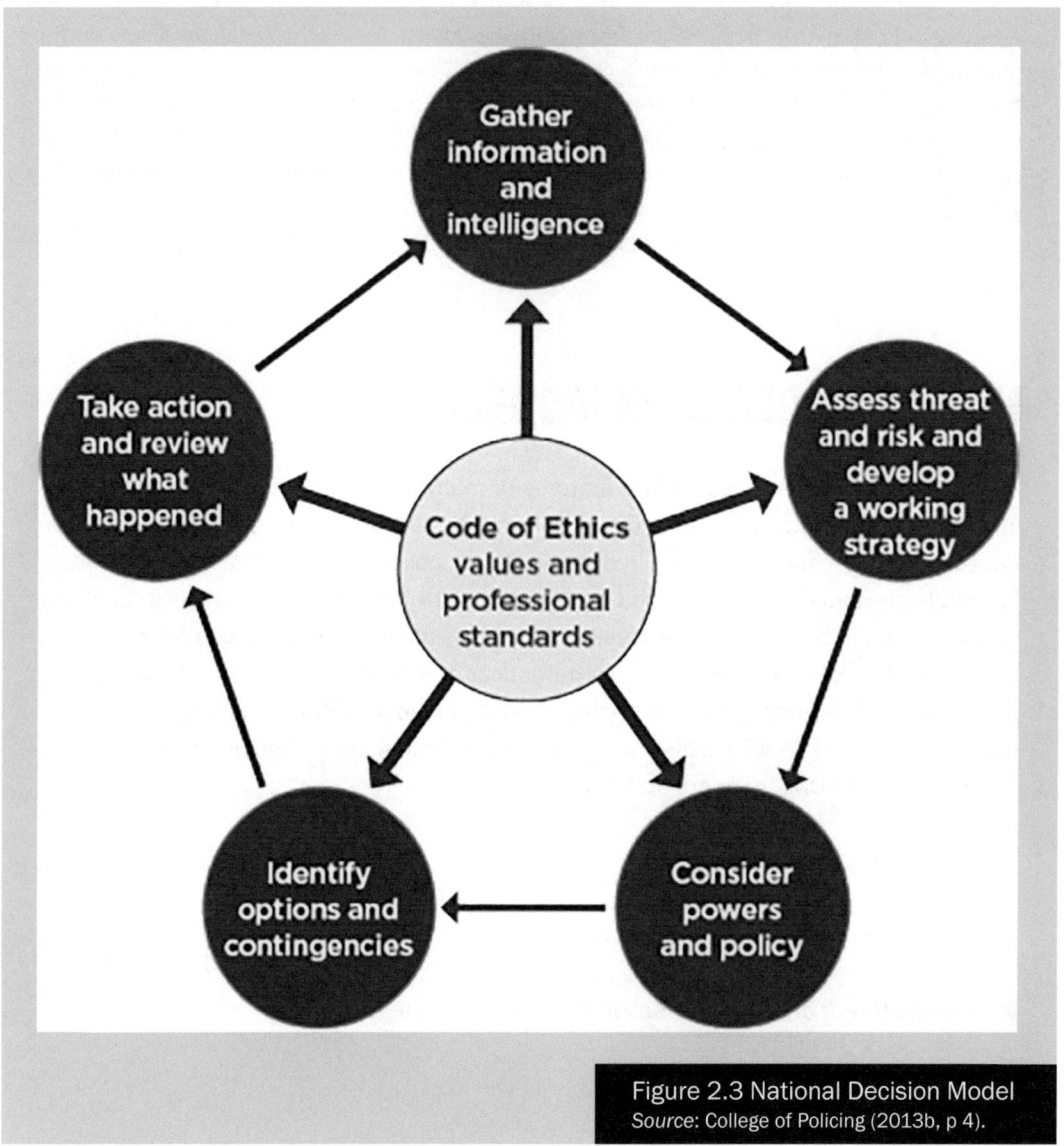

Figure 2.3 National Decision Model
Source: College of Policing (2013b, p 4).

FOLLOW THE CODE OF ETHICS

The fundamental principles of the NDM expect decision-makers to question whether their intended course of action is compliant with the Code of Ethics; whether those affected by the decision, such as the victim, their families or the community, would understand why the decision was made; whether the decision would reflect positively on policing; and whether the decision-maker could defend their actions publicly if the need arose (College of Policing, 2013a).

GATHER INFORMATION AND INTELLIGENCE

This element of the NDM requires the decision-maker to record what is known at the time the decision is made. This is important because the context in which the decision was made may change over time. Therefore, what is known, what is not known and what information may be needed to be better informed may influence the decision-making process.

ASSESSMENT OF THREAT AND RISK, AND DEVELOPING A WORKING STRATEGY

This element involves an assessment of threat, harm and risk to victims, members of the community and police officers who may be impacted by the decision. Questions to consider include the following.

- Is there a need for more information?

- What is the level of risk?

- Will action make the situation worse?

- Is the level of risk acceptable?

- Does the decision-maker have the appropriate knowledge and experience to deal with the situation?

In developing a 'working strategy', or a way forward, decision-makers should consider whether they need to take action immediately, whether they should defer a decision until more information is known, what more information may be readily available and the risks and consequences of their decision.

POWERS AND POLICY

This stage of the model requires decision-makers to consider the available powers and policies that will help manage the level of threat. This may include consideration of legislation, such as powers of stop and search, powers of entry and arrest; it may include local and national policies or guidelines. In some situations, the decision-maker may not follow local or national policies; however, when this happens, their decision would need to be fully justified.

OPTIONS AND CONTINGENCIES

This stage of the model focuses attention on the different ways in which the decision-maker can respond to the threat. Considerations will include the immediacy of the threat, the timescales involved, resource availability, the potential for escalation and whether any intended action is lawful, necessary and proportionate to the aims the decision-maker seeks to achieve. In these circumstances, there is a requirement to strike a balance between risk and reward; for example, decision-makers may decide to take positive action in the knowledge that their action may increase risk in one sense but reduce risk in another. This follows the principle of risk-based decisions, which accepts that risk can never be completely eliminated, but that consideration must be given to all parties affected by the decision.

TAKING ACTION AND REVIEWING WHAT HAPPENED

This element of the model has two stages; the first involves taking action, recording the reasons and justification for the action and monitoring the outcome. The second element requires some reflection on the outcome; if the situation has been resolved and the threat reduced, consider what worked well and which elements could have been improved. In the event the situation has not been resolved, repeat the NDM cycle and consider alternative responses.

The NDM and the principles of risk-based decision making provide the foundation for practitioners to make ethical decisions that stand scrutiny in the event they are challenged. The investigation of major and serious crime often requires decision-makers to carry significant risk and the model helps provide a framework and structure to the decision-making process. The ultimate aim is to improve the quality of decision making and protect communities from harm.

REFLECTIVE PRACTICE 2.2

LEVEL 5

Imagine you are the investigating officer in a serious assault contrary to section 18 of the Offences Against the Persons Act (1861). The complainant is currently in a critical condition at hospital and has been unable to make a formal statement. You have traced and interviewed several witnesses who have provided evidence that suggests the complainant was assaulted without provocation by an individual who is well-known to them. There are no concerns with the identification of the alleged offender. A weapon was used during the assault, and evidence suggests there is likely forensic evidence in the form of blood on the clothing of the perpetrator. Research on the alleged offender indicates there is a history of violence.

- Applying the NDM as an aid to your decision making, consider what, if any, action you would take.

Sample answers are provided at the end of this book.

POLICY FILES AND RECORD KEEPING

A key element of investigative decision making requires the decision-maker to record their rationale, or their reasons that demonstrate how and why they arrived at their decision. This is a crucial exercise if there is to be transparency in the investigative process. Key decisions such as the parameter setting for house-to-house and CCTV enquiries, reasonable lines of enquiry, victim and witness interviews, nomination of suspects, whether and when to arrest, forensic recovery and examination, and decisions to involve the media in the investigation need to be recorded. This is not limited to the investigation of major and serious crime because good practice would suggest all investigators should record how and why they made their decisions.

For major and serious crime, SIOs are expected to maintain a specific policy file, which is a written record of their decisions that influence and direct the investigation. Policy files are also required to comply with the Criminal Procedure and Investigations Act (CPIA, 1996), in that investigators are required to '*record, retain and reveal*' to the prosecutor any '*material*' that is relevant to the investigation (MoJ, 2015, p 4). In this case, each policy file would constitute '*material*' for the purposes of disclosure. (See Chapter 5 for more details on disclosure.)

Policy files should follow a chronological order and be written in a format that stands scrutiny in the event the integrity of the document is challenged, for example, in a paginated policy book or an electronic register that has a digital footprint. Policy files should include the name of the decision-maker, the nature of the decision, the time and date it was made, and importantly the rationale underpinning the decision. At the conclusion of the investigation, policy files should be stored with other case papers in a retrievable and accessible manner.

According to the National Police Chiefs' Council (NPCC, 2021a, pp 165–6), areas to consider the use of a policy file to record decisions include the following.

1. *'Instigation and initial response'* to an investigation, such as why the investigation has been initiated; strategies outlining the strategic aims and objectives; the structure of the investigative team; victim and witness management; fast-track actions; intelligence development; and crime scene management.

2. *'Enquiry management'*, including key roles such as the identity of the SIO and their deputy and other roles such as family liaison, exhibits, disclosure and CCTV officers.

3. *'Investigative strategies'*, such as the overarching aims of the family liaison officer, the aims of the disclosure officer, digital media, intelligence and how the media will be used to support the investigation.

4. *'Administration'* surrounding the investigation, such as the location of the major incident room, resource levels, financial implications and engagement with the CPS.

POLICING SPOTLIGHT

A typical policy file may look like this.

Policy file			
Victim/operation name: *A N Other/Operation Harkin*		Policy decision number	1
Decision:	*Initiate an investigation into the death of A N Other*		
Rationale:	*At xxxx hours on xxxxxxxx an anonymous call was received at the police control room to report a male deceased in a wooded area adjacent to the A561 between junctions 8 and 9 of the M35 motorway. This is a secluded area, which is only accessible on foot from the A561 approximately 300 metres from the scene.*		
	On arrival at the scene, response officers found the deceased, now identified as A N Other, with a significant head injury and evidence to suggest there had been a violent exchange. A blood-stained baseball bat was recovered near the deceased.		
	Initial research would indicate that A N Other is involved in serious and organised crime. Credible intelligence suggests they are in dispute with a rival organised crime group and their family have raised concerns for their safety.		

	The existing threat and the circumstances surrounding the death of A N Other would tend to indicate third party involvement. It is therefore necessary to initiate an investigation in order to ascertain whether a crime has been committed with a view to the possible institution of criminal proceedings. A major incident room has been established and key roles have been identified. Strategies and decisions designed to progress this investigation will follow.		
Officer making entry:	*Richard Carr*	Time and date:	xxxxxxxxx
Officer making decision:	*Richard Carr*	Time and date:	xxxxxxxxx

COVERT POLICY FILES

The investigation of major and serious crime will often generate sensitive material or involve the deployment of covert resources, such as surveillance operatives and covert human intelligence sources (CHIS). Therefore, a separate policy file should be used for recording covert strategies and decisions related to sensitive elements of the investigation. This will ensure appropriate management of material under the provisions of public interest immunity (PII) (see Chapter 5 for more details on PII).

Decisions relating to covert policing tactics, engagement with the European Convention on Human Rights and details that may expose the identification or involvement of a CHIS should be treated with care to avoid unnecessary disclosure.

DEVELOPING HYPOTHESES

Building on the discussions in Chapter 3 of the *Criminal Investigation* edition, during the initial stages of an investigation, there may be limited information from which to generate definitive lines of enquiry. In these circumstances, the SIO may need to use their experience to develop hypotheses or plausible explanations in terms of the circumstances surrounding the offence. This may require consideration of routine activity, relationships, associates, lifestyle, precursor incidents and victim vulnerability or exposure to harm. For example, in the policy file above, intelligence indicated the deceased was involved in serious and organised crime and was in dispute with a rival crime group. On this basis, a reasonable hypothesis would propose the death may in some way be connected to this dispute; therefore, it would be reasonable to generate lines of enquiry to either support or undermine this theory. The process of hypothesis development is not about speculation or guesswork; there is a subtle difference between the two. One involves considered thought and reasoned argument, the other involves casting a net and waiting to see what you catch.

When hypotheses are developed objectively, they can provide a strong foundation for investigative decision making; however, there are inherent risks, and SIOs should recognise the dangers of generating lines of enquiry to bridge gaps in knowledge. It is inevitable that SIOs will make wrong choices. Therefore the NPCC (2021a, pp 32–3) proposes ways that are designed to militate against errors in hypothesis development, such as:

- understanding of the relevance and reliability of material gathered;

- ensuring investigative and evidential evaluation has been applied to material;

- ensuring there is sufficient knowledge of the subject matter to interpret the material correctly;

- defining a clear objective for the hypothesis;

- developing hypotheses that reflect known material;

- consulting with colleagues and experts when formulating hypotheses;

- ensuring there are sufficient resources available to develop and test hypotheses;

- ensuring hypotheses development is proportionate to the seriousness of the offence.

CRITICAL THINKING ACTIVITY 2.2

LEVEL 6

As the SIO, you are asked to investigate an allegation of child abduction, contrary to section 1, Child Abduction Act (1984). Following a breakdown in their relationship, the natural parents of child A, who is six years old, have separated and are currently involved in a dispute over custody and access arrangements to their child. Interim arrangements have been agreed upon for child A to live with her mother while her father has access at weekends.

Child A fails to return home after an access visit with her father, and her mother reports her concerns to the police. Following the correct procedure, the matter is recorded as a crime for further investigation.

There is no additional information at this stage of the investigation to support your decision making, and you are required to develop hypotheses to generate lines of enquiry.

- What hypotheses might be developed in a case of this nature?

- What are the risks and opportunities associated with your decision making?

Sample answers are provided at the end of this book.

CONCLUSION

All crime has reduced significantly since the mid-1990s; however, recent escalations in offending categories associated with major and serious crime mean communities are exposed to an increased risk of harm. Crime such as murder, manslaughter, serious sexual offences and the criminal use of firearms cause significant harm to victims and wider communities, and there is a reasonable expectation that investigators involved in this field have the skills, qualities and expertise to solve these crimes when they occur and bring offenders to justice.

A diminishing trend in positive outcomes would tend to suggest that investigators are falling short in their capabilities to effectively investigate this area of criminality. This is reinforced by the HMICFRS (2022) in its review of serious acquisitive crime, which highlighted how initial responses to crime failed to meet levels of acceptability, how missed opportunities and failure to secure forensic evidence undermined the potential for positive outcomes and how excessive demands on resources mean there are failures to gather basic information from victims of crime. It is, therefore, more important than ever for everyone in the investigative process, from the call handler through to the senior investigating officer, to have a thorough understanding of the fundamental principles associated with investigation.

SUMMARY OF KEY CONCEPTS

This chapter has outlined the fundamental principles of investigation and how they are applied to major and serious crime; the chapter has considered investigative decision-making and how the concept of risk can never be completely eliminated from decisions associated with this area of criminality. This chapter concluded with a discussion on hypothesis development, which involves using experience and intuition to develop lines of enquiry that are supported by reasoned argument. The content of this chapter enables you to:

- describe the sequential process of investigations associated with major and serious crime;

- apply a variety of concepts, such as the investigative mindset, golden hour, ABC and the five building blocks principle, which help maximise efficiency and ensure appropriate scrutiny is placed on material gathered through the investigative process;

- recognise how risk can never be eliminated from investigative decision making, how the context in which decisions are made is important and how a methodical approach will minimise risk and allow you to be transparent in your decision-making process;

- evaluate how intuition and judgement, which may improve with experience, are important elements in the development of an investigation.

CHECK YOUR KNOWLEDGE

1. What are the three stages of investigative practice, as defined by Newburn, Williamson and Wright (2007)?

2. What are the five building blocks of investigation?

3. What does the golden hour mean in practice?

4. The National Decision Model (NDM) is intended to shape professional judgement and decision making in the operational policing environment. What are the six elements of the NDM cycle?

5. What does the term 'hypotheses development' mean for investigators?

FURTHER READING

Cook, T (2019) *Senior Investigating Officers' Handbook*, 5th edition. Oxford: Oxford University Press.
This book offers a detailed insight into the responsibilities associated with the role of the senior investigating officer, including key skills, leadership, victim, witness and suspect management and wider investigative practice.

Cook, T, Hibbitt, S and Hill, M (2016) *Crime Investigators' Handbook*, 2nd edition. Oxford: Oxford University Press.
This book provides the basic principles of a wide range of investigative techniques and crime scene management.

College of Policing (2013) Risk. [online] Available at: www.college.police.uk/app/risk/risk (accessed 22 October 2023).
Drawn from the official source of professional practice for policing, this text outlines the ten principles associated with risk-based decisions.

Wright, M (2013) Homicide Detectives' Intuition. *Journal of Investigative Psychology and Offender Profiling*, 10(2): 182–99.
This research develops the evidence base and illustrates how intuition and judgement used when making decisions can develop with experience.

CHAPTER 3
MANAGEMENT OF MAJOR AND SERIOUS CRIME

LEARNING OBJECTIVES

AFTER READING THIS CHAPTER YOU WILL BE ABLE TO:

- describe the concept of a major incident room (MIR) and explain the key roles and functions associated with an investigation into major and serious crime;

- understand how an investigation into major and serious crime develops;

- understand concepts of 'vulnerable' and 'intimidated' victims and witnesses and the facilities afforded by the criminal justice system (CJS) allowing witnesses to provide their 'best evidence';

- outline the challenges associated with reluctant and hostile witnesses and discuss the approach to witness protection;

- critically examine the impact on those involved in major and serious crime investigation.

INTRODUCTION

In May 1981, Sir Lawrence Byford was appointed to review the investigation into Peter Sutcliffe, who became known as the Yorkshire Ripper. Sutcliffe was responsible for the murder of 13 women and the attempted murder of seven others between 1975 and 1980 in the regions of Greater Manchester and West Yorkshire. The review identified serious errors of judgement, negligence and indifference by senior officers as well as other mistakes made by officers at all levels of the investigation. A series of recommendations to bring about change included the standardisation of major incident room (MIR) procedures and the computerisation of records across the policing landscape. This was a fundamental change for investigative practice, which also introduced the Home Office Large Major Enquiry System (Holmes), which computerised records and, as a result, provided swift and efficient access to information for personnel engaged in major and serious crime investigations.

The MIR is the hub of all major and serious crime investigations. It is the 'wheelhouse' that co-ordinates the investigative response by providing a structured and methodical approach to the management of material that flows into and out of the MIR. Activity within the MIR provides a balance between 'investigation management' and 'information management' (Innes, 2003, p 97), which is designed to support the senior investigating officer (SIO) or lead investigator in directing the course of an investigation. The MIR should support the management of resources; allow for timely and effective disclosure of investigation relevant material; identify investigative 'actions' to ensure all reasonable lines of enquiry are followed; and provide an audit trail of their progression and results (NPCC, 2021b).

This chapter describes the Major Incident Room Standardised Administrative Procedures (MIRSAP), which outline all operating procedures used during major and serious crime investigations. It considers some of the key roles used to deliver an effective and efficient MIR; it explores the strengths and limitations of Holmes and explains how investigations into major and serious crime are developed; and it critically evaluates the risks encountered when the role or 'status' of an individual changes during an investigation.

This chapter considers the value of early engagement with the Crown Prosecution Service (CPS) and explores the Code of Practice for Victims of Crime in England and Wales (MoJ, 2020a), which sets out entitlements victims and their families can expect as they navigate their way through the CJS. The concept of 'vulnerable' and 'intimidated' victims and witnesses, which are often a central feature of major and serious crime investigations, will be examined with close attention paid to 'special measures', which are support facilities designed to support vulnerable and intimidated witnesses.

This chapter closes with an examination of the challenges associated with reluctant and hostile witnesses, explores witness protection schemes and concludes with an examination of the impact on those who are tasked with investigations of this nature.

THE MAJOR INCIDENT ROOM (MIR)

According to the National Police Chiefs' Council (NPCC, 2021b), MIRSAP provides the police service with information and guidance on the standardised administrative procedures associated with an MIR. In principle, the MIR is the central repository for material gathered during an investigation (NPCC, 2021b). Material such as written statements or accounts provided by victims and witnesses, information provided by enquiry officers and members of the public, reports associated with crime scene examinations, details of exhibits and CCTV images, SIO policy decisions, and much more are recorded and retained for investigative reference and compliance with the Criminal Procedure and Investigations Act (CPIA, 1996).

The scale of an MIR should be proportionate to the needs of the investigation and can be scaled up or down depending on the nature of the case. In principle, key roles within the MIR should remain the same; however, when there are limitations on resources, there is scope for 'role combination'. In other words, investigators can perform more than one key role in the enquiry. There are risks to this and care should be taken to avoid 'role corruption' where conflict or periods of high intensity can undermine quality, therefore appropriate checks and governance processes should be in place to prevent this (NPCC, 2021b).

A typical structure of a major and serious crime investigation makes it clear the MIR plays a central role. The investigative cycle illustrates how information flows between the MIR and the SIO; investigative direction is provided; investigative actions are raised and allocated to outside enquiry teams; and results are collated. The cyclical process continues, and in theory, the case progresses.

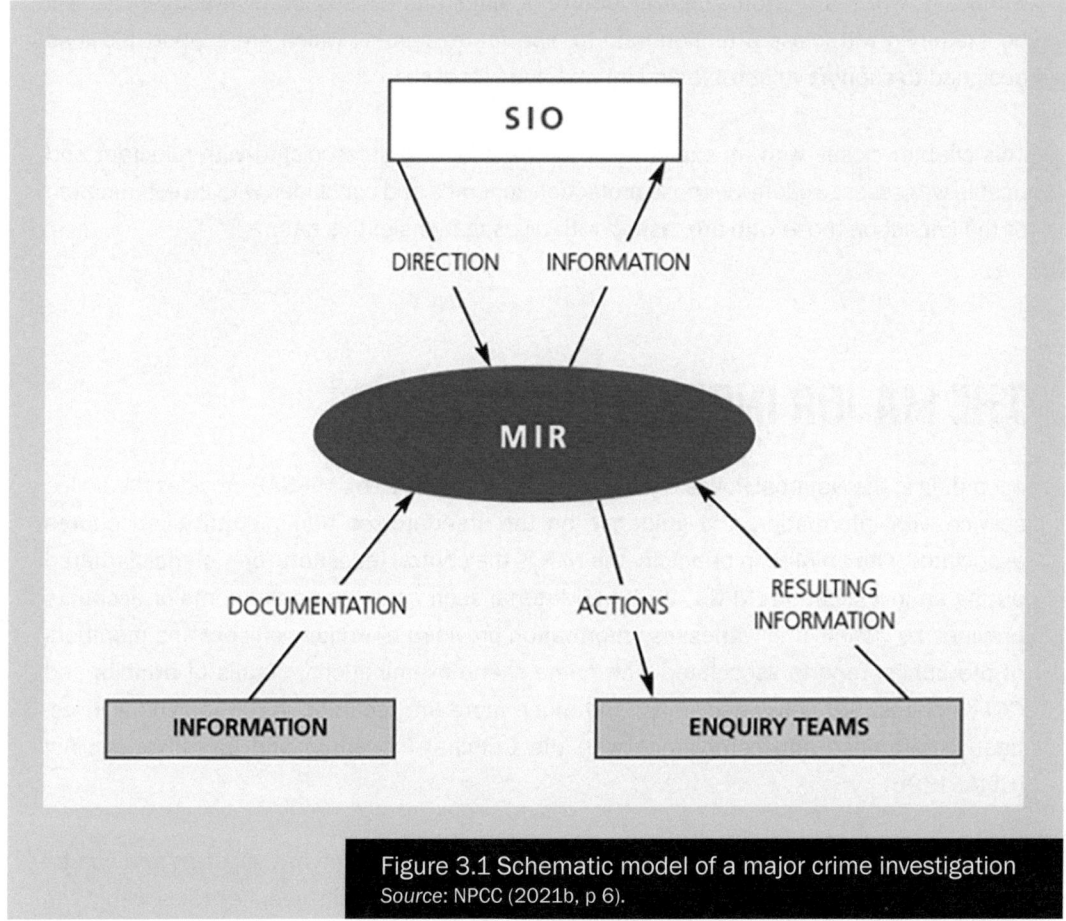

Figure 3.1 Schematic model of a major crime investigation
Source: NPCC (2021b, p 6).

In essence, the MIR allows the SIO to maintain an accurate record of material and delivers auditable functionality to manage the allocation and progression of investigative actions. Importantly, the MIR offers a facility through computerisation to retrospectively review an investigation or research individuals, vehicles, locations of interest and other material associated with the enquiry. This is particularly relevant with historic or extended investigations or when key personnel change.

KEY ROLES IN MAJOR AND SERIOUS CRIME INVESTIGATIONS

There are many roles drawn upon during a major and serious crime investigation, and a fully functional MIR relies on the skills and expertise of everyone involved (NPCC, 2021a, 2021b). Some roles involve leadership; some have a greater focus on the investigation itself, while others provide broader administrative support. The following are selected key roles that would generally form part of any MIR.

- The **senior investigating officer** (SIO) is the officer in overall command of the investigation. They are responsible for the investigation and setting strategic direction, implementing investigative methodology, setting lines of enquiry and making key decisions regarding case progression (Innes, 2003; Newburn, Williamson and Wright, 2007; Stelfox, 2009). Accredited to level 3 under the Professionalising Investigations Programme (PIP), the SIO carries ultimate accountability for the success or failure of the investigation.

- The **office manager** has delegated responsibility to direct and control the day-to-day running of the incident room. They have the responsibility to implement SIO decisions; monitor the progression of investigative actions and record outcomes; ensure administrative updates are indexed; and advise the SIO on operational demands against the sufficiency of resources.

- The **receiver** is responsible for receiving and reading all material entering the MIR to understand relevance and impact on the investigation. The receiver should be the first point of contact for new information; they have the responsibility to assess information and make decisions on case progression.

- The **action manager** has the responsibility to allocate investigative actions, monitor their return and review outstanding actions. They should work closely with the receiver and at times the roles may be combined as they can make decisions on case progression.

- The **disclosure officer** is an integral part of the investigation team. They carry a significant burden of responsibility to comply with the disclosure obligations as laid out by the CPIA (1996). Poor functionality in this role can lead to case failure or miscarriages of justice. (See Chapter 5 for more detail on disclosure.)

- The **exhibits officer** is expected to maintain a record of all items of property seized during an investigation and ensure each item is considered for its evidential value and investigative opportunities. They must ensure all exhibits are preserved in such a way that their integrity is assured, and records demonstrate effective continuity of transfer between investigators and forensic examiners.

- The **family liaison officer (FLO)** is used in a range of investigations, including murder, manslaughter, fatal road traffic collisions, mass fatalities and other critical incidents where the deployment of a FLO might enhance the police response (College of Policing, 2021a). The role requires the FLO to demonstrate a professional and compassionate persona towards victims' families, respecting their cultural beliefs as they bridge the gap between the family and the investigation.

Challenges associated with the role include the fact victims' families are likely in a time of crisis themselves; families may be estranged, which may frustrate channels of communication; there may be a suspect in the family; and there may be hostility towards the FLO and the investigative team. This means FLOs are susceptible to cognitive fatigue and, therefore, the SIO has a duty of care towards them and their selection should take account of the victims' family's cultural and ethnic background, training and experience, workload and resilience, family needs and scale and nature of the incident (ACPO/Centrex, 2006).

- The **outside enquiry team** are investigators responsible for the progression of investigative actions raised through the MIR. They are the ones operating 'in the field', interviewing victims and witnesses, tracing suspects, recovering CCTV, conducting house-to-house enquiries and developing lines of enquiry.

- The **media lead/officers** play an important role in major and serious crime investigations; they are responsible for managing the demands of the media and ensuring the communication strategy is delivered. This may include preparing media statements to generate leads, delivering messages of reassurance and facilitating interviews with the SIO or family members who are often used to appeal for information.

REFLECTIVE PRACTICE 3.1

LEVEL 4

The roles described here are just some of those used in major and serious crime investigations, and it takes the collective effort of many to deliver the investigative capacity and capability required to solve the most complex cases.

- Research the other roles involved and reflect on how they contribute; they can be found at: https://library.college.police.uk/docs/NPCC/MIRSAP_V1_Nov_2021.pdf

Sample answers are provided at the end of this book.

HOME OFFICE LARGE MAJOR ENQUIRY SYSTEM (HOLMES)

Following the requirement to computerise records to support the management of major crime investigations (Home Office, 1981), in 1986 Holmes was introduced, and now in its second iteration, Holmes 2 is routinely used by police forces across the United Kingdom (UK) and allows for the digital retention and retrieval of high-volume information gathered during the investigative process (Newburn, Williamson and Wright, 2007; Gooch and Williams, 2015). Employed during investigations into homicide, mass fatalities, acts of terrorism and more, Holmes 2 links across law enforcement agencies and provides functionality which makes the searching and recovery of information much easier and faster, meaning there is greater efficiency in the investigative process and reduced potential for missed opportunities. Storage and retention facilities provided by Holmes 2 mean unsolved cases can be revisited when new information comes to light; there is longevity in organisational memory, and it brings greater transparency to the investigative process.

While computerisation has brought benefits, there are limitations; Holmes 2 is like a 'super tanker'. In other words, it takes a while to get going; it is bureaucratic and very labour intensive. For this reason, not all major and serious crime investigations are managed by using a fully resourced MIR or Holmes 2. When circumstances allow, SIOs may decide to adopt the principles of an MIR but use local resources and an 'in force' incident management system (IMS) to record their actions and decision making. Lastly, despite the developments in artificial intelligence, Holmes 2 does not yet have the capability to 'think', it cannot analyse or interpret the evidence and it cannot make decisions; these require the skills and expertise of those leading the investigations.

CRITICAL THINKING ACTIVITY 3.1

LEVEL 5

You are the investigating officer into an offence of aggravated burglary, contrary to section 10, Theft Act (1968). Offenders forced entry into a residential property; armed with a firearm, they threatened the occupier before stealing jewellery to the value of £500,000. This offence is considered a serious crime by virtue of the fact that violence was used during the commission of the crime, the substantial financial gain for the offenders, and likely sentencing for those responsible. Research indicates similar offences have been committed in areas outside of your force boundary.

→

Consider your approach to this investigation and evaluate your response. When making your decisions, consider:

- whether you implement a full MIR managed through Holmes or manage the investigation using local resources and an 'in force' IMS;

- whether there is a requirement for all key roles to be nominated;

- the risks if the scale of the investigation escalates.

Sample answers are provided at the end of this book.

DEVELOPING THE INVESTIGATION

A successful prosecution relies on a careful search for evidence; it is a search for the truth, and the police have a duty to fairly and thoroughly progress all reasonable lines of enquiry, even if the evidence exonerates the suspect (Runciman, 1993; CPIA, 1996) (see Chapter 6 of the *Police Procedure and Evidence in the Criminal Justice System* title in this series). To reach this objective, investigators are expected to identify and progress a series of *actions* or in the event of urgency, *fast-track actions* to develop the case. The terms *actions* and *fast-track actions* are frequently used in major and serious crime investigations and are defined in the Murder Investigation Manual as follows.

- Actions: '*any activity which, if pursued, is likely to establish significant facts, preserve material or lead to the resolution of the investigation*' (ACPO/Centrex, 2005, p 77).

- Fast-track actions: '*any investigative actions which, if pursued immediately, are likely to establish important facts, preserve evidence or lead to the early resolution of the investigation*' (ACPO/Centrex, 2006, p 51).

During the early stages of an investigation, actions and fast-track actions are likely to fall within the same definition because any action during this period will likely establish important facts that will progress the enquiry. Many actions during this period may constitute a general trawl for information because details about the offence and those responsible may be unclear in the early stages. According to the NPCC (2021a, p 27) actions/ fast-track actions may include:

- *identifying suspects;*

- *witness search and assessment;*

- *crime scene identification and assessment;*

- *safeguarding actions;*

- *scene forensics, including where appropriate post-mortems;*

- *victim enquiries including possible motives;*

- *intelligence opportunities;*

- *CCTV opportunities;*

- *passive data and digital media opportunities;*

- *initial house-to-house (HTOH) enquiries;*

- *media opportunities.*

As an investigation develops, 'main lines of enquiry' may become apparent; these are described by ACPO/Centrex (2005, p 60) as lines of enquiry that 'appear to have the potential to lead to the suspect', and therefore they are given a higher priority than others. They may be 'evidence specific' and include tracing a named suspect; identifying and locating potential witnesses who need interviewing; or pursuing significant information that requires further investigation.

REFLECTIVE PRACTICE 3.2

LEVEL 5

You are a detective called to the scene of a robbery, contrary to section 8(1) of the Theft Act (1968). When you arrive at the scene, you are informed that the offender threatened the victim with a knife before stealing a bag containing money, a mobile telephone and other personal possessions. The offence was committed at a shopping centre on a busy Saturday afternoon.

- Apply your response to this offence and decide what initial or fast-track actions you would implement to generate lines of enquiry that may identify the offender.

Sample answers are provided at the end of this book.

TRANSITION FROM WITNESS TO SUSPECT

The priority should always be to identify the suspect and, at times during an investigation, a *nominal*, which is a term used to describe an individual who in some way features in an investigation, may transition between witness and suspect. The *nominal* may be known or unknown; they may be a victim, witness, suspect, offender or someone unidentified who may have witnessed the crime.

Either way, they will hold a *nominal record* which categorises their role or *status* in the investigation. The nominal record should contain personal information such as name, address and date of birth if they are known and other descriptive text that may help with the identification of unknown witnesses.

The status of a nominal within an investigation must be clear as this may determine how they are treated if they are interviewed in connection with the case. In some circumstances, it may be appropriate to afford them the protections provided under the Police and Criminal Evidence Act (PACE, 1984). According to PACE (1984), Code C paragraph 10.1, a caution must be given to a person before they are asked questions about an offence if there are grounds to suspect them of committing an offence. This makes it clear that when a suspect is identified before they are interviewed about the offence, they must be cautioned. There are times, however, when there is less clarity about an individual's role in the offence. In these circumstances, a distinction needs to be drawn between whether they are a *suspect* or a *person of interest*, which is someone who may be the offender but there is insufficient evidence for them to be formally nominated as a suspect. This is an important distinction to make because it will determine whether the individual is cautioned before an interview takes place.

In the event the SIO decides further enquiries are needed to determine a person's status in an investigation, an action may be raised to 'trace, interview, evaluate' (TIE) a person of interest (NPCC, 2021a, p 128). Interestingly, the choice of words associated with the term TIE fluctuates; sometimes referred to as 'trace, interview, eliminate' (NPCC, 2021a, p 128) or 'trace, implicate, eliminate' (College of Policing, 2013c, p 1) but essentially, they mean further enquires are considered necessary to confirm an individual's status in the offence.

POLICING SPOTLIGHT

There is a delicate balance when making decisions to treat an individual as a *suspect* or a *person of interest*, and careful thought needs to be applied because flawed decision-making may risk important evidence being excluded from a prosecution case. This was tested in the case of *Shillibier v R* (2006).

During the investigation, the SIO nominated Shillibier as a person of interest and interviewed him as a nominal subject to TIE. During the interview, incriminating evidence was disclosed, which was later used as part of the prosecution case.

An appeal against conviction suggested Shillibier should have been treated as a suspect and cautioned in accordance with PACE (1984) Code C paragraph 10.1. It was argued the evidence gathered should have been excluded from trial in accordance with section 78, PACE (1984), on the basis that the admission of the evidence had an adverse effect on the fairness of proceedings. Lord Justice Richards held there was insufficient evidence to treat Shillibier as a suspect and confirmed the SIO acted lawfully in categorising Shillibier as a TIE nominal.

The NPCC (2021a, p 130) summarises this by saying: '*The test is simple; are there reasonable grounds to suspect the individual committed the offence? If not, then the use of TIE is a legitimate and lawful tactic.*'

For more information, see *Shillibier v R* (2006).

EARLY INVOLVEMENT WITH THE CROWN PROSECUTION SERVICE

The Crown Prosecution Service (CPS), as the prosecuting authority in England and Wales, plays an important role in the conduct of criminal investigations and prosecutions. The CPS's duty is to ensure the right person is prosecuted for the right offence and to bring offenders to justice. The CPS decides which cases should be prosecuted, determines the appropriate charges in more serious and complex cases, and can advise police during the early stages of investigations. Equally, the CPS has the responsibility to prepare cases and present them in court, as well as to provide information and support to victims and witnesses through the judicial process.

The Code for Crown Prosecutors (CPS, 2018a) encourages prosecutors to advise police investigators about evidential requirements, pre-charge procedures, disclosure management and overall strategy, including suggesting reasonable lines of inquiry. This advice can include decisions to develop or refine the scope of the investigation, which may aid the police in completing the investigation within a reasonable period and build the most effective case.

The Director of Public Prosecutions (DPP) Guidance on Charging (CPS, 2020a) stated that consultations should take place between police and prosecutors and will take place in the most serious, sensitive and complex cases, including:

- all cases involving a death;

- rape and serious sexual offences;

- child abuse;

- large-scale or long-term fraud;

- cases with substantial or complex visual, audio or other key evidence;

- cases expected to take substantially longer than 90 minutes in consultation.

There are advantages to investigators through early engagement with the CPS, particularly in complex or serious crime investigations. Examples of this include investigations which raise issues involving:

- cross-border challenges including securing evidence from outside the UK or extradition;

- confiscation and money laundering;

- disclosure and the acquisition of digital material;

- covert investigations;

- witness status and anonymity.

The College of Policing recognises the importance of early engagement with the CPS and much Authorised Professional Practice (APP) contains guidance on the advantages of early engagement with the CPS.

While it is not the role of the CPS to direct the police on their investigation, early engagement with the prosecutor will ensure they are best placed to make charging decisions. By working together, effective strategies can be developed to build strong and robust cases.

REFLECTIVE PRACTICE 3.3

LEVEL 4

- Put yourself in the role of a crown prosecutor; from your perspective, consider the advantages of early engagement.

Sample answers are provided at the end of this book.

MANAGEMENT OF VULNERABLE OR INTIMIDATED VICTIMS AND WITNESSES

The CJS depends on witnesses who are willing to provide information to the police and to give evidence in court. However, for a variety of reasons, including stress, fear, intimidation, vulnerabilities or a lack of confidence in the CJS, some witnesses may be reluctant to engage with the police or the courts.

Supporting and encouraging victims and witnesses to engage with the CJS is therefore vital, including from the first contact they have with the police through to court proceedings.

The Code of Practice for Victims of Crime in England and Wales (MoJ, 2020a), referred to as 'the Code', sets out the services and minimum standards in 12 'rights' that victims of crime are entitled to receive, as shown in Table 3.1.

Table 3.1 Victims' rights

1	To be able to understand and be understood.
2	To have the details of the crime recorded without unjustified delay.
3	To be provided with information when reporting the crime.
4	To be referred to services that support victims and have services tailored to their needs.
5	To be provided with information about compensation.
6	To be provided with information about the investigation and prosecution.

$\longrightarrow$

(continued)

nake a Victim Personal Statement.

8   To be given information about the trial, the trial process and their role as a witness.

9   To be given information about the outcome of the case and any appeals.

10   To be paid expenses and to have property returned.

11   To be given information about the offender following a conviction.

12   To make a complaint about their rights not being met.

Source: MoJ (2020a, pp 1–2).

The Code defines a Victim (MoJ, 2020a, p 3) as:

- *a person who has suffered harm, including physical, mental or emotional harm or economic loss, which was directly caused by a criminal offence;*

- *a close relative (or nominated family spokesperson) of a person whose death was directly caused by a criminal offence.*

Additionally, rights under the Code can be extended to a person who is:

- *a parent or guardian of a victim if the victim is under 18; or*

- *a nominated family spokesperson if the victim has a mental impairment or has been so badly injured because of a criminal offence that they are unable to communicate or lacks the capacity to do so.*

The Code acknowledges that some victims who are considered vulnerable or intimidated are often victims of the most serious crimes (including a bereaved close relative) or have been persistently targeted and are more likely to require specialised assistance (some victims may fall into one or more of these categories). In those cases, the victim may be offered a referral to specialist support services.

Note: The Witness Charter (MoJ, 2013) contains similar rights given to witnesses to a crime.

REFLECTIVE PRACTICE 3.4

LEVEL 4

- Research the Code and identify who is entitled to enhanced rights.

Sample answers are provided at the end of this book.

SPECIAL MEASURES

Some witnesses may have difficulties attending court to give evidence due to their age, personal circumstances, fear of intimidation, or because of their individual needs. Where witnesses are vulnerable or intimidated, they may qualify for *special measures* under the Youth Justice and Criminal Evidence Act (YJCEA, 1999) to enhance the quality of their evidence and to allow them to give their best evidence in court. Special measures apply only to prosecution and defence witnesses but not to the defendant and are subject to the court's discretion.

Vulnerable and intimidated witnesses will be eligible for special measures, which are contained in sections 16–33 of the YJCEA (1999).

VULNERABLE WITNESSES

Section 16, YJCEA (1999) defines a vulnerable witness as:

- anyone under the age of 18;

- any witness whose quality of evidence is likely to be diminished because they:

  o   are suffering from a mental disorder as defined by section 1(2) of the Mental Health Act (1983); amended by section 1(2) of the Mental Health Act (2007);

  o   have a significant impairment of intelligence and social functioning; or

  o   have a physical disability or are suffering from a physical disorder.

It is, therefore, important that investigators and prosecutors should be aware of the possibility that a victim or witness may have a disability in order to allow an early application for special measures to be made.

INTIMIDATED WITNESSES

Section 17 of the YJCEA (1999) defines intimidated witnesses as those who are suffering from fear or distress in relation to testifying in the case. Complainants in certain sexual offences or certain offences involving the use of firearms or knives are automatically considered to be intimidated unless they choose to opt out.

Special measures are particularly important when considering cases of rape or other sexual offences due to the range of measures that are available and which may encourage victims of sexual offences to report those offences to the police and support a prosecution.

TYPES OF SPECIAL MEASURES

Special measures are available under sections 23–30 of the YJCEA (1999) and the court has discretion regarding which measures to grant, if it is satisfied the special measure or combination of measures is likely to enhance the quality of the evidence to be given. Among the special measures available are:

- screens;

- live links;

- evidence given in private;

- removal of wigs and gowns;

- pre-recorded evidence in chief;

- pre-recorded cross-examination/re-examination of a witness;

- examination by an intermediary;

- aids to communication.

There are other special measures available under the YJCEA (1999), which are intended to enable intimidated or vulnerable witnesses to give their best evidence, including:

- prohibiting a defendant charged with a sexual offence from personally cross-examining the complainant;

- prohibiting an unrepresented defendant from cross-examining child witnesses, complainants and certain classes of witnesses (for example, intimidated witnesses);

- prohibiting the publication of the name of a witness during the lifetime of the witness.

SEXUAL OFFENCES AND SPECIAL MEASURES

The End-to-End Rape Review (MoJ, 2021a) highlighted challenges associated with investigating and prosecuting rape cases.

> *The trauma of the crime and their subsequent experience leads many victims to disengage from the criminal justice process. Without the victim's engagement, prosecution and conviction is very difficult. But when cases are prosecuted, and victims stay engaged with their case, we see results: in 2019–20, 27% of rape defendants pled guilty, and we had an overall 69% conviction rate.*
>
> (MoJ, 2021a, p 5)

A number of special measures are of importance when investigating rape and other sexual offences. Complainants in rape and other sexual offences automatically fall within the definition of an intimidated witness. They are protected from being named unless they opt out, and the video of their interviews can be used as the evidence in chief (YJCEA, 1999, section 27). Section 28 of the YJCEA (1999) allows the cross-examination of complainants to be pre-recorded as well as any re-examination, meaning the complainant does not have to attend court itself. Additionally, section 41 of the YJCEA (1999) provides protection to complainants in proceedings for sexual offences by restricting evidence being given or questions being asked about previous sexual history.

In summary, the restrictions imposed through special measures are intended to act as a balance between the protection of the complainant and the right to a fair trial for the defendant.

EVIDENCE-BASED POLICING

The ethos behind special measures is to enhance the quality of evidence given by vulnerable and intimidated witnesses. An examination of special measures by Hamlyn et al (2004), where more than 1100 vulnerable and intimidated witnesses were interviewed, indicated reduced levels of anxiety and improved levels of satisfaction in the CJS. Similarly, research by Kebbell, O'Kelly and Gilchrist (2007) indicated that while victims of rape experienced a lack of consistency in the provision of special measures, they suggested special measures may reduce stress and help increase successful prosecutions.

There are, however, limitations – including a failure to recognise vulnerability, a lack of informed choice and poor-quality technology – which serve to create barriers to the effectiveness of special measures (Fairclough, 2020).

CRITICAL THINKING ACTIVITY 3.2

LEVEL 6

There is a consensus that special measures are effective in reducing a sense of anxiety and fear within vulnerable and intimidated witnesses; however, there are limitations.

* Using the available literature, critically evaluate the effectiveness of special measures.

Sample answers are provided at the end of this book.

RELUCTANT AND HOSTILE WITNESSES

Despite the existence of special measures, some potential witnesses may refuse to engage with investigators or are reluctant to testify, perhaps because of fear of reprisals or being identified as suspects or defendants. One possible opportunity is to consider applying for a Witness Anonymity Order (WAO) in cases where the witness has provided a statement.

The Coroners and Justice Act (CAJA, 2009) defines a WAO as an order requiring measures to be taken concerning court proceedings, which the court considers appropriate to ensure the witness's identity is not disclosed. The measures might include:

* withholding the witness's name;

* the use of a pseudonym;

* the use of screens;

* modification of the witness's voice;

* limiting or prohibiting questions that might identify the witness.

Investigators should advise the CPS of the need to apply for a WAO at the earliest opportunity; the CPS will then follow the Witness Protection and Anonymity guidance (CPS, 2022c).

Section 88 of the CAJA (2009) sets out the conditions that must be met before a WAO can be granted, including the following.

Condition A is that the proposed order is necessary—

(a) in order to protect the safety of the witness or another person or to prevent any serious damage to property, or

(b) in order to prevent real harm to the public interest (whether affecting the carrying on of any activities in the public interest or the safety of a person involved in carrying on such activities, or otherwise).

Condition B is that, having regard to all the circumstances, the effect of the proposed order would be consistent with the defendant receiving a fair trial.

Condition C is that the importance of the witness's testimony is such that in the interests of justice the witness ought to testify and—

(a) the witness would not testify if the proposed order were not made, or

(b) there would be real harm to the public interest if the witness were to testify without the proposed order being made.

In making any application, the prosecution must ensure they disclose any relevant information about the witness which would meet the test for disclosure under the CPIA (1996) (see Chapter 5).

WITNESS ANONYMITY

In certain circumstances, an application may be made by the police or the CPS for an Investigation Anonymity Order (IAO). An IAO is an order by the court which prevents, subject to certain exceptions, the disclosure of information that may identify the person named in the application as being someone who is or was able or willing to assist in the investigation. Such an order may provide reassurance to people who may have relevant information or evidence.

Section 78 limits the circumstances in which an IAO can be granted, including:

- offences of murder or manslaughter where a knife or firearm was used;

- when the person likely to have committed the offence was at least 11 but under 30 at the time of the offence;

- the person likely to have committed the offence is a member of a group which can be identified from the criminal activity they appear to engage in, and it appears the majority of the group are at least 11 and under 30;

- the person in respect of whom the order is sought has reasonable grounds to fear intimidation or harm if they are identified as able or willing to assist the investigation; and

- the person in respect of whom the order is sought can provide information that would assist the investigation and is more likely than not, as a consequence of making the order, to provide such information.

In some investigations, the police may be aware that a reluctant witness may be able to provide relevant evidence or exhibits but is refusing to assist. Consideration can be given to utilising the provisions in the Magistrates' Court Act (MCA, 1980) and the CPIA (1996), which allows a court to issue a witness summons or warrant in respect of a reluctant witness who is believed able to provide material evidence and it is in the interests of justice to require a reluctant witness to attend court to provide evidence.

There may also be the opportunity to use hearsay provisions contained in the Criminal Justice Act (CJA, 2003) in cases where a witness cannot attend court to give evidence. Hearsay is defined as a representation of fact or opinion made by a person, otherwise than in oral evidence in the proceedings in question, when tendered as evidence of any matter stated therein.

Section 114 of the CJA (2003) provides four circumstances in which hearsay evidence may be admissible in criminal proceedings.

1. The CJA (2003) or any other statutory provision makes it admissible.

2. It is covered by a common law exception.

3. All the parties to the proceedings agree it is admissible.

4. It is in the interests of justice to admit the evidence.

Section 116 of the CJA (2003) provides that where the witness is identified and is unable to attend court to give evidence for one of the following reasons, a statement made by the witness may be admissible.

- The witness is dead.

- The witness is unable to attend court because of their bodily or mental condition.

- The person is outside the UK and it is not practicable to secure their attendance.

- The person cannot be located although reasonable steps have been taken to find them.

- The person does not give (or does not continue to give) evidence through fear.

The court can only permit evidence where the person does not give evidence through fear when it is in the interests of justice to do so and the fear has not been provoked by the party seeking to adduce the evidence in question. The court must have regard to any relevant circumstances, including the statement's contents, the risk of unfairness and the availability of special measures. The Court of Appeal in *R v Riat* (2012) highlighted the need for the court to ensure that the evidence of fear was rigorously tested and that all the possibilities of the witness giving oral evidence were investigated.

It is therefore important for officers to ascertain why a witness is reluctant to give evidence and to record the reasons for the refusal as well as obtaining the details of the witness's account of the events.

POLICING SPOTLIGHT

The validity of evidence delivered under the provisions of a WAO was tested in the case of *R v Mayers and Others* (2008) and emphasised in *R v Donovan and Kafunda* (2012).

In the face of reluctant and hostile witnesses, in both cases the prosecution relied on evidence provided under a WAO, which allowed key witnesses to provide their evidence anonymously, meaning the defendants did not know and could not know the identity of their accusers, nor could they confront the witnesses who incriminated them.

Successful convictions followed. However, both cases attracted appeals on the basis that the defendants were denied a fair trial. In each case, the appeals were upheld, and convictions were quashed with the appeal courts affirming '*a witness anonymity order is to be regarded as a special measure of the last practicable resort*' (*R v Mayers and Others*, 2008, para 8).

WITNESS PROTECTION SCHEMES

Witnesses are vital to the functioning of the CJS and will often provide crucial testimony in criminal cases. Therefore, there may be the temptation for suspects or defendants to seek to intimidate witnesses to prevent them from giving evidence, which can undermine the justice system.

In the early 1990s, there was growing concern about the intimidation of witnesses and its impact in terms of undermining both '*public confidence in the criminal justice system and its effectiveness*' (Elliott, 1998, p 111). In some cases, the risk to a witness is so great that they may need to be relocated or change their identity. Witness protection schemes have an important role to play when there is a substantial risk to the safety of a witness. Witness protection is the means of providing protection measures for people involved in the criminal justice system who find themselves at risk of serious harm as a result of that involvement.

Witness protection is defined by the Serious Organised Crime and Police Act (SOCPA, 2005) and is generally directed to those persons who have provided crucial evidence and against whom there is a substantial threat. The definition in SOCPA (2005) does not preclude local forces from offering protection measures to witnesses and others who are at risk. There are considerable ramifications for individuals who participate in witness protection.

The UK Protected Persons Service (UKPPS) is a national service with a regional footprint which serves the National Crime Agency (NCA), national policing and other bodies. The UKPPS works closely with the Metropolitan Police Service, Police Scotland and the Police Service in Northern Ireland and provides protection to those who are judged to be at serious risk of harm where the protection arrangements required by the individual are not available to the local police force. Protection is bespoke and will depend on the threat level to the individual.

THE IMPACT ON THOSE INVOLVED IN THE INVESTIGATIVE PROCESS

It is well documented that policing as a profession exposes officers and staff to trauma in ways the general population may find difficult to understand (Velazquez and Hernandez, 2019). This, however, is not unique to policing; lawyers and other legal professionals are also exposed to similar organisational and environmental factors (Léonard, Saumier and Brunet, 2020; Léonard et al, 2021). This means there are increased risks to police and criminal justice professionals in developing trauma-related mental health disorders, such as post-traumatic stress disorder (PTSD) and depression, when compared to the wider population (Brewin et al, 2022; Bell, Palmer-Conn and Kealey, 2022). While there is now more openness towards mental health, there remains a stigma associated with disclosing mental health problems, which is a barrier to gaining access to mental health care (Velazquez and Hernandez, 2019; Bell, Palmer-Conn and Kealey, 2022).

The investigation of major and serious crime requires those involved to work under pressure for extended periods, most likely during the early stages of the investigation or during the arrest and interview phases of the enquiry. Equally, pressure may be exacerbated during high-profile cases that attract the media's attention and intense public scrutiny. The NPCC (2021a) is clear that the SIO has a duty of care towards the resilience and well-being of the whole investigation team to ensure there are no adverse effects on the mental health of themselves and their wider team.

EVIDENCE-BASED POLICING

Much research associated with mental health in policing relates to officers engaged on the front line, who are directly exposed to traumatic situations. MacEachern et al (2019, p 174) examined the concept of 'secondary traumatic stress' (STS), also known as 'compassion fatigue', affecting detective officers who are indirectly exposed to traumatic events. Defined by Bride and Kintzle (2011, p 22),

> STS refers to the occurrence of posttraumatic stress symptoms following indirect exposure to traumatic events. The indirect exposure typically occurs via a close personal or professional relationship with one or more traumatized persons who recount, often repetitively, the traumatic experience.

Using a self-completion questionnaire containing both qualitative and quantitative elements, MacEachern et al (2019) explored the experience of STS in detective officers engaged in major and serious crime investigations. Results indicated that all participants recognised their role exposed them to some form of trauma, and more than half (51 per cent) experienced some symptoms of STS, such as sleeping difficulties, emotional response to work and burnout.

CONCLUSION

This chapter has explored the concept of the MIR and examined some of the key roles required to service major and serious crime investigations. Effectiveness is dependent on organisation, structure, expertise and the collective effort of all involved. The introduction of MIRSAP, the MIR and Holmes offer much of the organisation and structure, while investigators, prosecuting lawyers and other legal professionals provide the expertise required to manage investigations of this nature.

Major and serious crime investigations are rewarding, but they vicariously expose those involved to traumatic events, which, if not careful, can lead to post-traumatic stress disorders and other mental health conditions. This, however, is not limited to investigators, lawyers and legal professionals; victims and witnesses are also exposed to trauma, meaning they can suffer with a sense of fear, anxiety and intimidation. Facilities and legislation designed to encourage and support vulnerable and intimidated victims and witnesses through the CJS have their challenges but on the whole, they are effective and are a measure that should be familiar to those who are involved in investigations of this nature.

SUMMARY OF KEY CONCEPTS

This chapter has considered the concept of an MIR and explored some of the fundamental challenges associated with case management. The contents of this chapter have allowed you to:

⚙ understand the structure and processes applied to the formulation of a MIR and the key roles that serve to administer the management and development of an investigation;

⚙ consider the difference between *actions* and *fast-track actions* and apply this terminology to the development of an investigation;

⚙ critically evaluate the concept of 'trace, interview, eliminate' and in particular the challenges this may bring to the decision-making process when making decisions to treat individuals involved as victims, witnesses, persons of interest or suspects;

⚙ apply policy and legislation associated with victim and witness management, which are designed to enable vulnerable and intimidated witnesses to deliver their 'best evidence';

⚙ understand the impact on police, lawyers and other criminal justice professionals who are concerned with the investigation of major and serious crime.

CHECK YOUR KNOWLEDGE

1. What is the role and function of a major incident room?

2. What are *fast-track actions*?

3. What are the advantages of early engagement with the CPS?

4. What special measures are available in criminal cases?

5. What provisions are available when dealing with reluctant witnesses?

6. What are the barriers faced by police officers and investigators in reporting mental ill health?

FURTHER READING

Bell, S, Palmer-Conn, S and Kealey, N (2022) 'Swinging the Lead and Working the Head': An Explanation as to Why Mental Illness Stigma is Prevalent in Policing. *The Police Journal*, 95(1): 4–23.
This article examines the challenges associated with police officer disclosure of mental ill health.

Fairclough, S (2020) Special Measures Literature Review. [online] Available at: https://cloud-platform-e218f50a4812967ba1215eaecede923f.s3.amazonaws.com/uploads/sites/6/2021/12/OVC-Special-Measures-Literature-Review-July-2020.pdf (accessed 22 October 2023).
This is a comprehensive review of literature, which provides a consolidated picture of the effectiveness of special measures, introduced under the YJCEA (1999). Designed to support vulnerable and intimidated witnesses and enhance the quality of their evidence during the judicial process, this literature review examines the strengths and limitations of each of the available special measures.

National Police Chiefs' Council (NPCC) (2021) Major Incident Room Standardised Administrative Procedures (MIRSAP 2021). [online] Available at: https://library.college.police.uk/docs/NPCC/MIRSAP_V1_Nov_2021.pdf (accessed 22 October 2023).
A record of all key roles associated with an MIR are outlined within the manual of guidance.

CHAPTER 4
ROLES AND RESPONSIBILITIES OF THE CROWN PROSECUTION SERVICE

LEARNING OBJECTIVES

AFTER READING THIS CHAPTER YOU WILL BE ABLE TO:

⚙ understand the history and development of the Crown Prosecution Service (CPS);

⚙ outline the principles that underpin the charging decisions made by the CPS;

⚙ recognise the advantages of engagement with the CPS, including pre-charge engagement;

⚙ understand pre-trial and trial preparation;

⚙ understand case management, including the acceptance of pleas.

INTRODUCTION

The Crown Prosecution Service (CPS) was established in 1986 following the Report of the Royal Commission on Criminal Procedure (RCCP) (HM Government and Philips, 1981), which led to two major pieces of legislation: the Police and Criminal Evidence Act (PACE, 1984) and the Prosecution of Offences Act (POA, 1985).

Part II of the RCCP Report (HM Government, 1981) focused on the prosecution of offenders, examining the arrangements that existed in England and Wales, and went on to make a series of recommendations about how prosecutions should be handled. Save for a limited number of cases that were dealt with by the office of the Director of Public Prosecutions (DPP), the vast majority of criminal prosecutions were prosecuted by the police and were essentially local to each of the 43 police forces, with the arrangements largely at the discretion and control of local chief constables.

The majority of forces had prosecuting solicitors' departments, which employed lawyers directly to act on behalf of the police, advising on prosecution decisions and presenting cases in court on which the police had decided to proceed. However, some forces employed local firms of solicitors from private practice to advise and act for them. The relationship between the chief constable and the prosecuting solicitor was one of client and solicitor. The solicitor acted on the instructions of the police; the solicitor could advise the police, but they were not bound to accept the advice.

Research conducted by the RCCP identified that in 1978, 19 per cent of all acquittals in the Crown Court were ordered by the judge because there were problems with the prosecution case and the Crown offered no evidence, and in 24 per cent of the cases, the judge directed the jury to acquit after the prosecution had called evidence. Thus 43 per cent of the cases failed because the prosecution was unable to establish a prima facie case. This is a significant proportion of cases that reached the Crown Court and failed to even reach the stage of a jury being asked to consider a verdict. In the magistrates' courts, 50 per cent of defendants were acquitted (HM Government, 1981, p 130). The research highlighted by the RCCP also identified that in about 20 per cent of cases, an acquittal should have been identified in advance of the trial (HM Government, 1981, p 131). The RCCP considered a number of related issues about prosecutions, including the theoretical principles that related to prosecutions, including the question of fairness. The RCCP analysis confirmed that:

> The proper objective of a fair prosecution system is not therefore simply to prosecute the guilty and avoid prosecuting the innocent. It is rather to ensure that prosecutions are initiated only in those cases in which there is adequate evidence and where prosecution is justified in the public interest. This requires a high

standard of competence, impartiality, and integrity in those who operate the system. The guilty should not escape prosecution nor the innocent be prosecuted because those who make the decisions or collect the necessary evidence, upon which the decisions can be made are inefficient or are motivated, by sectional political, social, or economic interests, or are corrupt. That is essential to public confidence in the system.

(HM Government, 1981, p 128)

The RCCP concluded that there should be a separation of the investigator's and lawyer's roles. It can be suggested that it is unsatisfactory for the person responsible for the decision to prosecute to be the person who has carried out or been concerned in the investigation (HM Government, 1981).

The RCCP (HM Government, 1981) recommended that:

- there should be a legally based prosecution service to cover every police force;

- it should be structured in such a way as to recognise the importance of independent legal expertise in the decision to prosecute and to make the conduct of prosecution the responsibility of someone who is both legally qualified and not identified with the investigative process;

- the service should be locally based.

CROWN PROSECUTION SERVICE (CPS)

Following the RCCP report, the government accepted the recommendation to create an independent prosecution service for England and Wales. However, it was decided that it would be a national organisation, although it would be locally based.

The Prosecution of Offences Act (POA, 1985) created the CPS, which is headed by the DPP. The CPS is superintended by the Attorney General, who is accountable to Parliament.

The police retained the power to charge suspects, but once a case had been charged, the CPS took over responsibility for all aspects of the prosecution. In 2001 Lord Justice Auld produced a Review of the Criminal Courts in England and Wales (MoJ, 2021b), which led to the government enacting the Criminal Justice Act (2003), which gave the CPS the power to charge offences other than offences which the police were allowed to continue to charge (CPS, 2020a). CPS lawyers were then deployed to work in police stations where they would advise operational officers and make charging decisions. Following austerity cuts, CPS lawyers were withdrawn from deployment to police stations but continue to make charging decisions.

The CPS consists of 14 geographical areas plus CPS Direct (which is the out-of-hours service that provides out-of-hours charging decisions and supports the geographical areas in charging) each of which is headed by a Chief Crown Prosecutor (CCP), Central Casework Divisions and Proceeds of Crime and various Headquarters Directorates. The CPS employs 7000 staff, including 2800 lawyers (CPS, 2023). The vision of the CPS is to become 'a leading voice in transforming the criminal justice system, using our expertise and digital capability to make the public safer and build the confidence of our diverse communities' (CPS, 2023).

Table 4.1 CPS structure

CPS Geographical Areas and CPS Direct		
• Cymru/Wales	• Mersey–Cheshire	• Thames and Chiltern
• East of England	• North East	• Wessex
• East Midlands	• North West	• West Midlands
• London North	• South East	• Yorkshire and Humberside
• London South	• South West	• CPS Direct

Central Casework Divisions and Serious Economic, Organised Crime and International Directorate	
• International Justice and Organised Crime Division	• Special Crime and Counter Terrorism Division
• Specialist Fraud Division	• Serious Economic, Organised Crime and International Directorate
• Proceeds of Crime	

Headquarters Directorates

The CPS is independent and makes its decisions independently of the police or the government. Prosecutors must be fair and objective. The CPS (2018a):

• decides which cases should be prosecuted;

• determines the appropriate charges in more serious or complex cases and advises the police during the early stages of investigations;

- prepares cases and presents them in court; and

- provides information, assistance and support to victims and prosecution witnesses.

REFLECTIVE PRACTICE 4.1

LEVEL 4

- Research the CPS website and identify which of the CPS areas covers your police area and establish who is the CCP for your area.

Sample answers are provided at the end of this book.

CODE FOR CROWN PROSECUTORS

In making their charging decisions on cases, prosecutors will follow the Code for Crown Prosecutors (CPS, 2018a) referred to as 'the Code' from here on in. It is important to remember that it is not the role of the CPS to decide whether a person is guilty of a criminal offence but to make assessments on whether there is sufficient evidence to prosecute the offender and whether it is in the public interest to prosecute. The aim is to ensure that the right person is charged for the right offence and to bring offenders to justice (CPS, 2018a).

In more serious or complex cases, prosecutors will decide whether a person should be charged and will decide on the appropriate offence(s). Decisions will be based on the Code, the DPP's Guidance on Charging (CPS, 2020a) and any relevant legal guidance or policy. Police decision-makers (PDMs) follow the same principles when making their decisions on whether to prosecute.

Prosecutors should advise the police about possible reasonable lines of inquiry, evidential requirements, pre-charge procedures, disclosure management and overall strategy (CPS, 2018a, 3.2). This can include decisions to refine or narrow the scope of the investigation or the number of suspects under investigation. Such advice assists the police in completing the investigation within a reasonable period and building the most effective prosecution case (CPS, 2018a, 3.4).

Once a case is received by the CPS, the prosecutor will apply the Full Code Test when:

- *all outstanding reasonable lines of inquiry have been pursued; or*

- *prior to the investigation being completed, if the prosecutor is satisfied that any evidence of further material is unlikely to affect the application of the Full Code Test.*

(CPS, 2018a, 4.3)

The Criminal Procedure and Investigations Act (CPIA, 1996) requires investigators to pursue all reasonable lines of inquiry, whether they point towards or away from the guilt of an offender. Prosecutors should advise investigators of reasonable lines of inquiry to follow. However, if the further line of inquiry would be unlikely to impact on whether the prosecutor is satisfied that the Full Code Test is met, then the prosecutor can make a charging decision before any further lines of inquiry are completed.

Prosecutors should not start or continue with prosecution if their view is that it is highly likely that a court will rule that the case is an abuse of its process and stay the proceedings (CPS, 2018a, 3.5).

Review is a continuing process, and the prosecutor will keep the case under review throughout the lifetime of the case.

The Full Code consists of two stages:

1. the evidential stage;

2. the public interest stage.

THE EVIDENTIAL STAGE

Prosecutors must be satisfied that there is sufficient evidence to provide a realistic prospect of a conviction against each suspect on each charge. A realistic prospect of a conviction is an objective test and means that a jury or magistrates court, properly directed, is more likely than not to convict. In reaching that decision, the prosecutor will consider a number of questions, including:

Can the evidence be used in court?
Prosecutors should consider whether there is any question over the admissibility of certain evidence. In doing so, prosecutors should assess:

- *the likelihood of that evidence being held as inadmissible by the court; and*

- *the importance of that evidence in relation to the evidence as a whole.*

Is the evidence reliable?
Prosecutors should consider whether there are any reasons to question the reliability of the evidence, including its accuracy or integrity.

Is the evidence credible?
Prosecutors should consider whether there are any reasons to doubt the credibility of the evidence.

Is there any other material that might affect the sufficiency of evidence?
Prosecutors must consider at this stage and throughout the case whether there is any material that may affect the assessment of the sufficiency of evidence, including examined and unexamined material in the possession of the police, and material that may be obtained through further reasonable lines of inquiry.

(CPS, 2018a, 4.8)

The prosecutor will also consider any explanation the suspect gave in deciding whether the evidential stage of the Code has been met. Only if the evidential stage is met will the prosecutor go on to consider the public interest stage of the Code.

THE PUBLIC INTEREST STAGE

Not all offences require there to be a prosecution. Officers have discretion on whether they should arrest a person, and equally prosecutors have discretion on whether a particular case requires there to be a prosecution. When prosecutors are considering the public interest, they will consider the factors identified in the Code (CPS, 2018a, 4.14).

- **How serious is the offence committed?**

  Clearly, the more serious the offence, the more likely it is a prosecution will follow. Prosecutors will also consider the suspect's culpability and the harm caused.

- **What was the level of culpability of the offender?**

  Among the factors the prosecutor will consider are the level of involvement, the extent to which the offending was pre-planned or premeditated, what was the benefit obtained by the suspect, the previous criminal record of the suspect, whether the offending is likely to continue or to escalate, and the suspect's age. A suspect may have a much lower level of culpability if they have been coerced, compelled or exploited, particularly if they are a victim of a crime that is linked to their offending. The prosecutor will also consider whether the suspect is or was at the time of the offending suffering from mental or physical ill health or disability.

- **What are the circumstances of the harm caused to the victim?**

The more vulnerable the victim's situation, or the greater the perceived vulnerability of the victim, the more likely a prosecution is required. This includes where a position of trust or authority exists between the victim and suspect, or where the victim is serving the public. Cases which involve an element of prejudice are more likely to require a prosecution.

Prosecutors will also consider any adverse impact a prosecution may have on the victim's physical or mental health, while always taking account of the seriousness of the offence, the availability of special measures and the possibility of continuing the case without the participation of the victim. The prosecutor will also consider any views expressed by the victim, but the prosecutor will reach a decision based on an overall view of the public interest.

- **What was the suspect's age and maturity at the time of the offence?**

A prosecutor will consider the age of the suspect and take account of the principal aim of the youth justice system, which is to prevent offending by children and young people. The CPS will also consider the best interests of the child or young person. The younger the suspect, the less likely it is that a prosecution is required; however, the public interest may require a prosecution where the offence committed is serious, the suspect's past record suggests that there is no alternative to prosecution, and the absence of an admission means that out-of-court disposals are not available.

- **What is the impact on the community?**

The greater the impact of the offending, the more likely it is that prosecution is appropriate. Evidence of the impact on the community may be obtained by way of a community impact statement.

- **Is a prosecution a proportionate response to the offending?**

The prosecutor will consider the cost to the CPS and the wider CJS and whether it is proportionate to prosecute the suspect and will consider the likely penalty to be imposed by a court. Public interest will never be solely determined by the cost and the prosecutor should consider all aspects of public interest before reaching a decision.

- **Do sources of information require protecting?**

  In cases that do not involve public interest immunity issues (see Chapter 5), particular care may need to be taken where details may need to be given in public that could harm sources of information, ongoing investigations, international relations, or national security.

The factors identified in the Code are not an exhaustive list of public interest factors.

Only where the prosecutor is satisfied that it is in the public interest to prosecute will a prosecution be approved.

THE THRESHOLD TEST

In some investigations, particularly in serious or complex cases, there may not be sufficient evidence available to allow the Full Code Test to be applied, but because of the seriousness or the circumstances of the case, the making of an immediate charging decision is justified and there are substantial grounds to object to bail. In these situations, the CPS can apply the Threshold Test.

However, the prosecutor can only apply the Threshold Test if the following five conditions are met (CPS, 2018a, 5.3–5.10).

1. There are reasonable grounds to suspect that the person to be charged has committed the offence.

2. Further evidence can be obtained to provide a realistic prospect of a conviction. The prosecutor will have to consider a number of factors, including the nature of the evidence, why it is not readily available and how long it will take to secure the evidence.

3. The seriousness or the circumstances of the case justifies the making of an immediate charging decision.

4. There are continuing substantial grounds to object to bail under the Bail Act (1976), and it is appropriate in all of the circumstances of the case to object to bail.

5. It is in the public interest to charge the suspect.

The prosecutor must keep threshold cases under review and should be proactive with investigators to ensure that the outstanding evidence or relevant material is being actioned. The additional evidence will need to be provided before the formal service of the case in Crown Court cases.

RECONSIDERING A PROSECUTION DECISION

Normally once the CPS has reached a decision and informed a suspect that there will not be a prosecution or that the prosecution has been stopped, the case will not start again. However, there may be some cases where the CPS may alter the original decision, particularly if the case is serious. These cases may include:

- *cases where a further review of the original decision shows that it was wrong, and to maintain confidence in the criminal justice system, a prosecution should be brought despite the earlier decision;*

- *cases which are stopped so that further anticipated evidence, which is likely to be available in the near future, can be collected and prepared. In these cases, the prosecutor will tell the defendant that the prosecution may well start again;*

- *cases which are not prosecuted or are stopped because of a lack of evidence but where more significant evidence is discovered later; and*

- *cases involving a death in which a review following the findings of an inquest concludes that a prosecution should be brought, notwithstanding any earlier decision not to prosecute.*

(CPS, 2018a, 10.2)

Victims can seek a review of certain CPS decisions not to prosecute or to stop the case under the Victims' Right to Review Scheme (CPS, 2020b).

The police can also appeal any charging decision made by a prosecutor to a District Crown Prosecutor (DCP) and must comply with the following procedure (CPS, 2020a, 4.31):

- an inspector (or higher rank officer) must consider the relevant material, and the rationale for the prosecutors' decision, before initiating the escalation procedure;

- the grounds for the appeal and why it is believed the prosecutors' decision is wrong by reference to the specific facts of the case and the sufficiency of evidence under the Full Code Test;

- if the suspect is in custody, the appeal must be made before the expiry of the custody clock;

- if the suspect is in custody and the intention is to bail the suspect after charge, consideration should be given to either appealing during the PACE clock or, if appropriate, releasing the suspect (either under investigation or on bail) and appealing expeditiously.

POLICING SPOTLIGHT

An offender has been arrested on suspicion of kidnapping, rape and murder. The body of the deceased has been recovered. There is CCTV evidence of the abduction, which shows the suspect driving the deceased from the scene of the abduction, but at this stage, there is no direct evidence of rape or the actual murder of the complainant. The suspect has given a no-comment interview. The question is whether there is sufficient evidence to seek a charging decision at this stage.

Applying the Threshold Test, there would be sufficient evidence to charge the suspect with kidnapping and murder because it is likely that the evidence can be brought up to the Full Code Test (FCT) within a reasonable period. The other elements of the FCT are present, but there is insufficient evidence to charge rape at this stage because it is not clear when there would be sufficient evidence (such as DNA evidence) to meet the FCT. Once the additional evidence is provided, the CPS can add the additional charge of rape.

EVIDENCE-BASED POLICING

In 2021 a joint thematic inspection was conducted by the Criminal Justice Joint Inspectorates into the police and the CPS's response to rape, from report to the police or the CPS's decision to take no further action. The report made a series of recommendations in terms of actions to be taken by the police and the CPS, including the following.

Recommendation 4

Immediately, police forces and CPS Areas should work together at a local level to prioritise action to improve the effectiveness of case strategies and action plans, with rigorous target and review dates and a clear escalation and performance management process. The NPCC lead for adult sexual offences and the CPS lead should provide a national framework to help embed this activity.

$\longrightarrow$

Recommendation 5

Police forces and the CPS should work together at a local level to introduce appropriate ways to build a cohesive and seamless approach. This should improve relationships, communication and understanding of the roles of each organisation.

As a minimum, the following should be included:

- *considering early investigative advice in every case and recording reasons for not seeking it;*

- *the investigator and the reviewing prosecutor including their direct telephone and email contact details in all written communication;*

- *in cases referred to the CPS, a face-to-face meeting (virtual or in person) between the investigator and prosecutor before deciding to take no further action; and*

- *a clear escalation pathway available to both the police and the CPS in cases where the parties don't agree with decisions, subject to regular reviews to check effectiveness, and local results.*

Recommendation 6

The police and the CPS, in consultation with commissioned and non-commissioned services and advocates, and victims, should review the current process for communicating to victims the fact that a decision to take no further action has been made. They should implement any changes needed so that these difficult messages are conveyed in a timely way that best suits the victims' needs.

(Criminal Justice Joint Inspectorates, 2021, p 10)

REFLECTIVE PRACTICE 4.2

LEVEL 5

You have arrested a 20-year-old man on suspicion of rape contrary to section 1 of the Sexual Offences Act (2003). You have interviewed the man, and he has denied the offence. You want to seek a remand in custody, and you want to ask the CPS to apply the Threshold Test.

- Apply your knowledge to this scenario considering the points to prove and identify the elements you would need to satisfy the Threshold Test.

Sample answers are provided at the end of this book.

SELECTION OF CHARGES

The Code requires prosecutors to consider each suspect individually and each charge separately when they make a charging decision. Prosecutors will not always select the most serious charge where there is a choice and the interests of justice would be met by selecting a lesser charge. In reaching a decision, the prosecutor should select charges that:

- *reflect the seriousness and extent of the offending;*

- *give the court sufficient powers of sentencing and to impose post-conviction orders;*

- *allows the court to make a confiscation order where the defendant has benefitted from the crime; and*

- *enable the case to be presented in a clear and simple way.*

(CPS, 2018a, 6.1)

It is likely that there are a number of different offences which could be charged by a prosecutor in an investigation. The prosecutor will consider the above factors in reaching a decision on the appropriate offence(s) to charge. Guidance may be found in any charging standards contained in CPS legal guidance. An example can be found in the legal guidance on offences against the person (CPS, 2022b), where guidance is given on the appropriate offence to consider. However, it is important for prosecutors to remember that the charging standards are guidelines and not tramlines, so that if there are aggravating features present, a prosecutor can select a more serious charge to reflect the criminality of the suspect and to give the court sufficient powers of sentence to deal with the case.

Prosecutors should not proceed with more charges than are necessary just to encourage a defendant to plead guilty to some of the offences, nor should they proceed with a more serious charge just to encourage a defendant to plead guilty to a less serious offence.

POLICE SPOTLIGHT

An offender assaults the victim, knocks him to the ground, and repeatedly kicks the complainant to his body. Fortunately, the injuries sustained by the complainant consist only of bruising. Under the charging standards, the level of injury might suggest a charge of common assault or assault occasioning actual bodily harm, but the repeated kicking, which is akin to using a weapon, may justify a more serious charge such as attempted grievous bodily harm with intent contrary to the Criminal Attempts Act (1981).

EARLY ENGAGEMENT WITH THE CPS

Early engagement with the CPS can be of great benefit in complex and serious crime investigations. While it is for the police to investigate crime, the CPS can add value to the quality of the investigative process.

The DPP's Guidance on Charging (CPS, 2020a) recommends that early advice is appropriate in the following types of cases:

- *a death;*

- *rape or other serious sexual offences;*

- *modern slavery and human trafficking cases, including cases involving exploitation under the Modern Slavery Act 2015 are being considered, e.g. in the context of 'county lines' supply of controlled drugs;*

- *investigation of an institution with multiple victims and/or suspects;*

- *where the issues or the scale of material make it likely that a prosecutor's review will be significantly more than 90 minutes;*

- *A Memorandum of Understanding requires early consultation (e.g. Joint MOU on undercover operatives);*

- *requests for International Letters of Request. European Investigation Orders and other Mutual Legal Assistance;*

- *extensive volumes of electronic data, multi-media evidence, or third-party material;*

- *large scale fraud;*

- *major police operations including public disorder, public protests, or other civil events;*

- *cases where the preservation of assets through 'Restraint' may be required, should be referred to CPS POC regardless of case type, size or complexity.*
(CPS, 2020a, Annex 6)

Early involvement with the CPS helps the prosecutor to be best placed to make the charging decision and, by working closely together, develop effective strategies to build strong and robust cases and to build a prosecution team ethos. The Attorney General's Guidelines on Disclosure highlight that *'the conduct of an investigation provides the foundation for the entire case, and may even impact on linked cases'* (Attorney General's Office, 2022, p 4).

Equally, there are significant advantages to investigators in complex or serious and major crime cases which may raise issues, including in cases involving the following.

- Cross-border issues, where it may be necessary to secure evidence from outside the United Kingdom, which may require a request for Mutual Legal Assistance (MLA) which the CPS has to be involved in because prosecutors are a designated judicial authority permitted to make formal requests for MLA under the Crime (International Co-operation) Act (2003). The CPS can also advise on any extradition issues which may arise.

- Confiscation/money laundering investigations. CPS lawyers can advise on confiscation issues under the Proceeds of Crime Act (2002) and can apply for a Restraint Order, either pre-charge or post-charge, in appropriate cases.

- Disclosure issues /digital material. Chapters 5 and 6 will examine some of the issues involving disclosure of unused material and digital material. Annex A of the Attorney General's Guidelines (2022) encourages investigators to consult with prosecutors, preferably before seizing substantial amounts of digital material, and also about the possibility of seeking the advice of a digital forensic specialist on the strategy for the identification and review of digital material.

- Covert investigations. The CPS can advise on the implications of the use of covert techniques and the use of the powers contained in the Police Act (1997), the

Regulation of Investigatory Powers Act (2000) and the Investigatory Powers Act (2016).

- Witness status/anonymity. Chapter 3 examined some of the issues and the relevant legislation which apply when dealing with witnesses.

- Assisting offenders. There may be certain investigations where issues may arise about the status of offenders or suspects who may indicate a willingness to assist in the investigation but who may seek immunity from prosecution or an undertaking or wish to reach an agreement with the prosecution. Prosecutors may use sections 71–72 of the Serious Organised Crime and Police Act (SOCPA, 2005) and certain sections of the Sentencing Act (2020) to secure intelligence or evidence from offenders to assist in the investigation or prosecution (of an indictable or either way offence). Offenders who provide such assistance are known as 'assisting offenders' and may receive:

  o   immunity from prosecution – section 71, SOCPA (2005);

  o   restricted use undertakings – section 72, SOCPA (2005);

  o   reduction in sentence – section 74, Sentencing Act (2020);

  o   review of sentence – section 388, Sentencing Act (2020).

Further guidance can be found via the CPS legal guidance on assisting offenders (CPS, 2022a).

PRE-CHARGE ENGAGEMENT

Chapter 6 will cover pre-charge engagement (PCE) with the defence. PCE is encouraged by the Code (CPS, 2018a, 3.4), and it may impact the decision whether to charge or on the selection of charges.

PCE may take place in any case where it is agreed by the parties that it may assist the investigation. Depending on the circumstances of the case, it may be appropriate for the police investigator, a prosecutor, the suspect's representative or the suspect to initiate PCE.

Some benefits of PCE are listed in Chapter 6, but it is important to ensure that PCE is not used to frustrate or delay the investigation that is taking place.

Where PCE takes place, the investigator should provide information about PCE to the suspect or their representative either before or after the interview. A written record should be kept of any PCE discussions.

PRE-TRIAL AND TRIAL PREPARATION

Following a decision to charge a suspect, the case will have to be prepared for court and the relevant paperwork, which is required by the CPS under the National File Standard, Annex 5, Director's Guidance (CPS, 2020a) needs to be provided.

The CPS will prepare the case for court, including:

- reviewing all of the evidence and deciding which witness statements will be served on the defence;

- deciding which exhibits will be used in the case;

- disclosure of unused material;

- settling the indictment if the case is being dealt with at the Crown Court;

- requesting further evidence;

- instructing expert witnesses;

- dealing with the defence statement and advising the police about any further lines of inquiry;

- making applications for bad character, hearsay and special measures;

- instructing a prosecution advocate if the case is not being prosecuted by a CPS advocate.

Effective prosecution depends on the effective working partnership between investigators and the CPS to ensure that the right material is available at the right time and that the case can be managed proactively. The CPS and the police should manage case progression.

The court has a responsibility to oversee the management of the case. Both the police and the CPS have a joint responsibility to ensure:

- *compliance with court directions or orders within the relevant timescales;*

- *shared action plans are kept under continuous review and managed proactively;*

- *escalation arrangements are used appropriately and consistently;*

- *consistent application of the Guidance.*

Police officers have a responsibility to:

- *comply with the National File Standard;*

- *provide any additional material or information requested on time;*

- *inform the prosecutor when any deadline is at risk of being missed.*

Prosecutors have a specific responsibility to:

- *identify any additional evidence or information likely to be required as soon as possible;*

- *ensure that requests are proportionate and necessary in all cases;*

- *provide the rationale for the request (where it goes beyond mere NFS compliance);*

- *ensure that requests to the police are made promptly to allow the maximum time for compliance.*

(CPS, 2020a, 10.6)

The Code requires the prosecutor to continually review the case throughout its lifetime. It is important that the police provide any new material to the CPS and inform the CPS of any information or material which may mean that the Code is no longer met.

Some cases may attract considerable public and media interest. In those cases, it is likely to be important that the SIO and CPS work together to develop a joint media strategy which will also reinforce the prosecution team ethos.

DEAL OR NO DEAL? THE ACCEPTANCE OF PLEAS

In the United States, plea-bargaining is an accepted part of the CJS and is described by the American Bar Association (ABA): *'Many criminal cases are resolved out of court by having both sides come to an agreement. This process is known as negotiating a plea or plea bargaining. In most jurisdictions it resolves most of the criminal cases filed'* (ABA, 2021, p 1).

Either party to the proceedings can initiate a plea bargain which usually involves the defendant pleading guilty to a lesser charge or to only one of several charges. It may also involve a guilty plea with the prosecution recommending a particular sentence. The judge is not bound to accept the recommendation. The US Supreme Court in *Brady v United States* (1970) has held that plea bargaining is constitutional, provided that the defendant's plea is voluntary and that defendants may only plead guilty if they know the consequences of doing so.

In England and Wales, there is no formal system of plea bargaining as understood in the United States. However, in criminal cases, defendants may indicate that they may wish to plead guilty to some, but not all, of the offences which have been charged, or they may offer to plead guilty to a different or less serious charge, because they are admitting only part of the offence.

In the event that pleas are offered, as part of the continuing review of the case, the CPS will have to consider whether it would be appropriate to accept or reject the offer of pleas from the defence.

Prosecutors should only accept the defendant's plea if:

- the court is able to pass a sentence that matches the seriousness of the offending, particularly where there are aggravating features;

- it enables a court to make a confiscation order in appropriate cases, where a defendant has benefitted from criminal conduct; and

- it provides the court with adequate powers to impose other ancillary orders (CPS, 2020a).

Care should be taken when considering pleas which would avoid the imposition of a mandatory minimum sentence. A prosecutor should never accept a plea because it is expedient to do so.

In considering the acceptance of a plea, the prosecutor should also ensure that the interests and, where possible, the views of the victim, or in appropriate cases, the views of the victim's family, are considered when deciding whether it is in the public interest to accept the plea. However, the decision will rest with the CPS.

In the event that the plea is accepted, it should be made clear to the court the basis of the plea, and in cases where the defendant pleads guilty to the charges but on the basis of facts which is different from the prosecution case and where this may significantly impact on the sentence to be imposed by the court, the court should be asked to hear evidence to determine what happened and sentence on the basis of those findings (*R v Newton*, 1982).

An example where the prosecution might accept offers of pleas would be where a defendant is charged with ten offences of burglary and pleads guilty to six of the offences but maintains a not guilty plea to the remaining four offences. It is likely that the prosecutor would accept the pleas because continuing with the four not-guilty charges would be unlikely to affect the sentence which the court would impose for the admitted criminality. In those circumstances, it would not be in the public interest to proceed to trial. However, if there were particularly aggravating factors in the remaining offences which would impact the sentence to be imposed by the court, the public interest would still require a prosecution.

A defendant can invite the judge to give an indication of the sentence in advance of a guilty plea if requested by the defendant in writing. The judge should not give an indication of sentence unless one has been sought by the defendant (*R v Goodyear*, 2005). The indication, if given, is binding but usually only for the day on which it is given or for such period as stated by the judge.

CONCLUSION

The CPS plays a pivotal role within the CJS, and it is important for operational officers to have an understanding of the constitutional role of the CPS and the information and material that prosecutors need from police officers in order to allow them to carry out their role, which is to ensure that the right offender is brought to justice for the right offence and to bring offenders to justice where possible. Decisions are taken fairly and with integrity, which helps to secure justice for the victims of crime, witnesses, suspects, defendants, and the public at large.

By working in close partnership with the CPS, robust cases can be built, which will lead to successful casework outcomes that enhance public confidence in the CJS.

This chapter has examined the background to the creation of the CPS and the prosecuting authority's role and responsibilities.

The chapter has analysed the Code for Crown Prosecutors, which is the Code applied in all cases by the CPS, and has examined the importance of working in partnership to strengthen the quality of cases.

The chapter also looked at trial preparation and the acceptance of pleas.

By working closely with the CPS and ensuring that the right cases are charged and prosecuted, the potential for miscarriages of justice is reduced and successful outcomes increased, which will enhance public confidence in the CJS.

SUMMARY OF KEY CONCEPTS

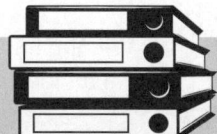

This chapter has examined the role of the CPS in England and Wales. The contents of this chapter allow you to:

- explain the rationale for the creation of the CPS;

- demonstrate your knowledge of the elements of the Code for Crown Prosecutors and to identify what the CPS are looking for in order to allow a charging decision to be made;

- identify the advantages to operational officers of early involvement with the CPS when dealing with major and serious crime;

- describe the key the features of preparation of cases for trial by the CPS;

- explain the approach taken by the CPS to the acceptance of pleas in criminal cases.

CHECK YOUR KNOWLEDGE

1. When was the CPS established?

2. How many parts are there to the Code for Crown Prosecutors?

3. How many elements are there to the Threshold Test?

4. Which part of the Attorney General's Guidelines (2022) deals with pre-charge engagement?

5. What is the name of the case which indicates that if there is a factual dispute to the basis of a guilty plea, which may impact on the sentence to be imposed, the court should hold a hearing to resolve the dispute?

6. What is the name of the case that allows a defendant to ask the judge to give an indication of sentence prior to entering a guilty plea?

FURTHER READING

Attorney General's Office (2022) Attorney General's Guidelines on Disclosure. [online] Available at: www.gov.uk/government/publications/attorney-generals-guidelines-on-disclosure (accessed 22 October 2023).
Annex B deals with pre-charge engagement with suspects, which may be beneficial to investigators.

Crown Prosecution Service (2018) Code for Crown Prosecutors. [online] Available at: www.cps.gov.uk/publication/code-crown-prosecutors (accessed 22 October 2023).
The Code for Crown Prosecutors is the Code applied in every case submitted by police investigators.

Crown Prosecution Service (2020) Charging (The Director's Guidance), 6th edition. [online] Available at: www.cps.gov.uk/legal-guidance/charging-directors-guidance-sixth-edition-december-2020-incorporating-national-file (accessed 22 October 2023).
Annex 5 of the Director's Guidance deals with the documentation that is required by the CPS from police officers.

CHAPTER 5
DISCLOSURE

LEARNING OBJECTIVES

AFTER READING THIS CHAPTER YOU WILL BE ABLE TO:

- explain why disclosure is important in major and serious crime investigations;

- analyse the legislative requirements relating to disclosure when investigating major and serious crimes;

- describe types of sensitive material;

- analyse how to apply the disclosure test;

- describe the issues involved when considering public interest immunity.

INTRODUCTION

A fundamental part of the criminal justice system (CJS) is the right to a fair trial, which is guaranteed by Article 6 of the European Convention on Human Rights (ECHR). The Attorney General's Guidelines on Disclosure highlight that the disclosure process helps to secure the right to a fair trial and is essential to avoid miscarriages of justice (Attorney General's Office, 2022).

In any criminal investigation, the police will generate material including witness statements, exhibits and information, including intelligence. Some of the material will be used as part of the prosecution, and some of the material will not be used in evidence.

Disclosure deals with material that may be relevant to the investigation, which has been retained but does not form part of the prosecution case against the accused (CPS, 2018d).

The Crown Prosecution Service (CPS) refers to disclosure as providing the defence with copies of, or access to, any material which might reasonably be considered capable of undermining the case for the prosecution against the accused or of assisting the case for the accused, which has not previously been disclosed (CPS, 2022).

Digital material is increasingly important in criminal investigations and any subsequent prosecution. The sheer volume of digital material poses challenges for investigators, and it is important to understand the issues that arise in seeking access to the digital material from complainants and witnesses and how digital material should be managed. Chapter 6 will examine digital material in more detail.

The importance of dealing with digital material correctly has been highlighted in two high-profile cases that considered significant failures to deal with digital material in accordance with the law relating to disclosure under the Criminal Procedure and Investigations Act (CPIA, 1996).

The first case involved the Post Office, which introduced a computer-based point of sales system (Horizon) which recorded sales remotely at sub-Post Office branches. The results often differed from the manual records, which were being kept by the sub-postmasters and sub-postmistresses. The Post Office, as part of the contracts with the postmasters and postmistresses, required any shortfall to be repaid. Based on the data from the Horizon system, the Post Office brought criminal proceedings against more than 750 people for offences of theft, fraud and false accounting. The Post Office maintained the accuracy of the Horizon system in the prosecutions and did not accept arguments from the defendants that the figures produced by the Horizon system were inaccurate or unreliable. However, although the Post Office was aware that the Horizon system was not always reliable, it failed to disclose this information to the defence. As a result of the stance taken by the Post Office and the non-disclosure of the information about Horizon, the defendants either pleaded guilty or were convicted after trial, often losing their liberty and their good character.

In civil proceedings brought against the Post Office by a number of sub-postmasters and sub-postmistresses, the failure to provide information about the reliability of Horizon and the failure to disclose the information was identified. The Judge commented:

> *In my judgment, the stance taken by the Post Office at the time in 2013 demonstrates the most dreadful complacency, and total lack of interest in investigating these serious issues, bordering on fearfulness of what might be found if they were properly investigated.*
>
> *(Bates and Others v Post Office Limited Group Litigation,*
> 2019, paragraph 219)

Following the decision of the High Court, the Criminal Cases Review Commission (CCRC) referred the cases of a number of postmasters and postmistresses who had been convicted to the Court of Appeal Criminal Division and in *Hamilton v Post Office* (2021), the Court allowed the appeals of 39 out of 42 appellants, due to the non-disclosure of the information about the potential unreliability of the Horizon system.

There is an ongoing public inquiry which has been set up by the government to investigate the failings associated with the Post Office Horizon IT system (Department for Business & Trade, 2020).

In the second case, Liam Allan, a criminology student, had been in a relationship which he believed had ended on amicable terms. However, his former partner made a complaint to the Metropolitan Police Service (MPS) that Allan had raped and sexually assaulted her on a number of occasions. Allan was interviewed under caution. He accepted that he had been in a consensual relationship but denied that he had raped or sexually assaulted the complainant. The issue in the case was clearly that of consent. Allan was charged with 12 offences of rape and sexual assault.

The complainant had voluntarily handed over her mobile phone to the MPS, and the investigating officer downloaded more than 57,000 lines of data. He did not identify any material that should be disclosed at that stage.

The case went to trial, and it was only during the trial that the download was disclosed to the defence, and it was identified that there were messages within the data that indicated that the intercourse had been with consent. The case was dropped, and there was a joint investigation by the MPS and the CPS into the disclosure failings in the case (MPS and CPS, 2018).

Following the collapse of the case, there were a number of reviews about disclosure including the House of Commons Justice Committee (2018) and the introduction of the

National Disclosure Improvement Plan which was agreed by the CPS, National Police Chiefs' Council (NPCC) and the College of Policing (2018) and a recognition that there was a need to drive-up performance on disclosure.

The House of Commons Justice Committee in its report said;

> It is fundamentally important that all police officers recognise both that they are searching for the truth; and that they have core disclosure duties which are central to the criminal justice process and not merely an administrative add-on. Nevertheless, we believe that there is more to do to ensure that this mindset is embedded across all police forces, and public confidence is improved.
>
> (House of Commons Justice Committee, 2018, p 51)

The increased focus on disclosure led to revised guidance from the Attorney General on disclosure (2022).

This chapter will provide a brief outline of the key elements of disclosure, examine how to apply the disclosure test to investigations, examine how to deal with cases involving sensitive material and provide a brief examination of the approach to be taken in cases which may involve public interest immunity (PII). Some of the material covered in this chapter is also covered in the *Police Procedure and Evidence in the Criminal Justice System* book in the series.

DISCLOSURE

According to Lord Justice Gross (2018), the law in relation to disclosure as contained in the Criminal Procedure and Investigations Act (CPIA, 1996) is satisfactory; however, the implementation of it is not. Disclosure should be integral to the criminal justice process and should not be viewed as a tiresome add-on.

Disclosure should therefore be at the heart of any criminal investigation, and compliance with the requirements of the CPIA should be an essential strategic consideration. Disclosure officers in serious and major crime investigations should have sufficient skills and authority, commensurate with the complexity of the investigation, to conduct their role (CPIA Code of Practice, 2020).

Disclosure under the CPIA relates solely to relevant unused material which is obtained or is inspected during the course of a criminal investigation. The CPIA Code of Practice (2020, p 4), referred to as 'the Code' from here on in defines a criminal investigation as:

- *investigations into crimes that have been committed;*

- *investigations whose purpose is to ascertain whether a crime has been committed, with a view to the possible institution of criminal proceedings; and*

- *investigations which begin in the belief a crime may be committed, for example when the police keep premises or individuals under observation for a period of time, with a view to the possible implementation of criminal proceedings.*

Accordingly, the Code applies when officers are dealing with reports of crimes that have been committed, such as attending a report of a burglary, investigating whether a crime has been committed following a report of suspicious behaviour and proactive covert investigations.

Material is defined by the Code as material of any kind, including information and objects, which is obtained or inspected in the course of a criminal investigation and which may be relevant to the investigation. According to the Code, material maybe relevant to the investigation when it appears to an investigator, or to the officer in the charge of an investigation, or the disclosure officer that it has some bearing on any offence under investigation, or on the surrounding circumstances of the case, unless it is incapable of having any impact on the case (CPIA Code of Practice, 2020, p 4).

An example of material that would be incapable of having any impact on the case is where a witness might have a conviction for speeding, and the case under investigation is an offence of theft. However, if the witness had convictions for dishonesty, then that would clearly be capable of impacting the credibility of the witness.

Disclosure is underpinned by five important principles, the five Rs, which can be summarised as shown in Table 5.1.

Table 5.1 The five Rs

Principle 1	**Reasonable lines of investigation**	
	In conducting an investigation, the investigator should pursue all reasonable lines of inquiry, whether these point towards or away from the guilt from the suspect. What is reasonable in each case will depend on the particular circumstances.	CPIA Code of Practice (2020, paragraph 3.5)
Principle 2	**Record material**	
	Material which may be relevant to an investigation must be recorded in a durable or retrievable form.	CPIA Code of Practice (2020, paragraph 4.1)

⟶

Table 5.1 (continued)

	If the material is part of a larger record which is to be destroyed, its contents should be transferred to a durable and more easily stored form before that happens.	(paragraph 4.2)
	Negative information, if it is relevant, must be recorded.	(paragraph 4.3)
Principle 3	**Retain material**	
	The investigator must retain material obtained in a criminal investigation which may be relevant to the investigation.	CPIA Code of Practice (2020, paragraph 5)
Principle 4	**Reveal material**	
	Revelation means to the CPS and is made by way of the Disclosure Schedules (MG6C, D and E)	CPIA Code of Practice (2020, paragraph 6)
	Certain items of material are presumed to meet the test for prosecution disclosure and copies of the items should be provided to the CPS.	(paragraph 6.6)
	Any other items of unused material which are believed to meet the test for disclosure should also be provided to the CPS.	(paragraph 6.6)
	Sensitive material should be listed on the MG6D.	(paragraph 6.14)
	Examples of sensitive material can be found in the Code of Practice.	(paragraphs 6.7–6.11)
	The items listed on the MG6C and MG6D should comply with the requirements of ˈParagraphs 6.7–6.11 COP and also the National Disclosure Standards.	National Disclosure Standards (CPS, 2018c)
	The disclosure officer is required to certify to the prosecutor that to the best of their knowledge and belief, all relevant material which has been retained and revealed to the disclosure officer, has been revealed to the prosecutor.	(paragraph 9.1)
Principle 5	**Review**	
	Disclosure is a continuing obligation, and any additional relevant unused material must be dealt with in according to the Code of Practice.	Section 7A, CPIA (1996) Attorney General's Guidelines on Disclosure (2022)

Investigators are responsible for conducting inquiries in connection with criminal investigations, but there may be advantages for investigators by early involvement with the CPS. The Code for Crown Prosecutors (CPS, 2018a), states that prosecutors should advise investigators of reasonable lines of inquiry, evidential requirements, pre-charge considerations, disclosure management, and overall investigation strategy.

The Attorney General's Guidelines on Disclosure (2022) emphasise the importance of considering, at the start of an investigation, the specific strategy and approach to be taken to disclosure.

THE DISCLOSURE TEST

The test for prosecution disclosure can be found in sections 3 and 7A of the CPIA (1996), which requires the prosecutor to:

Section 3

(a) disclose to the accused any prosecution material which has not been previously disclosed to the accused and might reasonably be considered capable of undermining the case for the prosecution against the accused or of assisting the accused, or

(b) give the accused a written statement that there is no material of a description mentioned in paragraph (a).

APPLYING THE DISCLOSURE TEST

The Attorney General's Guidelines on Disclosure (2022) highlight the need for disclosure to be conducted in a '*thinking*' manner in light of the issues in the case and this reinforces the guidance from the courts in *R v Olu and Others* (2010) and *R v R and Others* (2015).

In considering what material meets the test for disclosure, investigators and prosecutors should pay particular attention to material that has the potential to weaken the prosecution case, is inconsistent with it or assists the case for the defendant. This will include any material that goes towards an essential element of the offence(s) charged or that points away from the defendant having committed the offence(s) with the requisite intent.

According to Chapter 12 in the Disclosure Manual, factors which may suggest that material might satisfy the disclosure test will always require a consideration of the following factors;

- *the nature of the case against the accused;*

- *the essential elements of the offence alleged;*

- *the evidence upon which the prosecution relies;*

- *any explanation offered by the accused..., and*

- *what material or information has already been disclosed.*

(CPS, 2018d)

Chapter 12 of the Disclosure Manual also gives a number of examples of material which has the potential to weaken the prosecution case or to be inconsistent with it:

- *any material casting doubt upon the accuracy of any prosecution evidence;*

- *any material which may point towards another person, whether charged or not (including the co-accused) having involvement in the commission of the offence;*

- *any material which may cast doubt upon the reliability of a confession;*

- *information provided by an accused which indicates an explanation for the offence with which they have been charged;*

- *any other material that might go to the credibility of a prosecution witness;*

- *any material that might support a defence that is either raised by the defence or apparent from the prosecution papers...;*

- *any material which may have a bearing on the admissibility of any prosecution evidence;*

- *any material that might assist the accused to cross-examine prosecution witnesses, as to credit and/or to substance;*

- *the capacity of the material to have a bearing on scientific or medical evidence in the case;*

- *any material that might enable the accused to call evidence or advance a line of inquiry or argument; and*

- *any material that might explain or mitigate the accused's actions.*

(CPS, 2018d)

Any material which may lead to the exclusion of evidence by a court, or to a stay in the proceedings, or may indicate that a public authority (for example, the investigators) has acted incompatibly with the suspect's ECHR rights will meet the test for prosecution disclosure.

REFLECTIVE PRACTICE 5.1

LEVEL 5

You are investigating an offence of serious wounding, and you send off items of blood-stained clothing from the complainant for analysis. You have arrested James Smith for the offence based on eye-witness evidence which you obtained several days after the attack. Smith has been charged with section 18 wounding with intent, and the case has been sent for trial to the Crown Court. The result of the forensic examination reveals that there is DNA evidence on the clothing linked to Adam Jones, which was not previously known to the investigation.

- How do you deal with this fresh information?

Sample answers are provided at the end of this book.

SENSITIVE MATERIAL

During the course of major or serious crime investigations, it is likely that there will be sensitive, relevant unused material which will have been generated. An example of such material might be an intelligence report which, if it were to be disclosed to the defence, might compromise the source of the information. It is important to remember that due to the definition of material contained within the Code that information is caught by that definition, and accordingly, there is no such thing as 'off-the-record' information for the purpose of the Act (CPIA Code of Practice, 2020, p 4). If the intelligence provided meets the definition of material, it must be recorded. However, it will be sensitive material because it will meet the test for sensitive material.

DEFINITION OF SENSITIVE MATERIAL

The Code defines sensitive material as that which '*the disclosure officer believes would give rise to a real risk of serious prejudice to an important public interest*' (CPIA Code of Practice, 2020, 2.9). This was the test for sensitive material, which was identified by the House of Lords in *R v H & C* (2004).

Examples of types of sensitive material can be found in the Code (2020, 6.14). This is not an exhaustive list, but any item which is considered to be sensitive must meet the test for sensitive material. Certain items of material may contain both sensitive and non-sensitive material. For example, a senior investigating officer's (SIO) policy book may contain both types of material and it may be necessary to redact material to protect the sensitive material in the event that the non-sensitive material did meet the test for prosecution disclosure. While the sensitive parts can be listed on the sensitive material schedule (MG6D), the non-sensitive unused material would be listed on the MG6C schedule.

As indicated in Table 5.1, revelation to the CPS is made by way of nationally agreed forms. There are three main forms which are used when making the revelation, namely:

1. MG6C – relevant non-sensitive unused material;

2. MG6D – relevant sensitive unused material;

3. MG6E – disclosure officer's certificate.

It is important that the descriptions of the unused material contained on the MG6C and MG6D follow the requirements of the National Disclosure Standards (CPS, 2018c).

When the disclosure schedules are being completed, the disclosure officer should consider each item of sensitive material separately and identify how that specific item meets the definition of sensitive material. The prosecutor, when considering the MG6D, will also conduct the same exercise.

In the event that the sensitive unused material is too sensitive to list on the MG6D, the SIO must draw it to the attention of the prosecutor separately. The prosecutor is entitled to see all items of sensitive and non-sensitive material.

When applying the test for prosecution disclosure, it is likely that most items contained on an MG6D will not meet that test because the items are unlikely to undermine the case for the prosecution or assist the case for the accused. It is more likely that if the material could be used as part of the prosecution case, it would actually assist the case for the prosecution or would undermine the case for the accused.

It is only where the sensitive unused material meets the test for prosecution disclosure that issues of public interest immunity (PII) will arise (see below).

Working together with the CPS as a prosecution team is important to ensure that disclosure is at the heart of the criminal investigation and will reduce the risks of there being failures in disclosure which can impact the right to a fair trial and reduce public confidence in the criminal justice system.

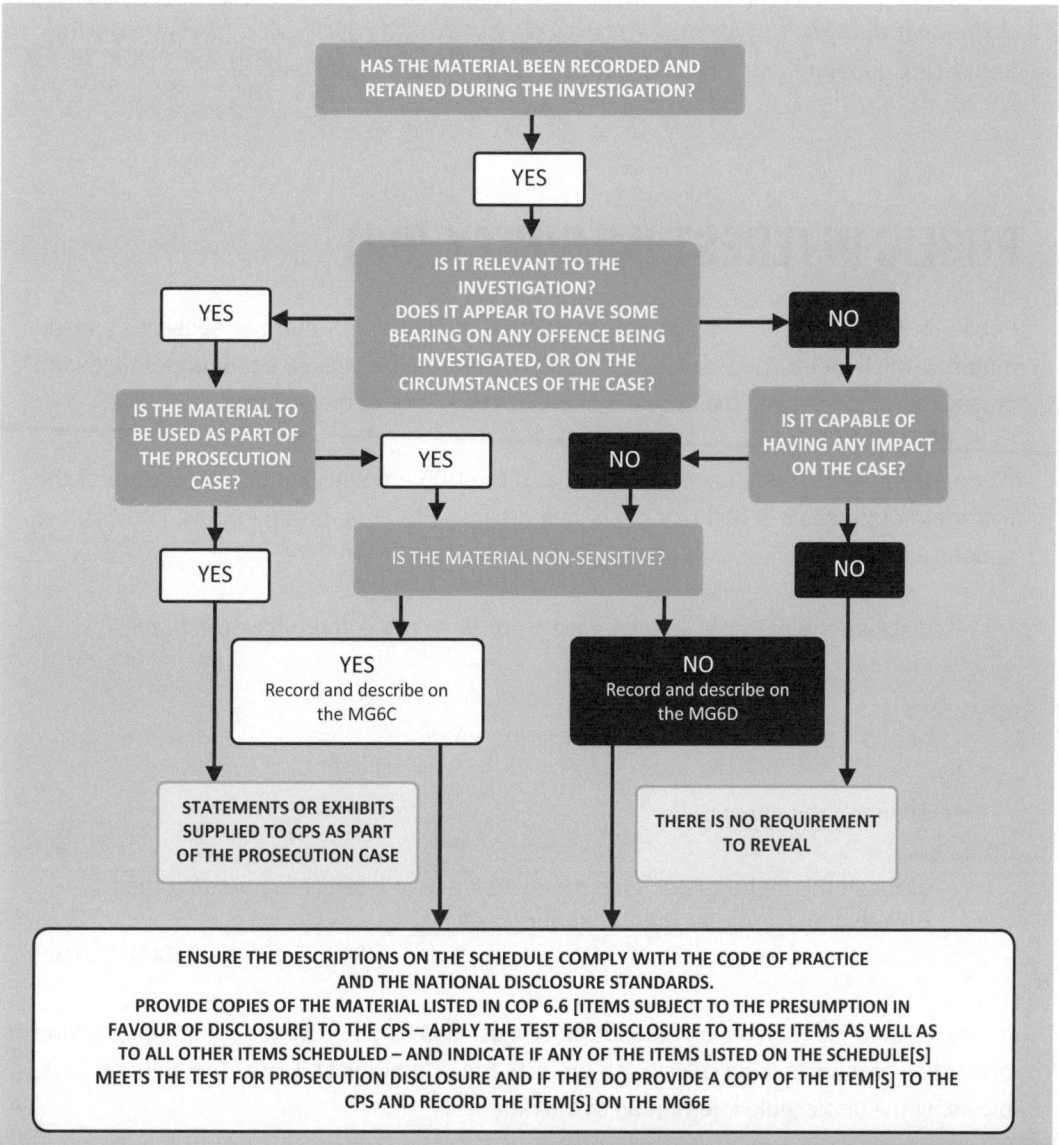

Figure 5.1 Unused material process map

POLICING SPOTLIGHT

While on duty, you have been assaulted by someone you have arrested for being drunk and disorderly. The suspect has been charged with offences of being drunk and disorderly and assaulting you in the execution of your duty. The suspect has pleaded not guilty, and the file needs to be prepared for court. You are asked to prepare the disclosure schedules for court and to act as the disclosure officer in the case.

You should not act as the disclosure officer in a case where there is likely to be a conflict of interest. Paragraph 3.3 of the CPIA Code of Practice (2020) precludes an individual from being appointed or continuing in the role in those circumstances.

PUBLIC INTEREST IMMUNITY (PII)

Public interest immunity (PII) is the process that arises when there is sensitive unused material which meets the test for prosecution disclosure because it either undermines the prosecution case against the accused or assists the case for the accused.

Where such material has been identified, and the CPS are satisfied that disclosure of the material would create a real risk of serious prejudice to an important public interest, the options are to:

- *disclose the material in such a way that does not compromise the public interest in issue;*

- *obtain a court order to withhold the material;*

- *abandon the case; or*

- *disclose the material because the overall public interest in pursuing the prosecution is greater than in abandoning it.*

(CPS, 2018d)

It may be possible to make a limited form of disclosure to the defence by agreeing a form of wording or redacting material which protects the underlying source of the material while providing the disclosable information to the defence.

Early consultation with the CPS is vital when dealing with issues of PII.

Following the decision in *R v H & C* (2004), applications for PII should only be made where:

- the CPS has identified material which meets the test for prosecution disclosure, disclosure of the material would create a real risk of prejudice to an important public interest, and the prosecutor believes that the public interest in withholding the material outweighs the public interest in disclosing it to the defence;

- the above conditions are not satisfied but the police or other investigating agency, after consultation at senior level, does not accept the CPS view; or

- in exceptional circumstances, the prosecutor has pursued all relevant enquiries of the police and the accused and is unable to determine whether the material meets the test for prosecution disclosure and seeks the guidance of the court.

Section 3(6) of the CPIA (1996) allows for applications to be made to the court to protect PII material. The Criminal Procedure Rules (HM Government, 2020, part 15) identify three different classes of PII applications.

- Type 1: Where the CPS gives notification to the defence and indicates the category of the material held. The defence have the opportunity to make representations, and there is a hearing in open court.

- Type 2: The CPS gives notice of the application to the defence but does not give details of the type of material because to do so would have the effect of disclosing the very material the prosecutor is seeking to protect. The defence are given the opportunity to make representations on the procedure to be adopted, but the hearing itself is made in the absence of the defence.

- Type 3: The CPS makes an application to the court without giving notice to the defence because to do so would have the effect of disclosing that which the prosecutor contends would not be in the public interest to disclose, which is 'a highly exceptional class'.

When an application for PII is made, the court will address a series of questions identified in *R v H & C* (2004).

- The court must first identify whether the material the prosecution seeks to withhold is material which may weaken the prosecution case or strengthen that of the accused. If the material cannot be so described, because, for instance, it is neutral or damaging to the accused, then it should not be disclosed.

- Is there a real risk of serious prejudice to an important public interest and if so, what, if full disclosure of the material is ordered? If the answer is no, full disclosure should be ordered.

- If the material does attract PII, can the accused's interests be protected without disclosure, or can disclosure be ordered in a way which will give adequate protection to the public interest in question and also afford protection to the interests of the defence? In considering whether limited disclosure is possible, the court should consider inviting the prosecution to make formal admissions or release summaries or redacted material.

- If the court considers making an order for limited disclosure, is it the minimum derogation necessary to protect the public interest in question? If not, it should order additional disclosure.

- If, however, the effect of limited disclosure may be to render the whole trial process unfair to the accused, fuller disclosure should be ordered even if this leads to the prosecution discontinuing the proceedings.

- The issue of disclosure should be kept under review as the trial unfolds and the evidence develops.

The Criminal Procedure Rules (HM Government, 2020, 3.11) set out a separate procedure to inform the court of sensitive material which the prosecutor has or is aware of, whose revelation to the public or the defendant would give rise to a real risk of serious prejudice to an important public interest but which the prosecutor does *not* consider meets the test for prosecution disclosure.

This procedure was formerly known as a 'notification hearing' and was considered by the Court of Appeal in *R v Ali* (2019), in which the court ruled that these hearings were required in exceptional circumstances where '*if the judge is not kept informed, there is a risk that the material in question will inadvertently impact on the fair management of the trial and thus run counter to the ends of justice*'.

Part 3.11 of the Criminal Procedure Rules further states that the CPS should ask for a hearing to inform the court of the sensitive material if they believe that it is necessary to avoid either (HM Government, 2020):

- *potential unfairness to the defendant in the conduct of the trial;*

- *potential prejudice to the fair management of the trial; or*

- *potential prejudice to that public interest.*

Part 3.11 does not provide specific examples and each case will have to be considered on its own merits; however, the following may be examples of appropriate cases:

- *where disclosure of the material is required to correct a misunderstanding of fact which could lead to potential unfairness to the defendant;*

- *where there is a Covert Human Intelligence Source [CHIS] whose name or identity appears on the face of the papers;*

- *where the defendant is a CHIS, particularly a participating CHIS; and*

- *where the line of defence may lead to the revelation of a covert operational technique which could undermine ongoing law enforcement activities in other investigations into serious offences.*

The Disclosure Manual (CPS, 2018d) provides more detailed guidance on PII applications.

POLICING SPOTLIGHT

On 19 July 2003, 'C' was attacked and raped in the early hours of the morning as she walked to her home address. On 10 February 2004, Andrew Malkinson was convicted of attempting to choke, suffocate or strangle C with intent to commit an indictable offence, namely rape and two other offences of rape. He had also been charged with attempted murder but was acquitted after trial. He was sentenced to life imprisonment.

C sustained a number of serious injuries and was examined by a police surgeon who recorded a number of injuries, including '*broken fingernail middle finger right hand*'. Photographs were also taken of C's injuries.

Some photographs of C's injuries were served on the defence, but two photographs showing C's hands were not provided.

Andrew Malkinson was arrested on 2 August 2003 and denied the allegations. He agreed to provide DNA samples.

On 3 August, C identified Malkinson at a video identification procedure. Two other people, B and M, had told the police that they had seen a man and woman near the scene of the crime and gave a description of the man. On 3 August, B initially identified another man whose image was part of the procedure but went on to tell the officer she had picked the wrong man, and the man was, in fact, the man in position four (Malkinson). On 14 January 2004, M took part in an identification procedure and identified Malkinson.

→

The defence requested details of the convictions of prosecution witnesses in the case. The defence was not supplied with the criminal records of B or M, although the records of some of the other prosecution witnesses were supplied.

The Criminal Cases Review Commission (CCRC) referred the case to the Court of Appeal due to the emergence of fresh DNA evidence which did not match Malkinson but did match another man.

The Court of Appeal was also asked to consider the failings in disclosure as separate grounds for appeal. The Court of Appeal allowed the appeal on the basis of the fresh DNA evidence.

The Court went on to consider the failings in disclosure of the previous convictions of B and M, who were two key witnesses in the case, and the non-disclosure of the two photographs. The Court held that they would have allowed the appeal based on the failures in disclosure.

Malkinson served a total of 17 years' imprisonment for an offence the court held he did not commit (*Malkinson v R*, 2023).

This case reinforces the importance of dealing with disclosure correctly to ensure the avoidance of miscarriages of justice.

REFLECTIVE PRACTICE 5.2

LEVEL 6

You are the disclosure officer in a murder investigation involving a group attack on the victim. Five suspects have been charged with murder and are awaiting trial at the Crown Court. On reviewing the unused material, you become aware of intelligence provided by a CHIS that another man, Scott Williams, was part of the group that carried out the attack. There is also information from Crimestoppers that a man, Michael Jones, was also involved in the attack.

- What are the disclosure implications, and how should you deal with the information?

Sample answers are provided at the end of this book.

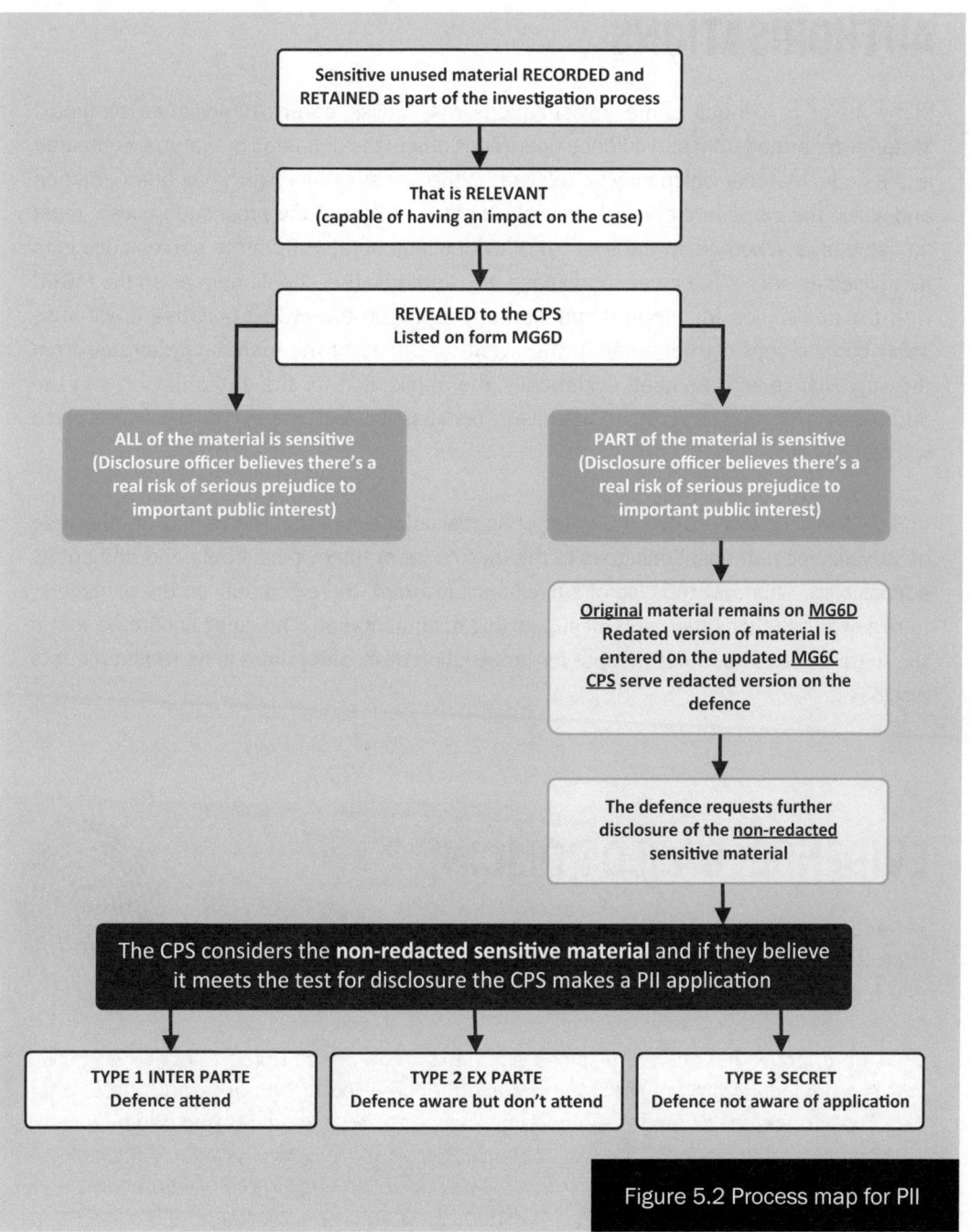

Figure 5.2 Process map for PII

AUTHORISATIONS

Many major or serious crime investigations may utilise covert surveillance methods. Material generated from surveillance operations meets the definition of material contained in the Code. Material which may be relevant to the investigation, which has been retained and which the disclosure officer believes will not form part of the prosecution case, must be listed on a schedule. In the event that evidence generated from the surveillance is to be utilised as part of the prosecution case, the authorisation should appear on the MG6C with the application for the authorisation appearing on the MG6D because it will inevitably contain sensitive material. In the event that none of the material generated from the surveillance is to be used evidentially, the application for the authorisation and the authorisation should be listed on the MG6D because the fact that surveillance took place will be sensitive.

In *R v GS and Others* (2005), the Court of Appeal established that the validity or otherwise of surveillance authorisations goes to the lawfulness of the evidence obtained and not its admissibility. Whatever the type of surveillance involved, there is a duty on the prosecutor to review the authorisation and all supporting documentation. The court confirmed that if the material does not meet the test for prosecution disclosure, there is no requirement to disclose it.

EVIDENCE-BASED POLICING

In December 2020, Her Majesty's Crown Prosecution Service Inspectorate (HMCPSI, 2020) reported on disclosure of material in the Crown Court and highlighted:

> The effective handling of disclosure is inextricably linked to the effectiveness of the prosecution team: that is, the performance of both the police and the CPS. The January 2020 report outlined improvements in case quality and compliance by both organisations, but noted that effective training was crucial if improvement was to be maintained. The report said, 'If the early signs of improvement found in this inspection are to be sustained, the focus on the National Disclosure Improvement Plan must be maintained and extended to ensure that activity by the police and CPS results in a cultural change at the operational as well as at the strategic level.'
>
> (HMCPSI, 2020, p 7)

DEFENCE STATEMENTS

Section 6 of the CPIA (1996) requires the defence in Crown Court cases to provide a defence statement (DS), following the provision of prosecution disclosure. In magistrates' court proceedings, the provision of a DS is optional.

The purpose of the DS is to assist in the management of the trial by identifying the issues which are in dispute in the case and provide additional information to the CPS, which may lead to the provision of additional disclosure of relevant unused material to the defence and may prompt additional lines of inquiry.

CONTENTS OF THE DEFENCE STATEMENT

The defence are required to provide the following information under section 6 of the CPIA (1996):

* the nature of the defence, and in particular any defences to be relied on;

* indicate the matters of fact the defendant takes issue with the prosecution;

* outline why the defence take issue with the prosecution;

* set out the particulars of the matters of fact the defence intend to rely on;

* indicate any points of law (including any point as to the admissibility of evidence) and details of any authority;

* details of any alibi; and

* details of any witnesses the defence propose to call.

Following receipt of the DS, the prosecution should examine the contents and consider whether there is any additional relevant unused material which meets the test for prosecution disclosure in light of the contents of the DS. The DS may also generate further lines of inquiry.

Following consideration of the DS, they will be notified accordingly if there is no additional material to be disclosed to the defence. In the event that there is additional non-sensitive material which has been identified as meeting the test for disclosure, the material will be provided to the defence.

If there is relevant sensitive material that meets the test for prosecution disclosure, it may be necessary to consider making an application for PII.

The defence can make an application to the Court under section 8 of the CPIA (1996) for an order for further disclosure if they can satisfy the court that they have reasonable cause to believe that there is prosecution material which meets the test for prosecution disclosure and which has not been disclosed.

The defence can only apply under section 8 of the CPIA in magistrate's proceedings when they have served a DS.

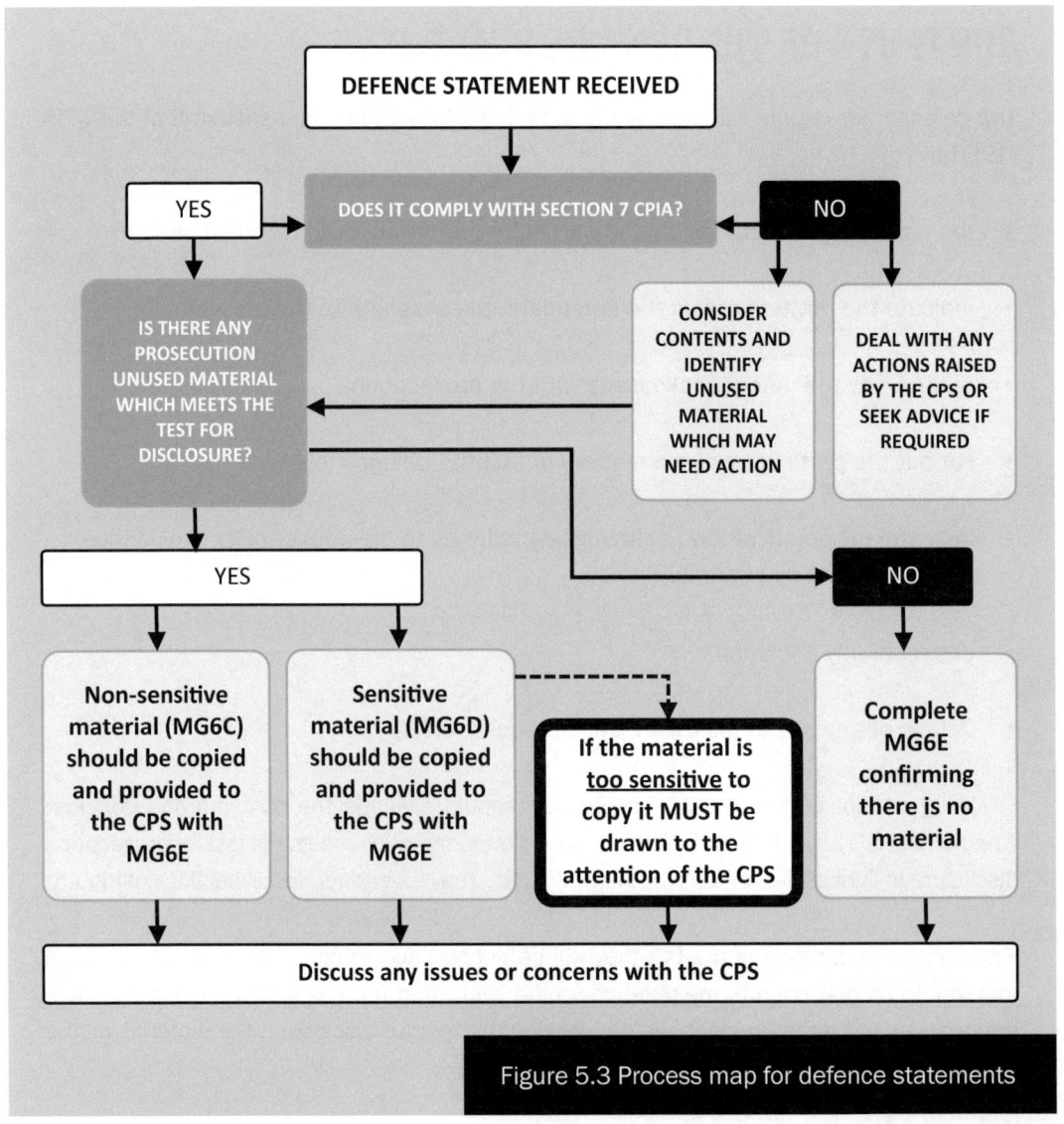

Figure 5.3 Process map for defence statements

REFLECTIVE PRACTICE 5.3

LEVEL 4

- Research the CPIA Code of Practice (2020) and identify the items that are subject to the presumption that they are likely to meet the test for prosecution disclosure.

Sample answers are provided at the end of this book.

CONCLUSION

Disclosure plays a vital part in the CJS and ensuring a fair trial for those accused of a crime in England and Wales. Disclosure of unused material should be regarded as being central to every criminal investigation, and ensuring that disclosure is dealt with correctly, in accordance with the CPIA, helps to reduce the risks of miscarriages of justice and ensures the right to a fair trial.

This chapter has examined the key concepts of disclosure and how to apply the test for prosecution disclosure. It has also considered the definition of sensitive material and applications for PII and how to deal with authorisations utilised in covert policing investigations.

SUMMARY OF KEY CONCEPTS

This chapter has examined the law relating to disclosure of unused material in England and Wales and has examined how failures in disclosure can impact public confidence in the CJS.

The chapter has also examined how to apply the disclosure test and to deal with cases involving sensitive material and PII. This chapter allows you to:

- understand and explain the importance of disclosure in major and serious crime investigations to ensure a fair trial;

- describe the test for disclosure contained in the CPIA;

$\longrightarrow$

- demonstrate how to apply the test for prosecution disclosure when considering unused material;

- demonstrate how to deal with sensitive material in major and serious crime investigations;

- describe the requirements of a defence statement and its importance in the trial process;

- demonstrate how to deal with PII.

CHECK YOUR KNOWLEDGE

1. What is the test for prosecution disclosure?

2. What are the five main principles which underpin the CPIA?

3. What are the defence required to include in a defence statement?

4. What is the definition of sensitive material?

5. What are the different types of hearing when a PII application is made?

6. What type of right is Article 6 ECHR?

FURTHER READING

Attorney General's Office (2022) Attorney General's Guidelines on Disclosure. [online] Available at: www.gov.uk/government/publications/attorney-generals-guidelines-on-disclosure (accessed 22 October 2023).
Provides guidance when dealing with disclosure.

Criminal Procedure and Investigations Act 1996 Code of Practice (2020) [online] Available at: www.gov.uk/government/publications/criminal-procedure-and-investigations-act-1996-section-231-code-of-practice (accessed 22 October 2023).
This is the statutory Code of Practice that police officers should follow when dealing with disclosure of unused material.

Crown Prosecution Service (2018) The National Disclosure Standards (2018). [online] Available at: www.cps.gov.uk/sites/default/files/documents/legal_guidance/National-Disclosure-Standards-2018.pdf (accessed 22 October 2023).
The standards provide guidance on how to schedule unused material.

CHAPTER 6
DIGITAL MATERIAL

LEARNING OBJECTIVES

AFTER READING THIS CHAPTER YOU WILL BE ABLE TO:

- explain why digital disclosure is important in major and serious crime investigations;

- analyse the legal basis for requests for access to digital data of complainants and witnesses;

- analyse the challenges when dealing with digital material;

- discuss the considerations under the ECHR which arise when dealing with investigations that involve digital material.

INTRODUCTION

Digital material is increasingly important in criminal investigations and any subsequent prosecution. The sheer volume of digital material poses challenges for investigators. It is important that there is an understanding of the issues that arise when dealing with large amounts of digital data, some of which will be used evidentially and some of which will be unused material in terms of the requirements contained within the Criminal Procedure and Investigations Act (CPIA, 1996), to help to develop confidence in the criminal justice system (CJS).

There are also additional sensitive considerations when dealing with certain types of investigations, such as rape and other sexual offences, when access to the digital data of complainants and witnesses is being sought. There has been major public concern about the extent of the nature of requests for access to digital material and whether such requests are lawful and can be justified.

In pursuing a criminal investigation, officers may want to access complainants' or witnesses' mobile data. Such access may lead to ethical challenges for investigators, which may revolve around the need to obtain digital material to ensure a fair trial for a suspect, Article 6 (ECHR), with the preservation of the Article 8 (ECHR) rights of the individual complainant or witness. Striking a balance between these two conflicting interests is crucial to ensuring justice and protecting the rights of all parties.

The Information Commissioner, John Edwards, issued an Opinion which called for an end to the excessive collection of personal information from the victims of rape and serious sexual assault: *'our investigation reveals an upsetting picture of how victims of rape and serious sexual assault feel treated. Victims are being treated as suspects and people feel revictimised by a system they expect to support them'* (Information Commissioner's Office, 2020b, p 1).

In an earlier report by the Information Commissioner, Mobile Phone Data Extraction by Police Forces in England and Wales, the then Information Commissioner Elizabeth Denham made a series of recommendations including the following.

- *[T]he introduction of better rules, ideally set out in a statutory code of practice, that will provide greater clarity and foreseeability about when, why and how the police and other law enforcement agencies use mobile phone extraction.*

- *[P]olice should revisit and clarify the lawful basis they rely upon to process data extracted from mobile phones.*

- *The police, Crown Prosecution Service and the Attorney General's Office should collaborate to improve the consistency of authorising of data extracts.*

- *Early engagement between the police and Crown Prosecution Service should be improved in order to allow the extraction, further processing and disclosure of mobile phone data to be more targeted such that privacy intrusion is minimised.*

- *[P]olice forces should make improvements to their engagement with individuals whose phones are to be examined, to ensure that they fully inform those individuals about what is being proposed and what their rights are.*

- *A national training standard should be introduced to ensure that all those involved in mobile phone extraction are aware of their legal obligations.*

- *Wider work being undertaken across the being undertaken across criminal justice, including revisions to the Victims' Code, the Attorney General's Guidelines on Disclosure and the Criminal Procedure and Investigations Act 1996 Code of Practice, should incorporate measures that address data protection and privacy concerns.*
  (Information Commissioner's Office, 2020a, pp 9–11)

Concerns have also been expressed about 'digital strip searches' where requests have routinely been made for access to complainants' mobile phone data and that unnecessary requests may contribute to the number of complainants withdrawing support for a prosecution case. Research from the Home Office (2020) shows an increase in withdrawals by complainants pre-charge, from 20 per cent in 2014/15 to 42 per cent in the year to September 2020. Dame Vera Baird, the Victims' Commissioner, in her briefing on the data extraction clauses in the Police, Crime, Sentencing and Courts Bill (Victims' Commissioner's Office, 2021, p 1) said:

> *I echo the concerns of many senior police chiefs that there has been a fall in public and victim confidence in the police, in particular in relation to rape cases. The issue of digital data extraction plays a big role in this.*

Big Brother Watch published research entitled Digital Strip Searches: The Police's Data Investigations of Victims:

> *Our research shows that these digital interrogations have been used almost exclusively for complainants of rape and serious sexual offences so far. But since police chiefs formalised this new approach to victims' data through a national policy in April 2019, they claim they can also be used for victims and witnesses of potentially any crime.*

> *The searches appear to be driven by a generalised suspicion of complainants, and mobile data trails are increasingly being seen as character references. By*

analysing victims' digital lives, police attempt to infer 'evidence' from information spanning years, analysing what kind of person they are, examining who they have relationships with, and even speculating about their state of mind.

Victims are faced with an impossible choice – the pursuit of justice or the protection of their privacy. No one should be faced with such a choice.

(Big Brother Watch, 2019, p 2)

This chapter considers the principles involved when seeking access to the mobile data of complainants and witnesses. Requests for access to digital material will raise issues under Article 8 ECHR, the right to respect for a family and private life of complainants and witnesses, and it is important that any requests are lawfully made.

The chapter also considers the law in relation to the access to digital data of complainants and witnesses contained in the Police, Crime, Sentencing and Courts Act (PCSCA, 2022) and the Extraction of Information from Electronic Devices: Code of Practice (Home Office, 2022b) hereinafter called 'the Code'.

The chapter concludes with an examination of how to deal with disclosure issues involving digital material, the documentation that should be kept, strategies and early involvement with the Crown Prosecution Service (CPS) and an examination of pre-charge engagement (PCE) with the defence.

POLICING SPOTLIGHT

One of the case studies in the Victims' Commissioner's report (2020) involved a complainant in a rape case who was asked to provide her mobile phone to the police. The police had declined to take her clothes from the night of the attack but made a number of requests for additional information, making her feel as if she was under suspicion and that she was a criminal. She declined to provide the material and said:

I felt anxious, confused and infuriated. I was under far deeper investigation than the rapist (who I have no doubt would have had questionable material had they searched the same). They had refused to take physical evidence – my clothing from the night of the attack - but wanted to investigate my private life. I asked them to justify each request but they could not, so I did not provide it.

(Victims' Commissioner's Office, 2020, p 27)

THE BALANCE BETWEEN ARTICLE 6 AND ARTICLE 8

All investigators must be aware of the sensitive issues that arise when both the right to a fair trial for the suspect (Article 6 ECHR) and the privacy rights of complainants and witnesses (Article 8 ECHR) are engaged. The CPIA Code of Practice (2020) requires investigators to pursue all reasonable lines of inquiry, whether they point towards or away from a suspect's guilt. An investigator or a prosecutor may decide that it is necessary to access or process personal or private information from a complainant or a witness to pursue a reasonable line of inquiry.

Pursuing reasonable lines of inquiry may engage the person's Article 8 rights and those rights in respect of other parties within that material. The Attorney General's Guidelines on Disclosure (2022, pp 4–6) deal with the general principles that should be applied when considering access to digital material:

a. *Collecting and/or processing personal or private material can only be done when in accordance with the law, strictly necessary, and proportionate.*

b. *In order to be in accordance with law and necessary, an investigator must be pursuing a reasonable line of inquiry... Seeking the personal or private information of a complainant or a witness will not be a reasonable line of inquiry in every case – an assessment of reasonableness is required...*

c. *The assessment of reasonableness should be made on a case-by-case basis and regard may be had to:*

   (i) *the prospect of obtaining relevant material; and*

   (ii) *what the perceived relevance of the material is to the identifiable facts and issues in the case.*

d. *If, by following a reasonable line of inquiry, it becomes necessary to obtain personal or private information, investigators will also need to consider:*

   (i) *what review is required;*

   (ii) *how the review of this material should be conducted;*

   (iii) *what is the least intrusive method which will nonetheless secure relevant material;*

   (iv) *are particular parameters for searching best suited to the identification of relevant material;*

   (v) *is provision of the material in its entirety strictly necessary; or alternatively, could the material be obtained from other sources...?*

e.   The rationale for pursuing the reasonable line of inquiry and the scope of the review it necessitates should be open and transparent.

f.   The refusal by a witness to provide private or personal material requires an investigator or prosecutor to consider the information the witness has provided (and could be provided) with regard to the use of their personal material, the reasons for the refusal, and how the trial process can address the absence of the material.

g.   Disclosure of such material to the defence is in accordance with the law and necessary if, but only if, the material meets the test for disclosure in the CPIA. Personal information which does not meet the test but is contained within the material to be disclosed should be redacted.

h.   Where there is a conflict between both of these rights, investigators and prosecutors should bear in mind that the right to a fair trial is an absolute right.

EVIDENCE-BASED POLICING

Liam Allan had been involved in a relationship which had ended. The complainant made a report to the Metropolitan Police that Allan had raped and sexually assaulted her on a number of occasions. She voluntarily allowed her mobile data to be downloaded by the investigating officer. There were over 57,000 lines of message data contained in the download.

Allan was interviewed under caution. He accepted that he had been involved in a consensual relationship with the complainant, and he denied that he had raped the complainant.

The CPS subsequently authorised 12 charges of rape and sexual assault in his case. The disclosure schedule (MG6C) provided by the MPS contained only three items.

No details of the contents of the download were provided to the CPS. The defence requested details of any social media or other material that met the test for prosecution disclosure. The prosecution was assured on a number of occasions that there was no material which met the test for disclosure, and it would be disproportionate to conduct the enquiries requested by the defence.

During the trial, the download was provided to the defence and among the messages was a message from the complainant to one of her friends which said, 'it wasn't against my will or anything' (MPS and CPS, 2018).

Following the identification of this material, the prosecution dropped the case because this information should have been disclosed to the defence as it clearly met the test for disclosure contained in the CPIA; it was material that undermined the prosecution case and/or assisted the defence case. The information should have been provided to the CPS when they were asked to make a charging decision applying the Code for Crown Prosecutors (see Chapter 4).

REFLECTIVE PRACTICE 6.1

LEVEL 5

You are interviewing a complainant who reports a sexual assault committed by a person she had met the same day the alleged assault took place. In the interview, the suspect accepts that he had met with the complainant that day. He also indicated that the only contact he had ever had with the complainant on his mobile phone was that day.

- What considerations do you have with regard to access to the complainant's mobile data?

Sample answers are provided at the end of this book.

DISCLOSURE

Chapter 5 examined disclosure in some detail. It is important to remember that the general provisions which relate to unused material contained in the CPIA (1996) and the CPIA Code of Practice (2020) equally apply to digital material.

In order to access a complainant's or witnesses' data, it must be a lawful request, and it must be necessary and proportionate to the case being investigated. The CPIA Code of Practice (2020) requires officers to pursue all reasonable lines of inquiry, whether they point towards or away from the guilt of the suspect. This must be considered on a case-by-case basis, taking into account the circumstances of the case. The Attorney General's Guidelines, Annex A (Attorney General's Office 2022) provide specific guidance with regard to digital material.

The CPS (2018b) gives additional guidance to officers on reasonable lines of enquiry when dealing with digital material.

EXTRACTION OF INFORMATION FROM ELECTRONIC DEVICES

Following widespread public concerns expressed about excessive requests for access to digital material, Chapter 3 of the Police, Crime, Sentencing and Courts Act (PCSCA, 2022) sets out the legal basis for the extraction of information from electronic devices. The Act is supported by the Extraction of Information from Electronic Devices: Code of Practice (Home Office, 2022b).

Section 37 of the PCSCA (2022) allows an authorised person to extract information stored on an electronic device from that device if the user of the device has voluntarily provided the device to an authorised person and the user has agreed to the extraction of the information from the device. The power in section 37 can only be exercised for the purpose of preventing, detecting or prosecuting crime, helping to locate a missing person, or protecting a child or an at-risk adult from neglect or physical, mental or emotional harm. The authorised person may exercise the power for the purpose of preventing, detecting or prosecuting crime where the authorised person reasonably believes the information stored on the electronic device is relevant to a reasonable line of enquiry which is being or is to be pursued. The authorising officer must also be satisfied that authorisation is necessary and proportionate and must take account of the provisions of the Code.

PCSCA: CODE OF PRACTICE

The Code (Home Office, 2022b) confirms that an authorised person can only exercise the powers under section 37 of the PCSCA for the purposes of preventing, detecting or prosecuting crime if they reasonably believe that information stored on the device is relevant to a reasonable line of enquiry which is being or is to be pursued by an authorised person. The CPS has issued Disclosure: A Guide to 'Reasonable Lines of Enquiry' and Communications Evidence (2018b).

In all cases, the authorised person must use the least intrusive means of processing the information as possible in the circumstances. This may be by selectively extracting the relevant material or, where this is not technically possible, by restricting the review of the excess information obtained (Home Office, 2022b, para 17).

The test of a reasonable belief that the information on the device is relevant is an objective one. Any decision to extract information from a device should be made having considered all of the information available at the time, considering the accuracy and provenance of the information and based on more than mere suspicion or speculation on the part of the authorised person (Home Office, 2022b, para 70).

The authorising officer is required to follow the guidance on reasonable lines of inquiry contained in the CPIA Code of Practice (2020) and the Attorney General's Guidelines on Disclosure (2022) (Home Office, 2022b, para 72).

The PCSCA Code (Home Office, 2022b, para 77) emphasises that there must be no presumption that information will be extracted from a device. If less intrusive means of obtaining the information are available, they must be considered and used where reasonably practicable to ensure that extraction meets the strict test of necessity and proportionality.

While each case must be carefully considered, it is highly unlikely that a full extraction from a device, such as a mobile phone, tablet, laptop or other computer and a review of all of the content will meet the necessity and proportionality test in most cases. This is due to the volume of material that may be stored on such devices and the unlikely event that all such information will be a relevant line of enquiry (Home Office, 2022b, para 80).

The PCSCA applies where the user of the device gives their voluntary permission to the police to access the device. There should be no undue pressure placed on the user, and the user should make a fully informed and conscious decision to access the device and have given informed permission to extract the information. The approval should be confirmed in writing. The Code does cover the circumstances where the user of the device cannot provide written confirmation.

Children and vulnerable adults without capacity cannot provide voluntary authorisation to access devices. In the case of a child, a parent, guardian or, if the child is in care, a representative of the relevant authority or voluntary organisation may give permission to access the device (Home Office, 2022b, para 6).

Access to digital material may be crucial for ensuring a fair trial, but it may need to be balanced with protecting the private rights of complainants and witnesses. By ensuring that access to digital data is only sought when it is a reasonable line of inquiry in the context of the case and that any material accessed is dealt with in accordance with the provisions of the CPIA, the investigation will be ethical and will stand scrutiny if there are any challenges about how disclosure has been managed.

MANAGEMENT OF DIGITAL MATERIAL

Annex A to the Attorney General's Guidelines on Disclosure (2022) outlines how relevant material and material that satisfies the test for prosecution disclosure can be identified, revealed and, if necessary, disclosed to the defence without imposing unrealistic or dispro-portionate demands on investigators and prosecutors.

SIOs in cases that involve a large amount of digital data should complete an investiga-tion management document (IMD), which will inform the disclosure management docu-ment (DMD) that prosecutors complete. The DMD means that prosecutors can be open and transparent with the defence and the court about how the prosecution has approached disclosure in the context of the case. As Chapter 5 made clear, disclosure is an inseparable part of the right to a fair trial, and by completing a DMD, the prosecution team is being open and transparent to the court and the defence how they have approached their disclosure obligations.

In cases involving substantial amounts of digital material, investigators should engage with the CPS about developing a digital material strategy and may wish to engage a forensic specialist.

Annex A (Attorney General's Office, 2022, para 39) makes it clear that it is not the duty of the prosecution to comb through all the material in its possession (eg, every word or byte of digital material) on the lookout for anything which conceivably or speculatively undermines the case or assists the defence case. The duty of the prosecution is to disclose material that might reasonably be considered capable of undermining the prosecution case or assisting the accused's case, which they become aware of, or to which their attention is drawn.

The defence must also play a part in defining the real issues in the case. This is a require-ment by the overriding objective under the Criminal Procedure Rules. The defence should be invited at an early stage (including consideration of pre-charge engagement) to define the scope of reasonable searches that may be made of digital material in order to identify any material that may meet the test for prosecution disclosure.

GENERAL PRINCIPLES

Annex A to the Attorney General's Guidelines on Disclosure deals with the general principles that should be followed by investigators when dealing with digital material.

- *No action should be taken which changes data on a device which may subsequently be relied on in court.*

- *If it is necessary to access original data, then that data should only be accessed by someone who is competent to do so and is able to explain the relevance and implications to a court.*

- *An audit trail should be kept of all processes followed. Another practitioner should be able to follow the audit trail and achieve the same results.*

- *The investigator in charge of the investigation has responsibility for ensuring that the law and these principles are followed.*

(Attorney General's Office, 2022, para 6)

It is important that a log or record of all digital material which is seized or imaged is retained as relevant to the investigation. The records should also include details of all persons who deal with the digital material, the date and times of any searches, the terms used and details of any strategy that is applied to the material.

Annex A (Attorney General's Office, 2022, para 50) makes it clear that the scheduling of relevant material should be carried out in accordance with the CPIA Code of Practice, and the scheduling should follow the guidance contained in the National Disclosure Standards (CPS, 2018c).

POLICING SPOTLIGHT

In the case of Liam Allan (see Chapter 5), over 57,000 lines of messages were downloaded from the complainant's mobile phone. The officer who downloaded the material failed to keep a record of the download or details of method of the search he conducted or of any material he examined. When the file was submitted to the CPS there were only three items on the MG6C, and he had recorded that there was no relevant data on the CRIS Report.

Following the collapse of the trial, when texts which suggested that the complainant had consented to intercourse with Allan, the CPS asked the officer in the case for his comments and he replied,

> *I've always made clear that there was a download but had told the CPS and the original prosecution counsel that I had looked through it and identified every-thing that was relevant. I can only read from this that because of the volume of analysis of phone downloads I deal with I wrongly assured myself that I had looked through the entire document.*

(MPS and CPS, 2018, para 41)

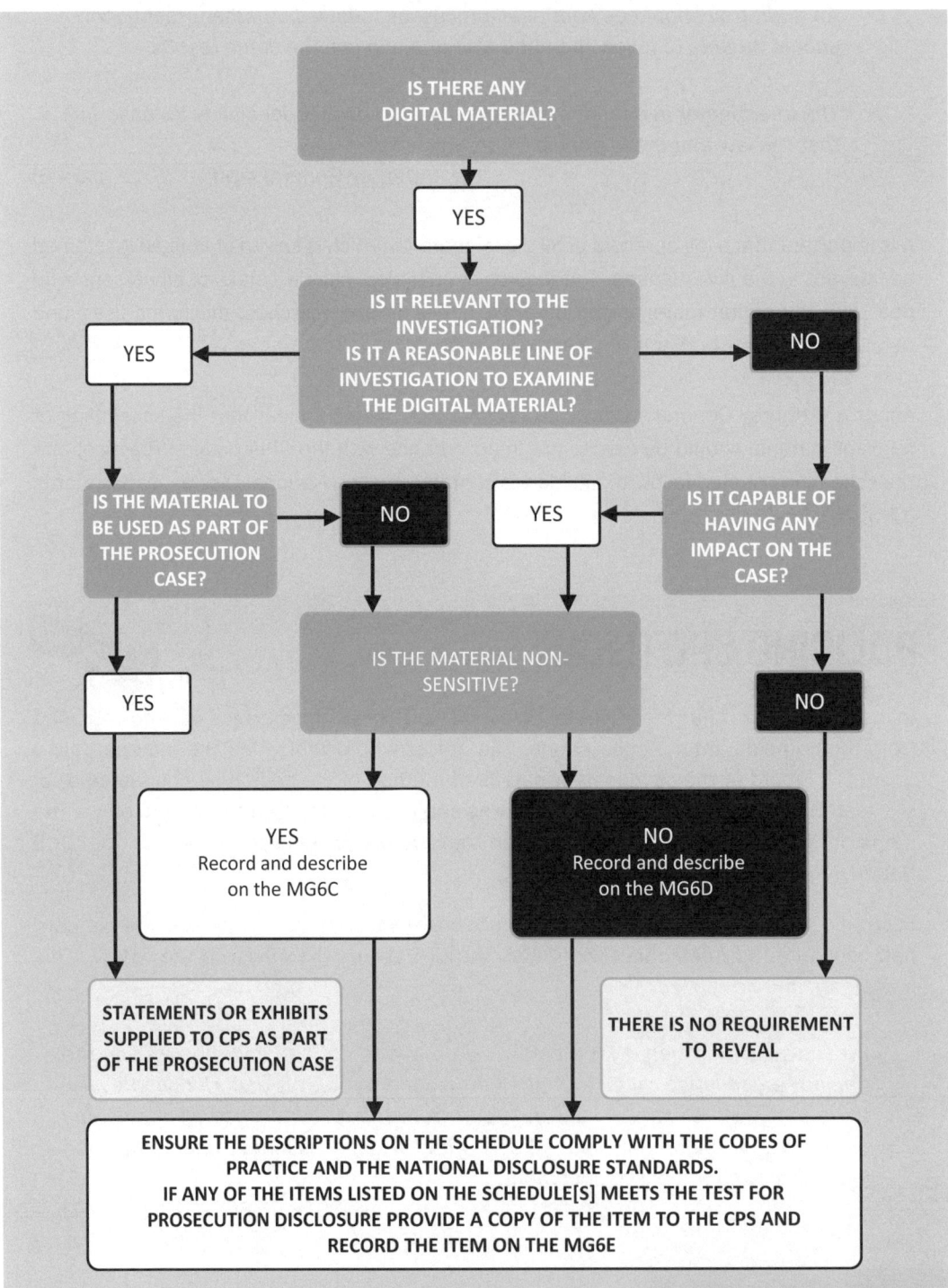

Figure 6.1 Process map

PRE-CHARGE ENGAGEMENT

Pre-charge engagement (PCE) refers to voluntary engagement between the parties to an investigation after the first PACE interview and before any suspect has been charged. PCE is voluntary and can be terminated at any time.

PCE may involve:

- giving the suspect the opportunity to comment on proposed further lines of inquiry;

- ascertaining whether the suspect can identify further lines of inquiry;

- asking whether the suspect is aware of, or can provide access to, digital material that has some bearing on the case;

- discussing ways to overcome barriers to obtaining potential evidence, such as revealing encryption keys;

- agreeing to any key word searches of digital material the suspect would like to be carried out;

- clarifying whether any expert evidence or forensic evidence is agreed and, if not, whether the suspect's representatives intend to instruct their own expert, and any timescales.

There are a number of potential benefits that may arise from PCE.

- Suspects who maintain their innocence will be aided by the early identification of lines of inquiry.

- PCE can help to inform the prosecutor's charging decision. It might avoid a case being charged that would otherwise be stopped when further information becomes available.

- The issues in dispute may be narrowed so that unnecessary inquiries are not pursued.

- Early resolution of the case may reduce anxiety and uncertainty for suspects and complainants.

- The cost to the criminal justice system may be reduced.

In all major and serious crime investigations, particularly those which may involve substantial amounts of digital material, early involvement with the CPS will be appropriate, and consideration should be given to the use of PCE.

REFLECTIVE PRACTICE 6.2

LEVEL 6

You are the investigating officer in a series of linked cyber fraud cases which involve the use of a number of digital devices and the use of different IP addresses. There is to be a strike day when it is intended to search a number of addresses connected with the investigation.

- With a focus on digital material, consider your strategy.

Sample answers are provided at the end of this book.

CONCLUSION

Digital material plays an increasingly important role as evidence in criminal investigations. There will often be conflicting issues to be considered by investigators in ensuring that all reasonable lines of inquiry are followed to ensure a fair trial, while seeking to balance the rights to privacy and a family life for witnesses and complainants.

Disclosure of unused material should be regarded as being central to every criminal investigation and ensuring that disclosure is dealt with correctly, in accordance with the CPIA, helps to reduce the risks of miscarriages of justice and ensures the right to a fair trial.

This chapter has examined the key concepts of disclosure and has considered the balance between the right to a fair trial under Article 6 ECHR and the right to respect for a private and family life under Article 8 ECHR.

The chapter has also considered the approach taken when dealing with requests for access to digital material and has highlighted that access to digital material should only take place where there is a lawful basis.

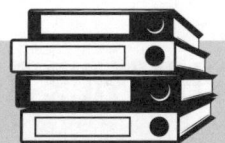

SUMMARY OF KEY CONCEPTS

This chapter has examined digital material and the surrounding issues, including the basis for seeking access to digital material of complainants and witnesses and issues relating to the balance between Articles 6 and 8 ECHR. The chapter has also examined how to deal with disclosure involving digital material and the use of pre-charge engagement. This chapter allows you to:

- describe why digital material is important in major and serious crime investigations;

- identify the legal basis for requests to access digital material to ensure compliance with the CPIA and to ensure a fair trial;

- describe how to balance the competing factors between Article 6 and Article 8 ECHR when dealing with digital material and to be able to justify requests for access to digital material;

- describe the pre-charge engagement process and to understand the benefits to major and serious crime investigations.

CHECK YOUR KNOWLEDGE

1. What are the conflicting principles which may arise when seeking access to digital material?

2. Which set of guidelines deal with digital material?

3. What type of right is Article 6 ECHR?

4. Which Act of Parliament deals with the access to digital material of complainants and witnesses?

FURTHER READING

Crown Prosecution Service (2018) Disclosure: A Guide to 'Reasonable Lines of Enquiry' and Communications Evidence. [online] Available at: www.cps.gov.uk/legal-guidance/disclosure-guide-reasonable-lines-enquiry-and-communications-evidence (accessed 22 October 2023).
This provides guidance on reasonable lines of inquiry when considering digital material.

Metropolitan Police Service and Crown Prosecution Service (2018) A Joint Review of the Disclosure Process in the Case of *R v Allan*. [online] Available at: www.cps.gov.uk/sites/default/files/documents/publications/joint-review-disclosure-Allan.pdf (accessed 22 October 2023).
This is the joint report that highlights some of the failures in the case of Liam Allan.

CHAPTER 7
COVERT APPROACHES TO THE INVESTIGATION OF MAJOR AND SERIOUS CRIME

LEARNING OBJECTIVES

AFTER READING THIS CHAPTER YOU WILL BE ABLE TO:

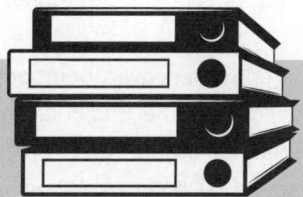

- understand the concept of covert investigation and how it can be applied to major and serious crime;

- describe the difference between directed surveillance, intrusive surveillance and property interference;

- critically evaluate how covert investigation conflicts with human rights;

→

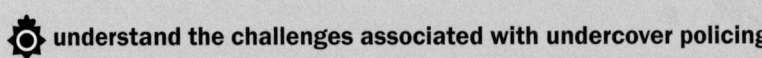

- understand the challenges associated with undercover policing;

- analyse the value of interception and communications data to major and serious crime;

- explain the role of the Investigatory Powers Commissioner.

INTRODUCTION

According to the Code of Practice for the Criminal Procedure and Investigations Act (CPIA, 1996), criminal investigations are required when crimes 'have been' committed, to establish whether a crime 'has been' committed and in situations when a crime 'may be' committed (MoJ, 2020b, p 4). Whether investigations are reactive and look backwards or they are proactive in looking forwards, covert techniques can be applied to most investigations into major and serious crime.

The Human Rights Act (HRA, 1998), the Regulation of Investigatory Powers Act (RIPA, 2000), the Investigatory Powers Act (IPA, 2016) and the Police Act (1997) provide the ethical and legal frameworks for covert techniques. Each area of legislation must operate in unison, they need to co-exist with one balancing the other, thereby protecting the rights and freedoms of not only those under investigation but also law-abiding citizens.

In principle, covert approaches to investigation transfer the process of gathering evidence away from the traditional notions, where victims and witnesses provide testimony about criminal events, and replace them with investigators trained in surveillance and other covert techniques. When used effectively, this can generate incontrovertible evidence, meaning this type of investigation is a very powerful tool in the investigation of major and serious crime.

This chapter outlines the concept of covert investigation, it examines the difference between directed and intrusive surveillance and the requirement to interfere with property to facilitate the deployment of intrusive surveillance techniques. This chapter discusses challenges associated with undercover policing and considers how covert techniques must balance the need for investigation against the rights and freedoms of those affected.

This chapter concludes with a discussion on the value of interception of communications, the importance of communications data in judicial proceedings and the oversight placed on operational practice to maintain control of intrusive investigative techniques.

COVERT INVESTIGATION

In a reactive sense, investigations are 'overt'; ostensibly they are conducted in the open with a high degree of transparency, and very often those responsible will be aware of or will certainly suspect police involvement. Offenders recognise the potential to escape punishment if no one testifies against them, and despite the introduction of legislation to support victims and witnesses through the criminal justice system (CJS), witness intimidation in major and serious crime investigations is a very real challenge. Whether intimidation is 'overt' through direct confrontation or 'implicit', which is the practice of non-co-operation with the police because of cultural traits (Sanders, 2019), investigators often turn to covert techniques to supplement evidential challenges.

In essence, an investigation is covert when it is conducted in a manner which is designed to ensure those under investigation are unaware of its existence (McKay, 2015; Harfield and Harfield, 2018; Home Office, 2018b). This is deemed necessary because individuals involved in major and serious crime operate at the high end of threat, risk and harm, and make it their business to familiarise themselves with investigative techniques. Therefore, covert investigators need to match this; they need to be innovative and at times audacious if they are to be successful against hard to reach criminals.

While always striving to adhere to the principles of the European Convention on Human Rights (ECHR), notably Article 6, right to a fair trial, and Article 8, right to respect for private and family life, covert investigation inevitably means the rights and freedoms of those who are targeted will to some extent be compromised. In fact, the reason for the introduction of the RIPA (2000) as the legal framework which regulates covert activity was to ensure surveillance and other covert techniques were compatible with the ECHR.

COVERT INVESTIGATION AND HUMAN RIGHTS

Human rights are firmly established within the CJS and the broad principles of 'Rights' and 'Freedoms' associated with the HRA (1998) are examined in other books in this series (also see Chapter 7 of the *Criminal Investigation* title). There is, however, an intrinsic link between the HRA (1998) and the broad spectrum of covert investigation and it is important to discuss them here.

RIGHT TO A FAIR TRIAL

Deceptive and non-deceptive techniques are utilised during the deployment of covert resources and technical surveillance equipment. Marx (1988, p 12) introduces the concept of:

- 'covert-non-deceptive' techniques, which include the use of audio and visual recording equipment, intercept facilities and tracking devices; and

- 'covert-deceptive' techniques, which involve the deployment of surveillance officers who pose as members of the public; undercover officers (UCOs) who often portray themselves as criminals to infiltrate criminal networks; and covert human intelligence sources (CHIS) who are tasked with developing and maintaining deceptive covert relationships to gather intelligence on criminal behaviour.

It is the convergence of 'covertness and deception' described by Marx (1988, p 13) that makes this approach to investigation both powerful and 'problematic', sometimes leading to challenges associated with the sense of 'fairness' in the way evidence is collected.

The underlying principles of Article 6, right to a fair trial, means those accused of criminal offences are presumed innocent until proven guilty. One of the primary functions of the prosecution is to preserve a defendant's right to a fair trial. In cases where the sense of 'fairness' is compromised, prosecutors have a duty to stop the case, regardless of how serious the allegations are (CPS, 2022c). In the normal order of events, suspects are informed at an early stage what they are accused of and told they have the right to remain silent, thus avoiding self-incrimination. Covert investigations remove these basic principles because they are built on secrecy; those who are believed to be involved in serious crime are unaware of the investigation into their conduct and therefore they are not offered the rights and protections of the CJS regarding self-incrimination. This, together with the deceptive manner of investigation, means there is potential for section 78 of the Police and Criminal Evidence Act (PACE, 1984), to apply, meaning valuable evidence may be excluded from trial or, in some cases, the court may 'stay' or stop the proceedings because of an abuse of judicial process.

RIGHT TO PRIVACY

Fundamentally, section 6(1) of the HRA (1998) makes it unlawful for public authorities to act in a way that is incompatible with the rights and freedoms associated with the ECHR. There are, however, exceptions to the rule. Rights and freedoms are categorised as *absolute* rights, such as Article 3, freedom from torture, inhumane and degrading treatment, meaning there can be no deviation from the right; similarly, Article 6, right to a fair trial, is also an absolute right, however in special circumstances (eg in times of war or national emergency) there can be some form of derogation from the right (Attorney General's Office, 2022). Equally, there are *qualified* rights, such as Article 8, right to respect for private and family life, which means public authorities may deviate from the right to protect the rights and freedoms of others. (The ECHR and the principles are included throughout all aspects of policing and are contained within most of the other titles in this series.)

By its very nature, covert surveillance is intended to gather private information, thus bringing the practice of surveillance into direct conflict with Article 8, right to respect for private and family life. Not only does covert surveillance capture private information from the individual subject of surveillance, but it is inevitable private information will also be gathered with respect to others who are not involved in criminality. For example, family, friends, acquaintances and broader members of the public may unwittingly be observed, photographed or have their conversations recorded without their knowledge or consent. This is known as *collateral intrusion*, which perhaps carries the greatest risk in deviating from Article 8, and every effort must be taken to minimise the intrusion on the privacy of those not subject to covert investigation (Home Office, 2018b).

COVERT SURVEILLANCE

According to Ball et al (2006, p 4), surveillance is defined as '*purposeful, routine, systematic and focused attention paid to personal details, for the sake of control, entitlement, management, influence or protection*'. A central feature of surveillance is the acquisition of information or data which is connected to the individual concerned (Marx, 2015). From a more contemporary perspective, the Covert Surveillance and Property Interference: Revised Code of Practice defines surveillance as the:

> *monitoring, observing or listening to persons, their movements, conversations or other activities and communications. Surveillance may be conducted with or without the assistance of a surveillance device and includes the recording of any information obtained.*
>
> *Surveillance is covert if, and only if, it is carried out in a manner calculated to ensure that any persons who are subject to the surveillance are unaware that it is or may be taking place.*
> (Home Office, 2018b, p 10; see also RIPA, 2000, sections 48(2) and 26(9))

DIRECTED AND INTRUSIVE SURVEILLANCE

There are two forms of surveillance that can be authorised under Part II of RIPA (2000), *directed* and *intrusive*. According to section 26(2), directed surveillance is covert surveillance which is not intrusive and is undertaken:

(a)   *for the purposes of a specific investigation or a specific operation;*

(b)   *in such a manner as is likely to result in the obtaining of private information about a person (whether or not one specifically identified for the purposes of the investigation or operation); and*

(c)   *otherwise than by way of an immediate response to events or circumstances the nature of which is such that it would not be reasonably practicable for an authorisation under this Part to be sought for the carrying out of the surveillance.*

Therefore, planned covert surveillance of a specific person, vehicle or location would fall within the definition of directed surveillance if the surveillance was likely to result in the acquisition of private information about the person or people within the vehicle or at the particular location.

In contrast, covert surveillance, which is intrusive, is defined under section 26(3) as surveillance which:

(a)   *is carried out in relation to anything taking place on any residential premises or in any private vehicle; and*

(b)   *involves the presence of an individual on the premises or in the vehicle or is carried out by means of a surveillance device.*

It is important to note a key element of intrusive surveillance is the fact it is conducted in or on residential premises or a private vehicle, where the expectation of privacy is greater and, therefore, the level of intrusion is much higher. An example of intrusive surveillance would be a listening device which is deployed into a suspect's home or vehicle to eavesdrop on conversations.

PROPERTY INTERFERENCE

Deployment of surveillance devices in some situations may require the commission of a crime or unlawful trespass on private property. Ordinarily, this would be unlawful, even for a public authority; however, Part III of the Police Act (1997) and Part 5 of the Investigatory Powers Act (2016) provide the legal framework to lawfully interfere with property belonging to another.

An authority for property interference is generally a prerequisite for intrusive surveillance; therefore, they need to co-exist because one facilitates the other. In these circumstances, a single authority can be combined; however, respective authorising officers must consider statutory provisions regarding necessity and proportionality independently of each other (Home Office, 2018b).

POLICING SPOTLIGHT

A covert investigation is commissioned into the unlawful activities of an organised crime group (OCG), believed to be involved in the large-scale distribution of Class A controlled drugs between Merseyside and Cumbria. Intelligence indicates the OCG use a white Ford Transit van to transport drugs between the two regions on a weekly basis.

The SIO sets the covert strategy, which involves the deployment of surveillance resources supported by a covert listening device and a tracking device in or on the subject vehicle.

A combined authority for directed surveillance, intrusive surveillance and property interference would be permissible in these circumstances. The directed surveillance authority allows for tactics such as foot and mobile surveillance, audio and visual recording equipment and perhaps aerial photography; similarly, authorities for property interference and intrusive surveillance allow for the entry into or onto the vehicle to deploy the surveillance device(s) and the subsequent tracking of the vehicle movements and monitoring of conversations.

STATUTORY OBLIGATIONS FOR SURVEILLANCE

The intrinsic link between covert surveillance and the HRA (1998) creates statutory obligations that must be considered by any person authorising surveillance activity. Section 28(2) of the RIPA (2000) for directed surveillance, section 32(2) of the RIPA (2000) for intrusive surveillance and section 93(2) of the Police Act (1997) for property interference require authorising officers to consider whether surveillance is *necessary* on one or more statutory grounds and *proportionate* to the aims the surveillance activity seeks to achieve (Home Office, 2018b, paras 4.4–4.5).

NECESSITY

The test for necessity is largely objective, meaning there is limited latitude for interpretation of the statutory grounds for granting surveillance. For the purposes of directed surveillance, surveillance is only considered necessary when:

- *in the interests of national security;*

- *for the purpose of preventing or detecting 'crime' or of preventing disorder;*

- *in the interests of the economic well-being of the UK;*

- *in the interests of public safety;*

- *for the purpose of protecting public health;*

- *for the purpose of assessing or collecting any tax, duty, levy or other imposition, contribution or charge payable to a government department; or*

- *for any other purpose prescribed by an order made by the Secretary of State.*
                    (RIPA, 2000, section 28(3); Home Office, 2018b, p 42)

For the purposes of intrusive surveillance, surveillance is considered necessary when:

- *in the interests of national security;*

- *for the purpose of preventing or detecting 'serious crime';*

- *in the interests of the economic well-being of the UK; or*

- *for the purpose of preventing or detecting an offence under section 188 of the Enterprise Act 2002.*
                    (RIPA, 2000, section 32(3); Home Office, 2018b, pp 48–9)

For the purposes of intrusive surveillance and property interference, the tests for '*serious crime*' are broadly outlined as:

(a)   *an offence which a person who has attained the age of twenty-one and has no previous convictions could reasonably be expected to be sentenced to a term of imprisonment for three years or more;*

(b)   *an offence which involves the use of violence, results in substantial financial gain or is conducted by a large number of persons in pursuit of a common purpose.*
                    (RIPA, 2000, section 81(3); Police Act, 1997;
                    section 93(2); Home Office, 2018b)

REFLECTIVE PRACTICE 7.1

LEVEL 4

You are investigating a series of burglaries, contrary to section 9(1)(b) of the Theft Act (1968). The offenders are stealing electrical equipment, such as computers, tablets and other mobile devices. Intelligence has identified second-hand shops as a potential outlet for the stolen property, and you believe covert surveillance may help identify those responsible.

- With a focus on the concept of *necessity*, consider whether you could justify an application for directed surveillance. As an additional measure, consider whether intrusive surveillance could be justified in these circumstances.

Sample answers are provided at the end of this book.

PROPORTIONALITY

The concept of proportionality restricts public authorities in the exercise of their powers, requiring them to strike a balance between the means used and the intended objectives. The test for proportionality is somewhat subjective. According to the Covert Surveillance and Property Interference: Revised Code of Practice, activity should not be excessive in the overall circumstances of the case, invoking the scenario which avoids using a sledge-hammer to crack a nut. Furthermore, proposed covert activity should be considered individually, having regard to the potential benefit it may bring to the investigation (Home Office, 2018b).

The severity or seriousness of crimes under investigation clearly influences decisions in terms of proportionality, particularly when deviating from Article 8 ECHR; however, seriousness alone does not automatically mean intrusive covert techniques are proportionate to the aims the investigation seeks to achieve. Other factors must be considered to meet the test for proportionality, namely:

- *balancing the size and scope of the proposed activity against the gravity and extent of the perceived crime or harm;*

- *explaining how and why the methods to be adopted will cause the least possible intrusion on the subject and others;*

- considering whether the activity is an appropriate use of the legislation and a reasonable way, having considered all reasonable alternatives, of obtaining the information sought;

- evidencing as far as reasonably practicable what other methods had been considered and why they were not implemented or have been implemented unsuccessfully.

(Home Office, 2018b, para 4.7)

The concepts of necessity and proportionality are essential elements when considering the use of covert resources. Understanding the fundamental principles and how they are applied to each investigation helps to provide justification when authorising activity which compromises an individual's right to privacy.

REFLECTIVE PRACTICE 7.2

LEVEL 6

You are investigating an offence of sexual communication with a child, contrary to section 15A of the Sexual Offences Act (2003). Intelligence indicates an unknown man, over the age of 18 years, has engaged in a virtual conversation of a sexual nature with a girl under the age of 16 years. It is clear from 'chat logs' that there is an intention to meet for the purposes of sexual activity. The identity of the man and girl are unknown; however, you know the location of the proposed meeting place.

- With a focus on the concept of 'proportionality', consider whether you could justify an application for directed surveillance.

Sample answers are provided at the end of this book.

UNDERCOVER POLICING

A range of covert tactics are available to law enforcement to prevent and detect crime or disorder and maintain public safety. Undercover policing is one such tactic, which, if applied correctly, is a proportionate, lawful and ethical way of gathering evidence and intelligence when perhaps other less intrusive methods of investigation have failed (College of Policing, 2021c).

Undercover officers (UCOs) fall within the definition of a CHIS and require authorisation under the provisions of RIPA (2000). Section 26(8) defines a CHIS as a person who is deployed to:

> (a)   establish or maintain a personal or other relationship with a person for the covert purpose of facilitating the doing of anything falling within paragraph (b) or (c);
>
> (b)   they covertly use such a relationship to obtain information or to provide access to any information to another person; or
>
> (c)   they covertly disclose information obtained by the use of such a relationship, or as a consequence of the existence of such a relationship.

Operating under a pseudonym or false identity with a remit to covertly gather intelligence and evidence of criminality, it follows the use and conduct of UCOs meet the definition of a CHIS. Their role is to form and maintain relationships, not just with those who are involved in criminality, but also with friends, associates and acquaintances who may not be connected to the offences under investigation. Again, this raises the concept of *collateral intrusion*, as there is a clear deviation from Article 8 ECHR, which means authorising officers must consider their *'use and conduct'* against the concepts of necessity and proportionality.

Grounds associated with necessity or the reason for their *use* largely mirror those associated with directed surveillance. Similarly, the concepts of proportionality and collateral intrusion follow a similar theme in so much as the *conduct*, or the behaviour and actions of UCOs, must not be excessive when balanced against the nature of offences under investigation (see RIPA, 2000, sections 28(3), 29(3); Home Office, 2018b, paras 4.4–4.16; Home Office, 2022c, paras 3.2–3.7, 3.18–3.21; College of Policing, 2021c, para 8.3).

ENGAGING IN CRIMINAL CONDUCT

For an undercover deployment to be effective, it may be necessary for a UCO to participate in criminal activity. For example, a UCO may be tasked to gather evidence of the sale and supply of controlled drugs, contrary to section 4 of the Misuse of Drugs Act (1971). In order to gather evidence, it may be necessary for the UCO to purchase and therefore possess a quantity of drugs. In these circumstances, the Covert Human Intelligence Sources (Criminal Conduct) Act (2021) allows the provision for a UCO to participate in criminal conduct.

Section 29B of the RIPA (2000) provides the framework which allows participation in criminal conduct, namely in circumstances when it is believed necessary:

1. *in the interests of national security;*

2. *for the purpose of preventing or detecting crime or of preventing disorder; or*

3. *in the interests of the economic well-being of the United Kingdom.*

Participation in criminal conduct must always be proportionate to the aims the investigation seeks to achieve and must have regard to the HRA (1998). Before granting a criminal conduct authorisation, consideration should be given to:

*   whether the aims sought to be achieved by the criminal conduct could reasonably be achieved by other conduct which would not constitute a crime;

*   whether the criminal conduct is part of efforts to prevent or detect more serious criminality;

*   whether the potential harm to the public interest from the criminal conduct would be outweighed by the potential benefit to the public interest and that the potential benefit would be proportionate to the criminal conduct in question (Home Office, 2022c).

Additional factors for consideration when authorising participation in criminal conduct suggest UCOs:

*   do not actively engage in planning and committing the crime;

*   are intended to play only a minor role;

*   participate only where essential to enable law enforcement to frustrate the principal criminals and arrest them (albeit for lesser offences such as attempt or conspiracy to commit crime or carrying offensive weapons) before injury is done to any person or serious damage is done to property (College of Policing, 2021c, para 7.3).

An important attribute of a UCO is the ability to portray an image of someone who is involved in criminality. There are, however, legal boundaries which are set by the authorising officer and underpinned by legal precedent, which, if adhered to, will maintain the integrity and admissibility of the intelligence or evidence gathered.

ENTRAPMENT

There is a delicate balance between the competing interests of tackling major and serious crime and holding offenders to account for their actions. The courts recognise the need for intrusive investigative techniques, which means Article 6 ECHR is not automatically breached by UCO deployments. That said, there are limits to what is considered acceptable in the eyes of the court before it crosses the threshold and becomes unacceptable, thereby breaching Article 6.

The fundamental principle behind undercover operations is the avoidance of state-created crime. In other words, agents of the state, or UCOs must not 'incite', 'lure', 'entice' or 'initiate' the commission of crime and then prosecute individuals for doing so. This would be entrapment, and case law has developed the judicial stance on levels of acceptability. The leading case is *R v Loosely* (2001), which builds on existing case law, such as *R v Mealey* (1974), *Teixeira de Castro v Portugal* (1999) and others, and helps set boundaries in levels of unacceptability. Lord Nichols, in his judgement in *R v Loosely* (2001), deals with what the courts consider acceptable practice in undercover policing operations.

In summarising, Lord Nichols reiterates a general acceptance that UCOs cannot simply act as passive observers and, therefore, must show at least some enthusiasm for the criminal activity they are investigating. This is considered essential to maintain their cover, but what they must not do is cause the offence to be committed by creating the opportunity for an individual to commit a crime they would otherwise not have committed. In other words, the police must do no more than present an '*unexceptional opportunity*' to commit a crime. The conduct of the UCO preceding the commission of the offence must be no more than might be expected from others in the circumstances. In these situations, conduct of this nature will not be regarded as inciting, instigating or luring a person into committing a crime and, therefore, it would not constitute entrapment (*R v Loosely*, 2001, para 23).

It is important to note that the concept of entrapment offers no legal defence; however, in circumstances where the level of acceptability is compromised to the extent entrapment exists, it may mean there is a potential breach of Article 6 ECHR, which may lead to a stay of the proceedings as amounting to an abuse of process or exclusion of evidence under the provisions of section 78(1) of the Police and Criminal Evidence Act (1984), which states:

> In any proceedings the court may refuse to allow evidence on which the prosecution proposes to rely to be given if it appears to the court that, having regard to all the circumstances, including the circumstances in which the evidence was obtained, the admission of the evidence would have such an adverse effect on the fairness of the proceedings that the court ought not to admit it.

The role of the UCO requires courage, skill and a high degree of expertise to infiltrate criminal networks operating at the highest levels of threat, risk and harm. This is not to say they are operating in isolation; there are many supporting resources and supervisory officers which are designed to ensure the safety of the UCO, help preserve the integrity of evidence and ensure any subsequent challenges regarding unnecessary deviation from Articles 6 and 8 ECHR are unsuccessful.

EVIDENCE-BASED POLICING

The legitimacy of investigative methods relies on the professionalism of those involved in the process. Mark Kennedy, a Metropolitan Police officer seconded to the National Public Order Intelligence Unit, was deployed to gather intelligence against environmentalist and protest groups between 2003 and 2010. Acting on information provided by Kennedy, on 13 April 2009, police arrested 114 activists and later charged 26 for conspiracy to commit aggravated trespass at the Ratcliffe-on-Soar Power Station, Nottingham. It was believed they intended to occupy the power station and disrupt the supply of energy to over 2 million homes.

Kennedy was later exposed as a UCO, and it became clear he had deceived several women into long-term sexual relationships, which clearly undermined trust and confidence in undercover policing as an investigative tactic. There followed a series of reviews into the use and conduct of Kennedy – see *A Review of National Police Units Which Provide Intelligence on Criminality Associated with Protest* (HMIC, 2012), *Ratcliffe-on-Soar Power Station Protest Inquiry into Disclosure* (Rose, 2011), *Ratcliffe-on-Soar Power Station (Operation Aeroscope) Disclosure, Nottingham Police* (IPCC, 2011) and the Investigatory Powers Tribunal, *Wilson v Commissioner of Police of the Metropolis and National Police Chiefs' Council* (2021) – which collectively identified poor supervision, a lack of control, breaches of rights under Articles 3, 8, 10, 11 and 14 ECHR and failings in investigative practice.

Such was the extent of the impact of Kennedy and others; notably, the exposure of a UCO deployed into an activist group which sought to influence the family of Stephen Lawrence in their campaign against the adequacy of the Metropolitan Police Service to investigate their son's murder (Ellison, 2014). The then Home Secretary, Theresa May, established a national Undercover Policing Inquiry in 2015, which continues to this date to investigate the validity of undercover policing operations across England and Wales since 1968.

INTERCEPTION OF COMMUNICATIONS

Communication is a necessary function in all walks of life, and this is no different for those who are engaged in major and serious crime. The ability to securely communicate is essential if criminals are to avoid detection; therefore, the interception of communications and

communications data play a vital role in the successful investigation of seriou
tection of the public and safeguarding of national security (Home Office, 20
Interception of communications traditionally amounted to a 'telephone tap',
development of technology, interception now extends to other forms of electror
cation such as mobile telephones, emails, text messages and internet calls.

To summarise, in section 4 of the Investigatory Powers Act (IPA, 2016), interception is defined as taking place when a person modifies, interferes with or monitors a communication which is sent via a telecommunication or postal system while in transmission and makes the content available to a person who is not the sender or intended recipient of the communication (Home Office, 2022d). This is clearly a very intrusive investigative tactic, which has the potential to impact ECHR Articles 6 and 8 and, in some circumstances, Article 10, freedom of expression, and is only made lawful by the provisions of a warrant authorised by the relevant Secretary of State under Part 2 or Chapter 1 of Part 6 of the IPA (2016) and approved by a judicial commissioner.

Again, those with the power to grant an authority to intercept communications must consider the necessity of such action, for example, being in the interests of national security, for the prevention and detection of serious crime or for the economic well-being of the UK (see IPA, 2016, section 20), as well as considering arguments relating to proportionality and the risk of collateral intrusion.

Interception of communication in the UK is used as a source of intelligence and provides the opportunity to identify and disrupt threats from terrorism and serious crime, as well as support the gathering of evidence and identification of opportunities to seize prohibited drugs, firearms and proceeds of crime (Home Office, 2014). That said, despite the value it brings to the investigative process, section 56 of the IPA (2016) prohibits the use of intercept material as evidence in criminal proceedings. This is contrary to practice in countries such as the USA, Canada and Australia. However, challenges associated with transcription, disclosure, retention and storage of material, balanced against an individual's right to a fair trial, means as far as the UK is concerned neither the prosecution nor defence can rely on intercept as evidence.

It should be noted, however, that intercept material from foreign jurisdictions is admissible in criminal proceedings in England and Wales because there is no statutory prohibition against its use.

COMMUNICATIONS DATA

Although material generated as a result of the interception of communications cannot be used as part of legal proceedings, communications data is used heavily during the investigative process. In fact according to Anderson (2016), it is used as evidence in 95 per cent of serious and organised crime prosecutions.

Communications data, defined as the '*who, when, where, and how of a communication, but not the content*' is material held by telecommunications and postal operators (Home Office, 2018c, p 10). This includes website providers if they deliver a telecommunications or messaging service, which means many businesses, such as online marketplaces, will be considered telecommunications operators in respect of some of their operations, even where the majority of their work is unrelated to telecommunications services or telecommunication systems (Home Office, 2018c).

In practical terms, communications data falls into two categories, *entity data*, which includes information about the subscriber or account holder, such as their name and address, connection and payment methods and apparatus details, and *events data*, which includes call or internet records, when and where communications were made, duration and recipient details and information about data uploads and downloads. Additionally, communications data includes details about the communication architecture, such as cell site or mast locations and Wi-Fi hotspots (Home Office, 2018c).

The acquisition, retention and use of communications data is governed by the IPA (2016), and section 61 provides authorising officers with the power to grant the acquisition of communications data when considered necessary in the:

- interests of national security;

- for the 'applicable' crime purpose, which is explained in sections 60A(8), 61(7A) and 61A(8) of the IPA (2016). In essence, where events data is sought, the applicable crime must be '*serious*' as defined in section 86(2A) of the IPA (2016); however, when entity data is sought, it can be for the purpose of preventing or detecting crime or of preventing disorder;

- in the interests of the economic well-being of the United Kingdom so far as those interests are also relevant to the interests of national security;

- in the interests of public safety;

- for the purpose of preventing death or injury or any damage to a person's physical or mental health, or of mitigating any injury or damage to a person's physical or mental health;

- to assist investigations into alleged miscarriages of justice; or

- where a person has died or is unable to identify themselves because or mental condition to (a) assist in identifying the person or (b) obtain about their next of kin or other persons connected with the person or reason for their death or condition.

As with interception of communication, surveillance and property interference, authorising officers are required to consider the concepts of proportionality and collateral intrusion when making decisions about whether to grant applications to deviate from Article 8 ECHR, right to private and family life.

OVERSIGHT

The IPA (2016) provides for an Investigatory Powers Commissioner (IPC), who has the responsibility to oversee the application and use of investigatory powers, which include covert surveillance, the interception of communications, property interference, the acquisition of communications data and the use of covert human intelligence sources. The IPC will be or have been a senior member of the judiciary and is independent to the government or other public authorities permitted to use investigatory powers.

The aim of the IPC is to ensure the privacy of those affected by investigatory powers are protected, safeguards are applied, and individual rights are maintained. The IPC has an obligation to conduct annual inspections, and in the event that serious errors in the application of investigatory powers are identified, if considered in the public interest, the individual affected should be informed of the error (Home Office, 2018b, 2018c, 2022c).

CONCLUSION

Those who commit major and serious crime are causing the greatest levels of threat, risk and harm to communities, and investigations of this nature can often be frustrated by a reluctance of victims and witnesses to provide the testimony required to prosecute those responsible; offenders know only too well that intimidation, either direct or implied, can make investigations of this nature a real challenge. This means law enforcement agencies must be bold and, at times, audacious in their response. This chapter has examined the concept of covert investigation and how it can enhance traditional forms of investigation by reducing the reliance on witness testimony and very often replacing it with incontrovertible evidence.

That said, the use of covert surveillance brings challenges. Naturally, there are infringements to an individual's right to privacy and, in some situations, their right to a fair trial. These issues are highlighted through an examination of undercover policing and the challenges associated with this tactic. This chapter has explored the interception of communications and the value of communications data in the investigation of major and serious crime.

Covert techniques not only impact the privacy of those subject to investigation; inevitably there will be an intrusion on the privacy of friends, family and acquaintances who are not subject to investigation. This is a very serious issue for authorising officers to consider. This chapter has examined their obligations to ensure the use of intrusive techniques is necessary for legitimate policing purposes and is proportionate to aims the investigative techniques aim to achieve.

This chapter has concluded with a discussion on the role of the IPC in providing oversight of investigatory powers, thereby ensuring the application and use of such intrusive techniques remain compliant with the law.

SUMMARY OF KEY CONCEPTS

This chapter has explored the following key concepts:

- the application of covert techniques to major and serious crime investigations;

- the key differences between directed and intrusive surveillance;

- how covert investigation impacts on the rights and privacies of those involved;

- the value of interception of communications and communications data;

- how the Investigatory Powers Commissioner provides oversight and governance to covert techniques.

CHECK YOUR KNOWLEDGE

1. What is the primary aim of covert investigation?

2. Describe the fundamental difference between directed surveillance and intrusive surveillance.

3. Which acts allow for the interference of property?

4. Section 29B of the RIPA (2000) provides the framework which allows participation in criminal conduct when it is believed necessary in the interests of national security, for the purpose of preventing or detecting crime or of preventing disorder, or in the interests of the economic well-being of the United Kingdom. What additional guidance do the Covert Human Intelligence Sources: Revised Code of Practice and the College of Policing Authorised Professional Practice offer on this subject?

5. What is the role of the Investigatory Powers Commissioner?

6. What is the case law that deals with entrapment?

FURTHER READING

Home Office (2018) Communications Data: Code of Practice. [online] Available at: https://assets.publishing.service.gov.uk/government/uploads/system/uploads/ attachment_data/file/822817/Communications_Data_Code_of_Practice.pdf (accessed 22 October 2023).
Provides detailed guidance on communications data, including scope and definitions, when it can be authorised, who performs the role of the authorising officers, urgent authorisations and duration, renewals and cancellations.

Home Office (2018) Covert Surveillance and Property Interference: Revised Code of Practice. [online] Available at: https://assets.publishing.service.gov.uk/government/ uploads/system/uploads/attachment_data/file/742041/201800802_CSPI_code.pdf (accessed 22 October 2023).
Outlines concepts of directed and intrusive surveillance, property interference and statutory provisions associated with necessity, proportionality and collateral intrusion. Details including authorisation levels, duration, reviews, renewals and cancellations are discussed.

CHAPTER 8
INVESTIGATIVE INTERVIEWING

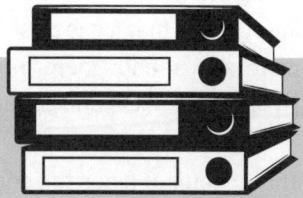

LEARNING OBJECTIVES

AFTER READING THIS CHAPTER YOU WILL BE ABLE TO:

- outline the principles that underpin the practice of investigative interviewing in England and Wales;

- describe the PEACE interview model and critically evaluate the benefits of an ethically driven approach to investigative interviewing;

- discuss the challenges associated with pre-interview briefings and understand how the strategic use of evidence may impact on an investigation;

- understand the concept of vulnerability;

- critically evaluate the role of the appropriate adult (AA);

- explain the concept of false confessions and their associated risk factors.

INTRODUCTION

Historically, victims and witnesses were interviewed because they were expected to co-operate as they were fundamentally inclined to assist an investigation; in contrast, suspects were expected to be unco-operative, and therefore, they were interrogated to obtain a confession (Shepherd, 2007). An admission of guilt held *primary status as evidence*', and investigators who acquired confessions were held in high regard (Shepherd, 2007, p14). While the significance of confessions should not be ignored, much has changed in terms of the approach to investigative interviewing in England and Wales.

A series of high-profile miscarriages of justice resulting from false confessions brought about reform through the Royal Commission on Criminal Procedure (1981). The legislative change introduced by the Police and Criminal Evidence Act (PACE, 1984) mandated the use of audio-recorded police interviews, which aimed to provide greater transparency to the interview process, and section 76 of PACE (1984) placed the evidential burden on the prosecution to show any confession made was voluntary and not acquired through oppression. Continued exposure of unethical, oppressive and biased interview techniques (Williamson, Milne and Savage, 2013) influenced the Home Office to change direction and move from a model of interviewing that focused on the acquisition of a confession (Shepherd, 2007) to one that was more ethical and where truth-searching and information-gathering were the central theme (Williamson, Milne and Savage, 2013).

This chapter outlines the concept of an investigative interview, explores the seven principles of investigative interviewing (College of Policing, 2022) and describes the PEACE interview model, which is used by investigators in England and Wales to interview victims, witnesses and suspects. This chapter examines the challenges associated with pre-interview briefings and considers how investigators can exploit opportunities to expose truth and lies in suspect interviews by strategically using the evidence they have available.

This chapter concludes with an examination of the concept of vulnerability. It considers the role of the AA within the interview setting and explores the concept of false confessions and the risk factors associated with those who have the potential to confess to crimes they have not committed.

INVESTIGATIVE INTERVIEWING

According to the College of Policing (2022), interviewing victims, witnesses and suspects is a fundamental part of any investigation; interviews that are conducted with professionalism can help:

- *direct an investigation and gather material, which in turn can lead to a prosecution or early release of an innocent person;*

- *support the prosecution case, thereby saving time, money and resources;*

- *increase public confidence in the police service, particularly with witnesses and victims of crimes who come into direct contact with the police.*

(College of Policing, 2022, para 3)

Investigative interviews are always going to be *'difficult conversations'* (Shepherd, 2007, p 18). They are conducted in circumstances which are psychologically challenging for those involved; however, without the accounts of those central to the investigation, other sources of material such as CCTV images, fingerprints and forensic evidence may have limited value (College of Policing, 2022).

A successful interview is underpinned by the seven principles of investigative interviewing, which are summarised in the College of Policing Authorised Professional Practice, as shown in Table 8.1.

Table 8.1 The seven principles of investigative interviewing

Principle 1	The aim of investigative interviewing is to obtain accurate and reliable accounts from victims, witnesses or suspects about matters under police investigation. Information should be as complete as possible, free from omissions or distortion, and should be capable of withstanding scrutiny if challenged at court.
Principle 2	Investigators must act fairly when questioning victims, witnesses or suspects, ensuring compliance with the Equality Act (2010) and the Human Rights Act (1998), and thereby safeguarding those who are perceived as vulnerable from being disadvantaged by the criminal justice system (CJS).
Principle 3	Investigative interviewing should be approached with an investigative mindset, which means being open-minded, being receptive to alternative explanations and being objective by challenging preconceptions or personal bias (ACPO/Centrex, 2005). Accounts obtained should always be tested against what the interviewer already knows or what can be reasonably established.
Principle 4	Investigators are free to ask a wide range of questions in an interview to obtain material which may assist an investigation. Interviewers are not bound by the same rules of evidence as lawyers in court, which means the rules of 'hearsay' evidence do not apply; however, the interviewing style must remain fair and free from oppression.

⟶

Table 8.1 *(continued)*

Principle 5	Investigators should recognise the positive impact of an early admission; this includes victim reassurance; reduced resource implications for the police, prosecution and wider CJS; financial savings; and a more complete picture of offending. Equally, the defendant may receive credit for an early admission.
Principle 6	Investigators are not bound to accept the first answer as they have a duty to obtain an accurate and reliable account from sometimes reluctant victims, witnesses and suspects. Probing and truth-searching questions require persistence which does not necessarily equate to unfairness unless it strays into the realms of oppression.
Principle 7	When a suspect exercises the right to silence, investigators have a responsibility to ask questions. In these circumstances, warnings may be appropriate regarding a suspect's refusal to answer questions, which may allow a court to draw adverse inferences, in accordance with sections 34, 36 and 37 of the Criminal Justice and Public Order Act (1994).

Source: College of Policing (2022).

REFLECTIVE PRACTICE 8.1

LEVEL 4

Interviews conducted with professionalism and high ethical standards bring many benefits to investigations; they can help direct an investigation, support the prosecution of offenders and improve legitimacy in policing.

- Consider the consequences of failing to demonstrate professionalism and high ethical standards during investigative interviews.

Sample answers are provided at the end of this book.

INTERVIEW MODEL: PEACE

An investigative interview requires the application of three core elements:

1. reciprocity, which applies to all social exchanges and is based on the premise '*if we receive something or we are asked a question we are obliged to reciprocate*';

2. mindful behaviours such as respect, empathy and a non-judgemental attitude; and

3. effective *'conversation management'* (Shepherd, 2007, p18).

Developed on these underlying principles, in 1992, the PEACE interview model was adopted by the police service in England and Wales (Clarke, Milne and Bull, 2011). The mnemonic PEACE is used to describe five sequential phases of the approach to investigative interviews (see Table 8.2).

Table 8.2 PEACE interview model

P	**Planning and preparation**
	According to the College of Policing (2022), planning and preparation is one of the most important elements of the interview. The planning process should involve reviewing the investigation, understanding the material or evidence already available and the aims and objectives the interview seeks to achieve. Planning and preparation should take account of the time and location of the interview, and the characteristics of the interviewee, such as their age, vulnerability, cultural background, domestic circumstances, health and well-being, gender and previous experience with the police.
	Regarding suspect interviews, consideration should be given at this stage to the pre-interview briefing and what material or evidence will be disclosed to a legal adviser before the interview (discussed in more detail later in this chapter).
E	**Engage and explain**
	This is the opening phase of the interview. While there is a sense of professional formality as the *'rules of engagement'* are explained, this is the first stage to developing a conversation and building a rapport with the interviewee. Rapport is considered the *'foundation for effective interaction'* (Abbe and Brandon, 2013, p 237). It is the *'bond'* or *'connection'* between the interviewer and the interviewee (Vallano et al, 2015, p 369) and is known to enhance witness recall, increase co-operation and build trust between parties (Macintosh, 2009; Collins, Lincoln and Frank, 2002; Bull and Soukara, 2010).
A	**Account, clarification and challenge**
	Beyond initial engagement, interviewees are asked to provide an account of the event, which may require clarification or challenge (Gudjonsson, 2003; Shepherd, 2007). Initiating the *account* phase with an open-ended question such as *'Tell me...'*, *'Describe...'* or *'Explain what happened...'*, the interviewee is allowed the opportunity to give an uninterrupted narrative. The account may then be broken down into more manageable topics for systematic probing through a combination of open or specific closed questions (College of Policing, 2022).
	Challenging the account of a victim, witness, or suspect is an important element of the interview. This should not create a sense of confrontation, it is simply designed to remove ambiguity or expose inconsistencies in the account provided.

→

Table 8.2 *(continued)*

C	**Closure**

On closing, the interviewer should summarise the contents of the interview and provide the interviewee with an opportunity to add or clarify anything they have said. Taking this as an opportunity to provide clarity in terms of next steps, the way the interview is closed has the capacity to reassure victims and witnesses that the police are taking a proactive approach to the investigation, reduce anxiety about what happens next in the judicial process (Snook, Eastwood and Barron, 2014) and help maintain the professional image of the investigator (Walsh and Milne, 2010).

E	**Evaluation**

Following an interview, the interviewer needs to evaluate what has been said in the context of the investigation to determine whether any further action is necessary, such as additional research or a supplementary interview, and to reflect on their own performance to support continued professional development (College of Policing, 2022).

The seven principles of investigative interviewing (College of Policing, 2022) combined with the PEACE interview model demonstrate an ethical shift from accusatorial styles of interviewing to one where truth-searching and information-gathering with impartiality are at the heart of any investigation.

CRITICAL THINKING ACTIVITY 8.1

LEVEL 6

- Evaluate the effectiveness of the PEACE interview model.

In answering this question, it may be prudent, first of all, to determine what constitutes 'effectiveness'. Then, once this has been determined, critically evaluate the approach to investigative interviewing in England and Wales.

Sample answers are provided at the end of this book.

POLICING SPOTLIGHT

Following the introduction of the PEACE interview model, it became clear that investigations into major and serious crime demanded interviewers with advanced levels of skill and competency (Griffiths and Milne, 2013). In 2002, the Association of Chief Police Officers (ACPO) approved a five-tiered structure of investigative interviewing, which held common standards in training, skills development and performance. This is now incorporated into the Professionalising Investigations Programme (PIP) (see Chapter 1 of this book) and means practitioners accredited at PIP levels 1, 2 and 3 have incremental skills and competency to conduct interviews with victims, witnesses and suspects in priority and volume crime (PIP 1) and more specialist interviews on investigations with greater complexity or gravity (PIP 2 and 3) (ACPO/NPIA, 2009).

PRE-INTERVIEW BRIEFINGS

It is likely that a legal adviser will represent the interests of a suspect in most investigations into major and serious crime. Their role is to act in the best interests of their clients by challenging the legal and procedural aspects of police action, advising whether to assist the investigation, intervening to seek clarification, challenging inappropriate question types, exploring alternative outcomes, and attempting to persuade investigators their client is not responsible for the offence(s) under investigation (Home Office, 2019; College of Policing, 2022).

The relationship between the investigators and a legal adviser is important, and there should be mutual respect for the role of each party (College of Policing, 2022). However, investigators need to recognise that each has competing priorities and objectives. Therefore, it is important that pre-interview briefings are considered and planned according to the strategy set by the senior investigating officer (SIO), perhaps in consultation with a specialist interview adviser.

According to the Home Office (2019, para 11.1A), prior to an interview, when a suspect is represented by a legal adviser, they must be provided with 'sufficient information' to enable them to understand the nature of the offence(s) under investigation 'in order to allow for the effective exercise of the rights of the defence'. This does not mean investigators must disclose details that may prejudice the investigation. Far from it, the disclosure of material in the pre-interview briefing must be balanced against the needs of the investigation and the requirement for an effective and productive interview (College of Policing, 2022).

Pre-interview briefings will be case-dependent and there are no hard and fast rules on what must be disclosed, but an initial disclosure must not be designed to deceive or misrepresent the evidence and may include details relating to the nature of the allegation, circumstances of the arrest, any significant statement and topics for discussion (College of Policing, 2022). In major and serious crime investigations, when there is likely to be more than one interview, a frequent approach is to adopt a strategy of 'staged disclosure', which effectively drip-feeds investigative material to a suspect in advance of each interview. Known as the strategic use of evidence (SUE), the tactical release of evidence at key stages of the interview process aims to test the veracity of details provided by innocent suspects and expose lies or inconsistencies in accounts provided by the guilty (Hartwig et al, 2006; Granhag and Hartwig, 2008; Vrij, Granhag and Verschuere, 2015).

POLICING SPOTLIGHT

The risks associated with deceit and misrepresentation of evidence are illustrated in the case R v Mason (1988), during which investigators intentionally fabricated evidence. Similarly, the concept of disclosing 'sufficient information' to enable a legal adviser to 'exercise the rights of the defence' was tested in R v Nottle (2004), when critical evidence was withheld during a pre-interview briefing.

The defendants provided confession evidence during their respective interviews, which was later used as part of a successful prosecution. On appeal, defence counsel applied to exclude the evidence under section 76(2) or alternatively section 78 of the Police and Criminal Evidence Act (PACE, 1984) on the basis that:

- the confession was obtained in consequence of anything said or done which was likely, in the circumstances existing at the time, to render unreliable any confession which might be made by him in consequence thereof (PACE, 1984, section 76(2)(b)); and

- having regard to all the circumstances, including the circumstances in which the evidence was obtained, the admission of the evidence would have such an adverse effect on the fairness of the proceedings that the court ought not to admit it (PACE, 1984, section 78(1)).

In the case of R v Mason (1988), the confession evidence was excluded under section 78 of PACE (1984), which gives the court discretion to exclude if it considers that the admission of the evidence would have an adverse effect on the fairness of the proceedings, meaning the conviction was quashed.

In the judgment of R v Nottle (2004), the appeal was upheld as it was found 'there was no trick or unfairness that led to the oral admission', concluding investigators were not required to disclose every piece of evidence, more so they voluntarily provide disclosure of material to counter any future arguments at trial that no adverse inferences should be drawn under section 34 of the Criminal Justice and Public Order Act (1994) from a suspect's failure to answer questions (R v Nottle, 2004, para 13).

ESTABLISHING VULNERABILITY

According to Her Majesty's Inspector of Constabulary (HMIC, 2015, p 16) *'police custody is the principal gateway to the criminal justice system'*, and a significant number of individuals pass through this gateway with pre-existing mental health conditions or drug and alcohol dependency (Hannan et al, 2010; Bradley, 2009). An estimated 30 per cent of those entering the CJS suffer from some form of learning disability (HMI Probation et al, 2014). As many as 60 per cent of young people in the youth justice system have speech, language and communication difficulties, and 25 per cent have special educational needs (APPGC, 2014).

The custody officer, who is generally a police officer at the rank of sergeant, has a responsibility to establish whether the person being brought into police custody under arrest or arrested at the police station having attended voluntarily for an interview:

- *is or might be in need of medical treatment or attention;*

- *is a juvenile (which is a term used to describe a child in detention) and/or vulnerable and therefore require the support of an AA [appropriate adult].*
  (Home Office, 2019, para 3.15c)

The term 'juvenile', for the purposes of the Police and Criminal Evidence Act (PACE, 1984) is relatively straightforward. The Home Office (2019, para 1.5) defines a juvenile as *'anyone who appears to be under 18, shall, in the absence of clear evidence that they are older, be treated as a juvenile'*.

The test for 'vulnerability' is much more subjective and is defined as any person who because of a mental health condition or mental disorder:

- *may have difficulty understanding or communicating effectively about the full implications for them of any procedures and processes connected with:*

  o *their arrest and detention (or as the case may be);*

  o *their voluntary attendance at a police station or their presence elsewhere, for the purpose of a voluntary interview and;*

  o *the exercise of their rights and entitlements;*

- *does not appear to understand the significance of what they are told, of questions they are asked or of their replies;*

- *appears to be particularly prone to:*
    - o   *becoming confused and unclear about their position;*
    - o   *providing unreliable, misleading or incriminating information without knowing or wishing to do so;*
    - o   *accepting or acting on suggestions from others without consciously knowing or wishing to do so or;*
    - o   *readily agreeing to suggestions or proposals without protest or question.*
                                                                (Home Office, 2019, para 1.13(d))

The term vulnerability may also include individuals with learning difficulties, physical illness or disability, alcohol and/or substance misuse (HMIC, 2015).

According to the Home Office (2019, para 1.4), if at any time an officer has any reason to suspect that a person of any age may be vulnerable, in the absence of clear evidence to the contrary, that person shall be treated as vulnerable. The custody officer in the case of a detained person, or any investigating officer of a person who has not been arrested or detained, shall make or cause reasonable enquiries to be made to establish what information is available which may be relevant to any factors indicating the person may be vulnerable.

In terms of assessing vulnerability, at the time of detention, the custody officer must initiate a risk assessment which is based on self-reports of the detainee's situation at the time, drawn on information held in police records and elicited in consultation with a medical practitioner or other professional or family member (HMIC, 2015). That said, while there is rigour around the assessment for vulnerability, the test is subjective, which means there is potential for error. In a review into the welfare of vulnerable people in police custody, it was established there was inconsistency in approaches. Police officers and staff relied on their own experiences and personal judgements, developing a '*gut feeling*' or '*sixth sense*' when identifying and responding to vulnerable people, rather than being able to refer to official training or guidance (HMIC, 2015; Dehaghani, 2016, p 401).

Failing to recognise vulnerability can lead to the exclusion of evidence under the provisions of sections 76 and 78 of the Police and Criminal Evidence Act (1984), which deal with the admissibility of confession evidence and, perhaps more importantly, increase the risk of miscarriages of justice as a result of evidence being obtained from vulnerable suspects which, by virtue of their vulnerability, may lead to unsafe and unjust convictions.

EVIDENCE-BASED POLICING

Research by McKinnon and Grubin (2013) examined the extent to which police health screening procedures successfully identified detainees who required further assessment or treatment by a health care professional (HCP), or who needed the involvement of an appropriate adult (AA) for support during their detention. From a participant group of 248 detainees, research detected an overrepresentation of health morbidity and intellectual disability when compared against the general population, and police screening procedures failed to identify mental health conditions, psychotic disorders and intellectual disabilities. Similarly, research by McKinnon et al (2013) established that police risk assessment screening failed to identify psychotic disorders in 42 per cent of detainees and 33 per cent of detainees with major depression, meaning there are many missed opportunities in the custody setting to identify vulnerability.

THE APPROPRIATE ADULT

An appropriate adult (AA) is an individual who provides support to a juvenile (child who appears under the age of 18 years) or a vulnerable person while in detention or being questioned about a criminal offence. Their role is to safeguard their interests, rights, entitlements and welfare by offering advice and guidance on procedural matters so they can participate effectively, ensure the police act appropriately and assist with communication during the detention and questioning process (Home Office, 2019, para. 1.7A).

In the case of a juvenile, subject to certain conditions, an AA may be a parent, guardian, a representative of a local authority or voluntary organisation, a social worker of a local authority or some other responsible adult over 18 years of age. In the case of a vulnerable person, similar criteria apply; for example, the AA could be a parent, guardian or other person over 18 years of age who is responsible for their care or custody, such as a care support worker and, when circumstances allow, someone with experience in dealing with vulnerable people (Home Office, 2019, para 1.7).

There are conditions in terms of those who are ineligible to perform the role of an AA, including:

- *a police officer or someone employed by the police;*

- *someone under the direction or control of the chief officer of police or;*

- *a person who provides services under contractual arrangements with a police force at the relevant time.*

(Home Office, 2019, para 1.7)

Individuals should not perform the role of an AA if they are suspected of involvement in the offence, they are the victim, a witness or involved in the investigation, or they have received admissions from the juvenile or vulnerable person prior to being involved as the AA (Home Office, 2019, note 1B).

Section 38(4) of the Crime and Disorder Act (1998) places the local authority under a statutory obligation to provide youth justice services, including the provision of resources to act as AAs to safeguard the interests of children and young people while they are detained or questioned by police. It is interesting to note that there are no such statutory obligations for vulnerable adults, which compounds the disadvantage these individuals experience in the CJS (Bath et al, 2015).

POLICING SPOTLIGHT

In 2015, the Home Secretary commissioned the National Appropriate Adult Network (NAAN) to review the provision of AAs for mentally vulnerable adults detained or interviewed by the police. The subsequent report, *There to Help*, concluded there were significant limitations to the provision of AAs for mentally vulnerable adult suspects, inadequate police practices in the identification of vulnerability, and limited availability and variable quality of AAs, which collectively '*undermines their welfare, inhibits the exercise of their legal rights, risks miscarriages of justice and lengthens custody times potentially increasing the risk of self-harm*' (Bath et al, 2015, p 4).

EVIDENCE-BASED POLICING

It is essential that those who perform the role of AAs are effective in the provision of support to vulnerable adults while they are detained or interviewed by the police. Medford, Gudjonsson and Pearse (2003) examined 501 audio-recorded interviews with vulnerable adults and juveniles, which established that while direct contribution from the AA was limited, their presence during the interview appeared to positively affect the behaviour of the police and the legal adviser, meaning the mere presence of an AA provides an additional safeguard for vulnerable suspects.

In contrast, Farrugia and Gabbert (2019) examined 27 real-world police interviews with vulnerable adults who were suspected of committing major and serious crimes, including murder, attempted murder, rape and sexual assaults. The research concluded that they often failed to intervene when guidance, according to PACE (1984), suggested they should have, meaning passivity in the role, together with the complexities of the vulnerable suspect, could present challenges to the CJS.

REFLECTIVE PRACTICE 8.2

LEVEL 5

You have arrested a 17-year-old man on suspicion of rape contrary to section 1 of the Sexual Offences Act (2003). You have brought him to the police station for the purpose of an interview.

- Apply your knowledge to this scenario and consider whether there is a need for an AA and, if so, who may perform the role.

Sample answers are provided at the end of this book.

FALSE CONFESSIONS

The transition from accusatorial interview techniques of the past, which focused on the acquisition of a confession, to an approach which seeks accurate and reliable information in a more balanced and ethical manner aims to reduce the risk of false confessions, which may result in miscarriages of justice. It is difficult to estimate the number of false confessions, but we know they exist through case histories, notably in the Maxwell Confait case (1972), Birmingham Six and Guildford Four (1974) and the Cardiff Three (1988), all of which were influenced by coercive interview techniques, self-report studies among the prison population (Gudjonsson, 2003) and laboratory-based research (Kassin and Kiechel, 1996). The unmistakable fact is that some people confess to crimes they have not committed.

The reason why people confess to crimes they have not committed is often a combination of situational factors such as the custodial environment or interview technique and the psychological vulnerabilities of the suspect (Gudjonsson, 2003, 2018; Kassin and Gudjonsson, 2004). In essence, there are three types of false confession, which are summarised by Gudjonsson (2003, 2018) as the following.

- *Voluntary false confessions*, which are offered by suspects with no external pressure, perhaps through a desire for notoriety, guilt associated with previous offending, inability to distinguish fact from fiction or a desire to protect the real criminal.

- *Coerced-compliant false confessions*, which result from the pressures of the interview and may be brought about by an inference of being allowed to go home after confessing, bringing the interview to an end or a means of coping with the demands of the interview when the perceived benefits in the short term are more desirable than the long-term implications.

- *Coerced-internalised false confessions*, which occur when the suspect comes to believe during police questioning that they have committed the crime, even though they have no memory of doing so.

The concept of *interrogative suggestibility* illustrates how leading questions, when phrased in a way that suggests an expected or desired answer, are intrinsically linked to false confessions (Stern, 1939; Gudjonsson, 2018). This can be influenced by various characteristics including age, gender, ethnicity, intelligence and experience with the CJS. Other factors heightening the risk of false confessions include:

- *the context of the investigation, such as the pressure on police to solve the case, the relationship between the suspect, victim and other suspects and the broader responsibilities of the suspect, for example, having dependents;*

- *the interview and custodial factors, such as the length of time in custody, number of interviews and tactics used;*

- *lack of understanding of the caution; which highlights the importance of ensuring the caution is explained and suspects understand the nature of the caution and its implications;*

- *age and mindset of the suspect, innocence itself may play its part;*

- *physical and mental or other developmental disorders;*

- *alcohol and substance abuse;*

- *absence of support while in custody and during interviews.*

(Gudjonsson, 2018, p 51)

Investigators need to be familiar with the fact that some people falsely confess to crimes they have not committed and take mitigating action to reduce the risks. Taking steps to ask probing questions through the 'Account, clarification and challenge' phase of the PEACE model to obtain corroborating evidence to support confessions; managing interview pressures and situational factors which may aggravate suspects' vulnerability; and approaching interviews in a balanced, non-judgemental and open-minded way will go some way to reduce the potential for false confessions and miscarriages of justice.

CRITICAL THINKING ACTIVITY 8.2

LEVEL 4

- Consider what you have learned through this chapter and describe how it can be applied to an investigative interview with a 17-year-old suspect who has been arrested in connection with an allegation of murder, contrary to common law.

Sample answers are provided at the end of this book.

CONCLUSION

Investigative interviews with victims, witnesses and suspects are a fundamental part of any investigation, which, when conducted professionally, have the potential to realise many benefits. This chapter has discussed how they can help direct an investigation, identify lines of enquiry which may lead to the prosecution of offenders or the early release of innocent suspects, save time, money and resources, and increase public confidence in the police service.

Coercive interview techniques of the past, which were confession-driven, have been replaced with an approach to investigative interviewing which seeks to establish the truth and to obtain accurate and reliable information in a balanced, non-judgemental way. This chapter has explored the seven principles of investigative interviewing described by the College of Policing (2022). It has examined the PEACE interview model, which provides the framework for an effective investigative interview with victims, witnesses and suspects.

A significant element of the interview process takes place before the questioning of a suspect begins. This chapter has examined the role of 'pre-interview briefings' and has considered how investigators can strategically use their evidence to maximise outcomes. By adopting a strategy of *staged disclosure*, which tactically releases evidence at key stages, investigators can test the reliability of information provided by the innocent and expose lies or inconsistencies in accounts provided by the guilty.

This chapter has explored the concept of vulnerability and considered the role of the AA, who has the responsibility to safeguard the rights and interests of juveniles under the age of 18 and vulnerable people while they are in detention or being questioned about a criminal offence.

This chapter has concluded with a discussion about the types of false confessions, the factors that heighten the risk of false confessions and the steps investigators can take to help reduce the potential for miscarriages of justice.

SUMMARY OF KEY CONCEPTS

This chapter has discussed the following key concepts:

- the underlying principles of investigative interviewing;

- the PEACE interview model;

- how the strategic use of evidence can add value to the outcomes of an investigative interview;

- the concept of vulnerability and how failing to recognise can impact on policing and the wider CJS;

- the types of false confessions and the reasons why they happen.

CHECK YOUR KNOWLEDGE

1. What are the benefits of conducting an investigative interview with professionalism?

2. How many principles of investigative interviewing are there?

3. PEACE is a mnemonic for a five-stage sequential model of investigative interviewing. Can you name the five stages?

4. What is the purpose of a pre-interview briefing?

5. What is the role of the AA?

6. What are the three types of false confession?

FURTHER READING

College of Policing (2022) Investigative Interviewing. [online] Available at: www.college.police.uk/app/investigation/investigative-interviewing (accessed 22 October 2023). This website outlines the College of Policing Authorised Professional Practice on investigative interviews.

Gudjonsson, G H (2003) The Psychology of Interrogations Confessions: A Handbook. Chichester: Wiley & Sons Ltd.
This book examines in detail interrogations, interviews and their propensity for false confessions. It explores the empirical evidence behind false confessions and those who are susceptible.

Shepherd, E (2007) *Investigative Interviewing: The Conversation Management Model*. Oxford: Oxford University Press.
This book provides a comprehensive account of the PEACE model of interviewing, its development and structure and the concept of conversation management.

Vallano, J P, Evans, J R, Schreiber Compo, N and Kieckhaefer, J M (2015) Rapport-Building During Witness and Suspect Interviews: A Survey of Law Enforcement. *Applied Cognitive Psychology*, 29(3): 369–80.
This journal examines the use and value of rapport during the interview process.

CHAPTER 9
THE USE OF CIVIL ORDERS

LEARNING OBJECTIVES

AFTER READING THIS CHAPTER YOU WILL BE ABLE TO:

- explain why civil orders are important in disrupting major and serious crime;

- analyse how theoretical principles underpin the use of civil orders;

- describe the criminal and civil burden of proof, how they differ and what this means for the standard of evidence required for civil orders;

- evaluate how civil orders impact on human rights;

- discuss the difference between a range of civil orders and how they are applied to major and serious crime.

INTRODUCTION

The traditional law enforcement response to the investigation of major and serious crime has limitations. The collection of evidence, the intimidation of victims and witnesses, the scale and reach of offending across international borders, the use of technology and the nature of individuals involved collectively means reaching the standard of proof required for criminal prosecutions is challenging.

The Serious and Organised Crime Strategy (Home Office, 2018a) encourages law enforcement agencies to adopt a holistic approach to investigation, one which not only *pursues* offenders but also *prevents* criminality from occurring in the first place, *protects* communities from harm and is *prepared* for when it happens. Despite the challenges and limitations, the *pursue* element of the strategy is often the first option investigators take. Less frequently will investigators look to alternative methods, ones that aim to prevent offending in the first place, thereby protecting communities from harm and, in some cases, protecting the individuals themselves.

Civil orders are a relatively new concept in legal proceedings, and they provide a viable alternative to investigation. They are not dependent on the strength of evidence required to meet the criminal standard of proof, they are not necessarily dependent on victim or witness testimony, and they can be applied both with and without conviction, meaning they present real opportunities to tackle high harm criminality in a different way.

This chapter explores the theoretical principles which underpin the use of civil orders; concepts such as deterrence, routine activity, rational choice and situational crime prevention and how these theories apply to civil orders will be discussed. It examines the *standard of proof*, how this differs between criminal and civil cases, and how the associated standards of evidence might affect an individual's right to a fair trial according to the European Convention on Human Rights (ECHR). Prominent civil orders relevant to the disruption of major and serious crime are explored in detail, and the chapter concludes with a summary of some broader civil orders which are available to investigators in their aim of disrupting and deterring some of the most serious forms of criminality.

THEORETICAL PRINCIPLES OF CIVIL ORDERS

Civil orders in the context of major and serious crime are reliant on a range of theoretical principles, which need to act together to increase their effectiveness. Some of these theories are discussed here.

DETERRENCE THEORY

General deterrence presents the notion that people are discouraged from committing crimes by the prospect of having to face some form of punishment (Miceli, Segerson and Earnhart, 2022). Individuals commit crimes when the perceived benefits outweigh the expected punishment. Therefore, when general deterrence fails, alternative measures are required. 'Specific' or 'special' deterrence is aimed at individuals who have already committed crimes and involves the application of sanctions in the hope that this will prevent them from committing more crimes in the future (Barnes et al, 2010). This form of deterrence is dependent on three key components, *severity* of sanction, *certainty* of arrest, prosecution and conviction, and *celerity* or swiftness of punishment. When one of the three components is missing, the deterrence effect will be reduced (Barnes et al, 2010; Sloan et al, 2013).

RATIONAL CHOICE THEORY

Despite how irrational some offending behaviour may seem, the assumption is that all offenders think before they act, even if this is momentarily based on the immediacy of the situation rather than through any longer-term strategic thinking (Newburn, 2007).

In criminological terms, the theory of rational choice proposes that individuals are responsible for their own behaviour, making conscious decisions to commit crime while balancing the risks against reward. Crimes are described as purposeful acts which benefit the offender in some way, such as material or financial gain, excitement, prestige or status, sexual gratification and, in some cases, the dominance of others (Clarke and Cornish, 1985; Newburn, 2007). Choices to commit crimes are influenced by psychological and social factors, where group behaviour can sometimes increase the level of risk associated with offending (Clarke and Cornish, 1985).

ROUTINE ACTIVITY THEORY

According to Cohen and Felson (1979, p 589) routine activity theory proposes that predatory crimes are committed when there is a convergence in time and space of three core ingredients:

1. *motivated offenders;*

2. *suitable targets;*

3. *absence of a capable guardian.*

Described by Felson and Eckert (2016, p 41) as the *'chemistry of crime'*, each crime has its own ingredients, and the absence of one core element may be sufficient to prevent the successful commission of a predatory crime (Cohen and Felson, 1979). One of the main propositions suggests that the rate of criminal victimisation increases when there is a convergence in time and space of the three core elements, which is aggravated when there are more people present who are motivated to commit the crime (Cohen and Felson, 1979; Newburn, 2007).

SITUATIONAL CRIME PREVENTION

Crimes are committed in response to situational conditions. Therefore the concept of *situational crime prevention* aims to build on rational choice and routine activity theory by reducing opportunities to commit crime by manipulating situation-specific behaviour and changing offending environments (Clarke, 1995; Wikström et al, 2010). Common examples of how situational conditions have been changed to affect offending behaviour include the introduction of close circuit television cameras (CCTV), burglar alarms, increased street lighting and controls on 'crime facilitators' such as guns, knives, cars, and telephones, and includes new and emerging technologies which facilitate most crimes (Clarke, 1995; Newburn, 2007).

Criminological theories have supported the development of a range of civil remedies which form the basis of alternative investigative strategies, which, when applied successfully against specific crime and disorder problems, have the potential to deter offending and reduce harm to victims of major and serious crime.

CRITICAL THINKING ACTIVITY 9.1

LEVEL 6

You are investigating a group of individuals who are involved in gang-related activity, including drug supply and the criminal use of firearms.

- Critically evaluate how deterrence, rational choice, routine activity theory and situational crime prevention strategies can be applied to their behaviour to disrupt criminality and encourage desistance from crime.

Sample answers are provided at the end of this book.

BURDEN AND STANDARDS OF PROOF

The golden thread running through criminal proceedings in England and Wales is clear: the onus or burden lies with the prosecution to prove a person is guilty. It is not for the defendant to prove their innocence (*Woolmington v DPP*, 1935). This concept is embedded into ECHR Article 6(2), right to a fair trial, which states '*everyone charged with a criminal offence shall be presumed innocent until proved guilty according to law*'. Furthermore, Article 6(1) ECHR outlines how the standard of proof in criminal cases is '*beyond reasonable doubt*'. In other words, there must be certainty of guilt to convict. This is summarised by Lord Denning in *Miller v Minister of Pensions* (1947, cited in Block and Hostettler, 2002, p 50):

> if the evidence is so strong against a man so as to leave only a remote possibility in his favour which can be dismissed with the sentence 'Of course it is possible, but not in the least probable', the case is proved beyond reasonable doubt, but nothing short of that will suffice.

In civil proceedings, the rules are very different. First, the Civil Evidence Act (1995) and the Civil Procedure Rules (Rule 33) govern the introduction of hearsay evidence in civil proceedings, which means information, intelligence, incident reports, and other material are admissible as evidence; second, the standard of proof is based on the '*balance of probabilities*', which means it is '*more probable than not*' (Redmayne, 1999, p 167), making it easier for claimants (prosecution) to meet the evidential threshold required in civil cases.

While preventative orders designed to tackle major and serious crime are available under the civil standard of proof, the crimes they aim to disrupt attract the criminal standard, namely '*beyond reasonable doubt*'. This brings into question whether civil orders attempt to circumvent due process and are therefore incompatible with ECHR Article 6, right to a fair trial.

This was tested in the context of anti-social behaviour orders (ASBOs), which established that proceedings for an ASBO are, in fact, 'civil' in nature, and they did not involve a charge under Article 6(1) ECHR. The House of Lords (2002) in *R v Manchester Crown Court ex parte McCann* (2002) held that the use of hearsay evidence in proceedings for an ASBO was not contrary to Article 6(1) and confirmed the standard of proof to be applied in deciding whether anti-social behaviour had taken place was equivalent to the criminal standard of beyond reasonable doubt. According to the Crown Prosecution Service (2022d, para 62), the court stated:

> the standard of proof to be applied to a defendant's conduct was the criminal standard. There were good reasons, in the interests of fairness, for applying that higher standard where allegations were made of criminal or quasi-criminal conduct which, if proved, would have serious consequences for the person against whom they were made.

It is therefore expected that applications for preventative civil orders, particularly in the context of major and serious crime, should reach a higher or *enhanced* standard of proof, perhaps based on a sliding scale depending on the severity of conditions sought to be imposed by the orders themselves.

POLICING SPOTLIGHT

The validity of applying the civil standard of proof was tested in the case of *Jones v Birmingham City Council* (2018). The case concerned the issuance of a gang injunction in 2016 against Jerome Jones, who was believed to be part of a criminal gang in the Birmingham area.

An appeal against the application of a civil standard of proof in what was suggested as criminal proceedings, thereby breaching Article 6 ECHR, was dismissed by the Court of Appeal. This was escalated to the Supreme Court in January 2023, and in judgment, the Supreme Court confirmed the application of the civil standard of proof did *not* engage Article 6 and upheld the decision made by the Court of Appeal.

SERIOUS CRIME PREVENTION ORDERS

Serious crime prevention orders (SCPOs) are a civil measure that may be imposed pre- and post-conviction. They are designed for use against individuals who are involved in the most serious forms of criminality (Home Office, 2015). They are issued by the Crown Court when sentencing a person over the age of 18 years (or in some situations corporate entities and partnerships) who has been convicted of a serious offence, or by the High Court without a conviction when they are satisfied there are reasonable grounds to believe the order would protect the public by preventing, restricting or disrupting involvement by the person in serious crime throughout England, Wales, Northern Ireland or elsewhere (Home Office, 2015).

Schedule 1 of the Serious Crime Act (2007), amended by section 47 of the Serious Crime Act (2015) and section 7 of the Modern Slavery Act (2015), provides a list of offences that constitute 'serious crime' for the purposes of an SCPO. These include offences associated with but not limited to drug trafficking, firearms, human trafficking, prostitution and child sex offences, computer misuse, money laundering and fraud.

The court has discretion in terms of the conditions that may be considered necessary to impose on an individual subject of an SCPO; examples include prohibitions or restrictions on or requirements in relation to:

- *an individual's financial, property or business dealings or holdings;*

- *an individual's working arrangements;*

- *the means by which an individual communicates or associates with others, or the persons with whom [they] communicate, or associates;*

- *the premises to which an individual has access;*

- *the use of any premises or item by an individual;*

- *an individual's travel (whether within the United Kingdom, between the United Kingdom and other places, or otherwise).*

(Serious Crime Act, 2007, section 5(3))

Additional conditions may require an individual subject of an SCPO to report to a law enforcement officer and answer questions or provide information or documentation at a time, place and location as described in the order (Serious Crime Act, 2007, section 5(5)).

The nature of SCPOs is such that applications for orders in England and Wales may only be made by the Director of Public Prosecutions (DPP), the Director of the Serious Fraud Office or, for terrorist-related offences, the Chief Officer of Police, on condition they have consulted with the DPP (Serious Crime Act, 2007, section 8). In considering whether to grant an order, the court should concern itself with future risk, not simply the possibility of risk. Still, it must be satisfied there is a real and significant risk that the individual will commit further serious offences (*R v Hancox and Duffy*, 2010).

In the event an order is granted, it can last for up to five years, and any breach of its conditions is deemed to be a criminal offence, which may be subject to a maximum penalty of five years' imprisonment.

Acting as a specific deterrence which is directly influenced by theories including routine activity, rational choice and situational crime prevention, SCPOs are described by the Home Office (2023b, para 1) as a '*powerful tool for preventing and disrupting the activities of the highest-harm criminals involved in serious crime*'. Despite this, the Home Office (2023b) directly criticised law enforcement agencies, claiming that SCPOs are not being used to maximum effect, and in January 2023, it commenced a period of consultation with relevant professionals and the public to inquire how improvements can be made to increase their use and effectiveness.

POLICING SPOTLIGHT

The practical application of a SCPO is illustrated in the case of Curtis Warren, reported in the media as the United Kingdom's answer to Pablo Escobar. Convicted of attempting to smuggle cocaine into the UK from Colombia and failing to comply with a confiscation order, following his release from prison in November 2022, an SCPO came into effect, which restricts his freedom to exercise everyday activities. The SCPO restricts his access to mobile telephones, social media platforms and the use of digital currency, limits his access to money and requires him to notify the National Crime Agency (NCA) of his intentions to travel, all of which are intended to prevent him committing further serious crime.

REFLECTIVE PRACTICE 9.1

LEVEL 4

You are the officer in charge of an investigation into an offence of possession of a firearm without a certificate, contrary to section 1 of the Firearms Act (1968). Your investigation has resulted in the conviction at the Crown Court of an individual who is known to be involved more broadly in drug trafficking and money laundering.

- Consider whether an SCPO might be appropriate in this case and, if so, what prohibitions, restrictions or conditions you may consider useful in disrupting their involvement in serious crime.

Sample answers are provided at the end of this book.

SERIOUS VIOLENCE REDUCTION ORDERS

Serious violence reduction orders (SVROs) are post-conviction orders introduced under section 342A of the Police, Crime, Sentencing and Courts Act (PCSCA, 2022), and provide police with powers to adopt a more proactive approach to tackling knife-enabled criminality (Home Office, 2022e). This new legislation aims to broaden the powers of stop and search because SVROs provide an 'automatic' right to search anyone who is the subject of an order, thereby increasing the risk of detection in the minds of those subject to an order.

Applying to adults (over the age of 18 years), a court may grant an order against an offender convicted of a particular offence where two conditions are achieved. First, the court is satisfied on the *balance of probabilities* that:

3 (a)   *a bladed article or offensive weapon was used by the offender in the commission of the offence, or*

   (b)   *the offender had a bladed article or offensive weapon with them when the offence was committed.*

(PCSCA, 2022, section 342A)

Second is that the court must be satisfied on the balance of probabilities that:

4 (a)   *a bladed article or offensive weapon was used by another person in the commission of the offence and the offender knew or ought to have known that this would be the case, or*

   (b)   *another person who committed the offence had a bladed article or offensive weapon with them when the offence was committed and the offender knew or ought to have known that this would be the case.*

(PCSCA, 2022, section 342A)

In the event that either of the two conditions are met, the court must then consider when sentencing for the original offence whether it is necessary to grant an order to:

5 (a)   *protect the public in England and Wales from the risk of harm involving a bladed article or offensive weapon,*

   (b)   *protect any particular members of the public in England and Wales (including the offender) from such risk, or*

   (c)   *prevent the offender from committing an offence involving a bladed article or offensive weapon.*

(PCSCA, 2022, section 342A)

SVROs are applicable to individuals who have been convicted of a relevant offence to the criminal standard; however, the order itself may be granted on evidence reaching the civil standard of proof, namely the balance of probabilities. If an SVRO is granted, it must last no less than six months and no longer than two years, although a court may defer the start date of an order beyond a term of imprisonment (Home Office, 2022e).

POWERS OF STOP AND SEARCH

Under the provisions of section 342E of the PCSCA (2022), SVROs remove the necessity for *'reasonable suspicion'*, which applies to powers of stop and search under section 1 of the Police and Criminal Evidence Act (1984) and allows a police constable the *'automatic'* right to stop and search an individual subject to an order, making it easier for police officers to search those who have previously been convicted of an offence involving a bladed article or an offensive weapon (Home Office, 2022e).

While there is an automatic right to stop and search, this is a discretionary power meaning officers are expected to apply their professional judgement when making decisions about whether to exercise their powers and should take account of the broader circumstances that may be relevant to the decision (Home Office, 2022e).

BREACH OF A SERIOUS VIOLENCE REDUCTION ORDER

One of the aims of SVROs is to reduce repeat offending, which accounts for 30 per cent of all knife or offensive weapon offences (MoJ, 2023), therefore the 'two strikes' rule, provided by section 315 of the Sentencing Act (2020), which proposes minimum prison sentences for those who repeatedly carry knives, becomes a significant factor in the minds of those with a propensity to carry knives. Offences committed by an individual subject of an SVRO include:

- *fail without reasonable excuse to comply with an order;*

- *do anything prohibited by the order;*

- *provide false information to the police with regards to compliance with the order;*

- *deny they are subject of an SVRO;*

- *obstruct the police in the exercise of their powers of stop and search under the provisions of an SVRO.*

(PCSCA, 2022, section 342G)

The 'two strikes' sentencing provisions mean that adults convicted more than once of being in possession of a bladed article or offensive weapon face a minimum six-month prison sentence and a maximum of four years, while young offenders, aged 16 and 17, face a minimum four-month detention and training order (Sentencing Act, 2020, section 315).

POLICING SPOTLIGHT

On 19 April 2023, SVROs were introduced as legislation for the first time. Under the requirements of section 141 of the Police, Crime, Sentencing and Courts Act (2022), it is necessary to '*pilot*' operational effectiveness before implementation more broadly across England and Wales. SVROs are currently being tested in four areas, Merseyside, Surrey, Thames Valley and West Midlands.

On their implementation, Emily Spurrell, the Police and Crime Commissioner in Merseyside said:

> *It's vital we do everything possible to prevent any more families from suffering the heart-break caused by knife crime and these new SVROs gives Merseyside Police another tool in its arsenal to tackle those who are known to hold and use these lethal weapons.*
>
> (Spurrell, 2023, para 13)

CRITICAL THINKING ACTIVITY 9.2

LEVEL 5/6

- Consider the automatic right to stop and search, which is applicable to an individual subject to an SVRO, and evaluate how this may impact trust and confidence in policing.

Sample answers are provided at the end of this book.

GANG INJUNCTIONS

Gang injunctions are a pre-conviction order introduced in 2011 as Part 4 of the Policing and Crime Act (2009) and allow the police and local authorities to apply to a County Court, High Court or Youth Court for an injunction when it is believed an individual over the age of 14 years is involved in, has encouraged or has assisted in gang-related violence or drug dealing activity and the injunction is necessary to prevent such activity or protect the individual from harm (HM Government, 2016).

In the event that these conditions are met, and the court is satisfied on the balance of probabilities, they may grant an injunction for a period of two years, which restricts movement, association and other ordinarily legal activities, thereby reducing the opportunity to cause harm or be exposed to harm because of the gang culture. Any breach of the injunction carries a maximum sentence of two years imprisonment (HM Government, 2016).

The legislation mandates that police or local authorities demonstrate that not only is an individual involved in drug dealing activity or violence, but their actions are 'gang related'. Section 34(5) of the Policing and Crime Act (2009) defines gang-related violence as that which:

occurs in the course of, or is otherwise related to, the activities of a group that:

   a)   *consists of at least 3 people; and,*

   b)   *has one or more characteristics that enable its members to be identified by others as a group.*

The principal aim of a gang injunction is to offer a *'specific deterrence'* to those engaged in serious gang-related violence, erode the gang culture and encourage desistence from a criminal lifestyle; however, they also affect routine activities and act as a form of situational crime as prohibitions in movement or restrictions in association place distance between gang members, thereby disrupting criminality.

EVIDENCE-BASED POLICING

The effectiveness of gang injunctions was tested by Carr, Slothower and Parkinson (2017) who examined the criminal histories of 36 gang members from four gangs for a 36-month period before and a 36-month period after their respective injunctions. Data included records of crimes committed against the gang members during the same time periods. Criminality was measured by arrests, police station interviews, fixed penalty notices and summonses. Time spent in custody during the gang injunction periods was removed from denominators' calculating rates, meaning estimates of changes in offender behaviour and victimisations were based on their days at liberty and out of prison.

Results across all 36 gang members indicated their individual offending counts dropped by 70 per cent in the three years after their gang injunctions and the level of harm associated with their offending reduced by 61 per cent. Fewer criminal events were attributed to 92 per cent of the individuals in the three-year period beyond the injunction and only 8 per cent of the individuals increased their detected criminal activity.

Interestingly, victimisation of the gang members in their three-year post-injunction period dropped by 60 per cent when compared to the pre-injunction period.

The evidence derived from this study illustrates gang injunctions offer police and local authorities across England and Wales an effective alternative strategy in the fight against gang-related criminality when perhaps more traditional forms of major and serious crime enforcement have failed.

Additionally, the service of the injunction on individual gang members may introduce a deterrence effect on the wider criminal group. Research suggests there may be some gang members who are not fully internalised into the gang culture and through their vicarious experience may feel more inhibited with regards to future participation in group offending. This proposal is theorised by Stafford and War (1993, cited by Paternoster and Pique, 1995), who discuss how the deterrence process involves a combination of personal and vicarious experiences, which serves to inform their perception of risk. In other words, if an individual or someone they know commits a crime and goes unpunished, their perception of risk will decrease; conversely if crimes are punished their perception of risk increases, thereby creating a specific deterrence effect through either direct or vicarious experience. It is therefore clear how the simple act of serving an injunction can start to deter offending immediately, not just with the principal subjects, but also with the wider group through their vicarious experience.

In turning to the theoretical concept of how gang injunctions can break the cycle of offending and encourage desistance from crime, it is key to understand the principles of how restrictions on movement, association and lifestyle can directly impact on routine activities of criminal gangs and their situational exposure to offending.

DOMESTIC VIOLENCE PROTECTION NOTICES AND ORDERS

Domestic violence has a damaging impact on victims and families and the police should always aim to prosecute for substantive offences; however, the complex nature of domestic violence means prosecution is not always possible. Implemented in 2014, domestic violence protection notices (DVPNs) and domestic violence protection orders (DVPOs) are civil orders that aim to fill a gap in providing protection to victims by enabling the police and magistrates' courts to put in place protective measures in the immediate aftermath of a domestic violence incident where there is insufficient evidence to charge the offender (Home Office, 2022f).

The Domestic Abuse Act (2021) allows for the provisions of DVPNs and subsequent DVPOs to be applied for in circumstances where the offender is over the age of 18, violence is used or threatened towards the victim and/or an associated person, the alleged offender is to be released subject to no further action, caution or bail without conditions, and the DVPN is considered necessary to protect the victim and/or associated person from violence or the threat of violence (Home Office, 2022f). The term 'associated person' carries particular meaning and includes someone who is linked to the alleged offender through marriage, civil partnership, intimate relationship of significance, as a cohabitant, a child or relative (Family Law Act, 1996, section 62).

A DVPN can only be authorised by a police superintendent or above if they have reasonable grounds to believe it is necessary to protect the person from violence or threat of violence (Crime and Security Act, 2010, section 24(2)). The standard of proof is deliberately low and only requires the authorising officer to have *reasonable cause to believe* the order is necessary and in these instances, evidence will generally derive from an officer's testimony, police incident records, body-worn camera footage and in some cases the victim themselves.

In the event a DVPN is authorised, prohibitions and restrictions may:

- *prohibit the individual from evicting or excluding from the relevant premises the person for whose protection the DVPN is issued;*

- *prohibit the individual from entering the relevant premises;*

- *require the individual to leave the relevant premises; or*

- *prohibit the individual from coming within such distance of the relevant premises as may be specified in the DVPN.*
                                                    (Crime and Security Act, 2010, section 24(8))

When a DVPN has been authorised, the police must make an application within 48 hours to the magistrate's court for a DVPO. The court must satisfy itself on the balance of probabilities that the individual has been violent towards or has threatened violence towards the victim and/or an associated person and the court thinks the DVPO is necessary to protect that person from violence or a threat of violence (Crime and Security Act, 2010, section 28(2)(3); Domestic Abuse Act, 2021, section 29). A DVPO may last between 14 and 28 days and any breach carries a penalty of a possible fine of £50 for every day while in breach, up to a maximum of £5,000, or two months' imprisonment (Domestic Abuse Act, 2021, section 39; Home Office, 2022f).

EVIDENCE-BASED POLICING

Preventing and reducing domestic violence and abuse is a national and international social priority (Cordier et al, 2021). Following the introduction of DVPOs in England and Wales, an evaluation of their effectiveness concluded that DVPOs brought modest reductions of re-victimisation when compared to incidents where the alleged offender had been arrested and released with no further action (Kelly et al, 2013).

Building on this, the concept of DVPOs was subject to a meta-analysis by Cordier et al (2021), who concluded that DVPOs brought a feeling of safety to victims of domestic violence and restored a sense of control to victims and the police by providing a power of arrest when offenders breached the terms of the DVPO.

BROADER PROTECTIVE MEASURES AND CIVIL ORDERS

The aim is to always investigate the primary offence and prosecute when there is sufficient material to meet the evidential threshold; however, in addition to those already discussed in this chapter there are a host of other protective civil orders for investigators to consider.

SEXUAL HARM PREVENTION ORDERS

SECTION 103A OF THE SEXUAL OFFENCES ACT (2003)

A sexual harm prevention order (SHPO) is intended to protect the public from offenders who pose a risk of sexual harm by placing restrictions or 'positive' requirements on their behaviour (Home Office, 2023a). The court may make an SHPO following a conviction for a sexual or violent offence or:

- *where it finds a person not guilty of a specified sexual or violent offence by reason of insanity;*

- *where it finds that the defendant has a disability and has done the act charged against the defendant in respect of such an offence;*

- *on the application of the police, in respect of a qualifying offender who poses a risk to the public.*

(College of Policing, 2021d)

A key factor when considering a SHPO is the risk presented by the individual. In this context, the court should consider the likelihood and imminence of future offending and the possible harm which may result (Home Office, 2023a). In the event that the court is satisfied the conditions are met and the individual poses a risk of sexual harm, they may grant a SHPO for a minimum of 5 years if considered necessary to protect children under 18, vulnerable adults or members of the public from sexual harm in the UK and abroad (Sexual Offences Act, 2003, section 103A(3)).

SEXUAL RISK ORDERS

SECTION 122A OF THE SEXUAL OFFENCES ACT (2003)

The police or NCA may apply to a magistrate's court for a sexual risk order (SRO) when it appears an individual, who has not been convicted of a relevant offence (Home Office, 2023a), has acted in a sexual nature and there is reasonable cause to believe they pose a risk to children under 18, vulnerable adults or members of the public in the UK and abroad. In the event the magistrate's court is satisfied to the 'enhanced' balance of probabilities the order is necessary, they may grant the order for a period of two years (Sexual Offences Act, 2003, section 122A).

SLAVERY AND TRAFFICKING PREVENTION ORDER

SECTION 14 OF THE MODERN SLAVERY ACT (2015)

A slavery and trafficking prevention order (STPO) aims to protect people from the physical and psychological harm caused by slavery and trafficking. A court may make an STPO against an individual following:

- *a conviction for a slavery or human trafficking offence;*

- *a finding that the defendant is not guilty of a slavery or human trafficking offence by reason of insanity; or*

- *a finding that the defendant is under a disability and has done the act charged against the defendant in respect of a slavery or human trafficking offence.*
  (Modern Slavery Act, 2015, section 14(1))

The court may make the order only for a period of at least five years if it is satisfied there is a risk the individual may commit a slavery or human trafficking offence, and it is necessary to make the order for the protection of others (Home Office, 2017b).

SLAVERY AND TRAFFICKING RISK ORDER

SECTION 23 OF THE MODERN SLAVERY ACT (2015)

A slavery and trafficking risk order (STRO) may be sought against an individual who has not been convicted of a slavery or trafficking offence but who is thought to pose a risk of harm. The police, NCA, Immigration Service Gangmasters Labour Abuse Authority (GLAA), or a labour abuse prevention officer (LAPO) may apply for an STRO to a magistrate's court and may grant the order if it is satisfied on the *'enhanced'* balance of probabilities that the defendant has acted in a way which means there is a risk that the defendant will commit a slavery or human trafficking offence and that it is necessary for the purpose of protecting the public from the harm likely to occur from the commission of the offence (Home Office, 2017b).

SHPOs, SROs, STPOs and STROs all have far-reaching powers and may prohibit some forms of employment or impose what is described by the Home Office (2023a, p 54) as *'positive'* actions or restrictions on movement, association, travel, access to the internet or reporting conditions which are deemed proportionate and tailored to the nature of the offending.

FEMALE GENITAL MUTILATION PREVENTION ORDER

SECTION 1 FEMALE GENITAL MUTILATION ACT, 2003

Female genital mutilation is the partial or total removal of the external female genitalia for non-medical reasons (CPS, 2021). Aimed at safeguarding victims and potential victims, section 1 of the Female Genital Mutilation Act (2003) allows a family court, having regard to all the circumstances, including the need to secure health, safety and well-being, to grant a female genital mutilation prevention order (FGMPO) when they are satisfied on the *'enhanced'* balance of probabilities the order is necessary to protect a girl against the commission of a genital mutilation offence or a girl against whom an offence has been committed.

In cases where an FGMPO is granted the court may impose prohibitions, restrictions or other requirements which are considered appropriate in the circumstances (Female Genital Mutilation Act, 2003, section 1(3)).

There is a wide variety of civil orders available to investigators, all of which are designed to offer some form of protection to victims of major and serious crime. The discussion here has highlighted just some of those available.

REFLECTIVE PRACTICE 9.2

LEVEL 5/6

Protective orders such as STROs and FGMPOs are often deemed necessary because victims decline to prosecute, which is often driven by a fear of retribution or a false sense of loyalty to the perpetrator.

- What steps can you take as an investigator to encourage victims of slavery, trafficking or female genital mutilation to pursue criminal prosecutions?

Sample answers are provided at the end of this book.

CONCLUSION

The investigation of major and serious crime is challenging. The availability of evidence, the intimidation of witnesses, the complexity of the crime and the nature of those involved means very often prosecutions fail to reach the criminal standard of proof. Civil orders should never be considered as a replacement for prosecution, and they are not a panacea; however, they offer a viable alternative when traditional methods of investigation have failed.

Despite their value, civil orders are an underused resource, which means there are missed opportunities to provide victims of major and serious crime the protection they need from the police and other law enforcement agencies.

This chapter has considered theories applicable to the effectiveness of civil orders. Concepts including deterrence, routine activity, rational choice and situational crime prevention and how they apply to the use of civil orders have been explored. By introducing a specific deterrence effect on those already engaged in criminality, civil orders seek to disrupt and deter offending. Restrictions and prohibitions act as a form of situational crime prevention by disrupting routine activities and by removing the reliance on victim and witness testimony. The balance of risk associated with offending acts as a Sword of Damocles in the minds of the offender.

This chapter has examined the burden and standard of proof, how this differs between criminal and civil cases and how this affects an individual's right to a fair trial. This chapter has examined a range of civil orders, which are considered most relevant to major and serious crime, and concluded with a discussion on some of the broader protective civil orders available to investigators.

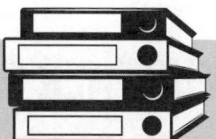

SUMMARY OF KEY CONCEPTS

This chapter has examined how civil orders are a viable alternative to prosecution in the fight against major and serious crime and explored the following key concepts:

- the key criminological theories that apply to civil orders;

- the difference between criminal and civil standards of proof, what this means for investigators in the collection of evidence and how this may affect an individual's right to a fair trial;

- the range of protective orders available to investigators and their propensity to protect victims of major and serious crime.

CHECK YOUR KNOWLEDGE

1. What are the three key elements of routine activity theory?

2. What is the difference between the criminal and civil standard of proof?

3. What is the aim of an SCPO?

4. What constitutes a 'gang' for the purposes of a gang injunction and what does a gang injunction seek to do?

5. How does a DVPN or a DVPO impact on major and serious crime?

FURTHER READING

Carr, R, Slothower, M and Parkinson, J (2017) Do Gang Injunctions Reduce Violent Crime? Four Tests in Merseyside, UK. *Cambridge Journal of Evidence-Based Policing*, 1: 195–210.
This article examines the effectiveness of gang injunctions on the propensity for offending by 36 individuals who were affiliated to four street gangs in Merseyside. A longitudinal examination 36 months before and 36 months after the introduction of gang injunctions saw their individual offending episodes reduce by 70 per cent and the harm associated with offending reduce by 61 per cent.

Home Office (2015) Serious Crime Act 2015. Fact Sheet: Improvements to Serious Crime Prevention Orders. [online] Available at: https://assets.publishing.service.gov.uk/government/uploads/system/uploads/attachment_data/file/415969/Fact_sheet_-_SCPOs_-_Act.pdf (accessed 22 October 2023).
This government report provides a short summary of the concept of serious crime prevention orders and discusses their value in disrupting serious crime.

Miceli, T, Segerson, K and Earnhart, D (2022) The Role of Experience in Deterring Crime: A Theory of Specific Versus General Deterrence. *Economic Inquiry*, 60(4): 1833–53.
A short discussion paper which illustrates the difference between general and specific deterrence theory.

SAMPLE ANSWERS

CHAPTER 1

CRITICAL THINKING ACTIVITY 1.1

An offence of sexual assault, contrary to section 3 of the Sexual Offences Act (2003), would not ordinarily be classed as a major crime; however, you are aware there is significant concern among the community, who are worried they may be at risk of being assaulted in a similar way. This means the offence could be classed as a major crime to ensure appropriate resources with the right skills and abilities are assigned to the case to ensure the crime is investigated effectively to maintain trust and confidence in the investigative process.

CRITICAL THINKING ACTIVITY 1.2

The Serious and Organised Crime Strategy requires police, wider law enforcement, education, health, social care and other governmental agencies use their collective powers and resources to *pursue* offenders, *prevent* individuals from being drawn into offending in the first place, and *protect* communities from harm, and are *prepared* to meet the challenges associated with serious and organised crime.

Applying this to a real world scenario, such as gun and gang criminality, the *pursue* element would see the police investigating offences and bringing to justice those responsible; the *prevent* element may involve educating children in school about the dangers of gun and gang crime or youth workers using diversionary methods to discourage offending; the *protect* element might involve high visibility police patrols in high risk areas; and the *prepare* element would require all agencies to have the resources and facilities in place to respond when necessary.

CRITICAL THINKING ACTIVITY 1.3

The potential for escalation of relatively minor crimes into major and serious crimes presents a significant risk for policing and, when it happens, trust and confidence in the service can be significantly undermined. Offences such as anti-social behaviour, sexual offences, domestic abuse, hate crime and other precursor events all have the potential for escalation, which means it is necessary the police have the right skills, qualities and training to effectively investigate crimes when they occur and also have the ability to recognise the threat, risk and harm associated with all incidents and investigations.

CHECK YOUR KNOWLEDGE

1. Major crime relates to any offence for which there is a need for the appointment of a senior investigating officer or the requirement of specialist resources. This means that it will be investigated by the appropriate person and resources will be committed to the investigation to minimise the risk to policing.

2. Police, Crime, Sentencing and Courts Act (2022): over the age of 18 years, convicted of child murders, substantial premeditation or an exceptional degree of seriousness. Sentencing Act (2020): convicted of specific violent, sexual or terrorist offences or a 'serious' offence, which is 'specified' under the act which carries a sentence of 10 years or more. Individual poses a significant risk to the public of serious harm and is considered dangerous.

3. Organised Crime Group Mapping.

4. Pursue all reasonable lines of inquiry, whether these point towards or away from the suspect.

5. Deliver a professional, ethical and effective investigation capacity for policing in the twenty-first century and provide a set of national benchmarked standards of practice at all levels of investigation.

CHAPTER 2

REFLECTIVE PRACTICE 2.1

The five building blocks principle asks you to preserve life, preserve crime scenes, secure evidence, identify victims and witnesses and identify suspects. In these circumstances you may consider the identification of a suspect has been achieved, certainly if you consider the presence of blood and a knife as an indicator that the individual has been involved in an act of violence.

Your priorities therefore would first be with the preservation of life, and you would take steps to establish whether someone in the vicinity has been injured or was in a life-threatening condition; second, you would treat the individual as a potential crime scene and take steps to preserve him and the evidence, perhaps also arranging a search of the area to identify any other potential crime scenes that would need to be preserved. These actions may help with the identification of a victim; if not this would be a priority, and you would also raise investigative actions to identify the anonymous caller and/or any other witnesses that may help you understand the nature of any offences that have been committed.

By applying the five building blocks in this way you can see how they form the basis of this and perhaps any other investigation.

CRITICAL THINKING ACTIVITY 2.1

Applying the principles of ABC to an investigation of grievous bodily harm with intent, contrary to section 18, Offences Against the Person Act (1861), your first action would be to interview the complainant to establish the nature of the assault. Further enquiries would include the recovery of

CCTV, house to house, a crime scene examination and perhaps an appeal for witnesses through the media.

If your enquiries revealed CCTV footage, which appeared to show the complainant acting aggressively towards another individual, which is inconsistent with the account provided, you would re-interview your complainant to give them an opportunity to explain the inconsistency. For example, the individual in the CCTV footage may not be the complainant; it may relate to a separate event or be a precursor incident before the assault. Seeking clarity is important and removes the possibility of making assumptions in terms of what may or may not have happened.

Questions that are intended to elicit an explanation for the investigative inconsistencies should be carefully planned, phrased tactfully and presented in a non-confrontational manner so as to reduce the potential for the complainant to lose trust and confidence in the investigation.

REFLECTIVE PRACTICE 2.2

Gather information and intelligence. You are investigating a serious assault, which is contrary to section 18 of the Offences Against the Persons Act (1861), and independent witnesses confirm the nature of the assault. There is an outstanding weapon and clothing worn by the perpetrator that are important for the investigation. Research indicates the suspected offender has a history of violence.

Assess the threat and risk and develop a working strategy. The complainant is in a critical condition at hospital and there is limited risk from the perpetrator. However, the suspect has a history of violence, which means there is potential for further acts of violence against other members of the public. Operating in the golden hour period, you know the sooner you act, forensic evidence is fresh and easier to recover and suspects are at their most vulnerable. Your working strategy would likely be to arrest the individual as soon as possible to maximise your opportunities to recover evidence.

Powers and policy. You are investigating a crime that falls within the criteria of an arrestable offence, but you would need to consider whether it was necessary to do so. In these circumstances you may feel it is necessary to arrest to allow for a prompt and effective investigation. You would need to consider your powers of search and recovery for the weapon and clothing; in these circumstances your power of seizure may come from a warrant or under the provisions of the Police and Criminal Evidence Act (PACE, 1984).

Identify options and contingencies. You decide your best option is to arrest the suspect at their home address, enter and search the premises under the provisions of section 32, PACE (1984) and recover any items you believe are evidence under section 19, PACE (1984). Contingencies may include having sufficient resources and equipment to manage the risks associated with the arrest.

Take action and review. The successful arrest and recovery of property, without incident, means your approach to this investigation has been thorough.

CRITICAL THINKING ACTIVITY 2.2

In these circumstances it is always important to maintain an open mind and recognise there may be alternative explanations; however, experience also may tell you these situations can be very serious. Appropriate hypotheses may be one of the following three statements.

1. The father has been delayed in returning Child A.

2. The father has abducted Child A with unharmful intent.

3. The father has abducted Child A with harmful intent.

Considering these hypotheses you may generate lines of enquiry to research the history of any previous incidents, medical and mental health, and previous threats, check the father's home address, trace and locate a vehicle, conduct house to house, recover CCTV, check ports and hospitals, and research mobile telephone and social media.

All of these enquiries present opportunities to the investigation; however, when there is 'harmful' intent, there may be risks attached. For example, directly approaching an address or vehicle associated with the father may escalate a situation and specialist resources may be needed to resolve what may be a very challenging situation.

CHECK YOUR KNOWLEDGE

1. According to Newburn, Williamson and Wright (2007) there are three stages to the investigative process. These are the '*identification and acquisition*' of material which is relevant to the case, the '*interpretation and understanding*' of information acquired during the investigation and the '*ordering and representation*' of evidence into a coherent reliable narrative, which tells the story of motive or reason for the criminal event or post event actions.

2. The five building blocks of investigation are:

    i.   preserve life;

    ii.   preservation of scenes;

    iii. securing evidence;

    iv.   identification of victims (and witnesses);

    v.   identification of suspects.

3. The golden hour is a notional 60 minutes beyond the commission of a crime when victims and witnesses are at their most cooperative; they are more likely to make spontaneous comments and they are less likely to have been contaminated by outside influences. This is the period when forensic evidence is fresh, meaning there are greater prospects for successful recovery, and suspects are at their most vulnerable.

4. The six elements of the NDM cycle are:

    i.   Code of Ethics;

    ii.   gather information and intelligence;

iii. assess threat and risk and develop a working strategy;

iv. consider powers and policy;

v. identify options and contingencies;

vi. take action and review what happened.

5. The term 'hypotheses development' means when there is a lack of information, investigators should draw on their experience to develop plausible explanations surrounding the nature of the crime under investigation to develop leads or lines of enquiry. An important element to consider is during this process errors can be made and investigators should remain open minded in terms of the validity of their decision making.

CHAPTER 3

REFLECTIVE PRACTICE 3.1

Other key roles that may contribute to an MIR include:

- the **deputy senior investigating officer** (DSIO) who has responsibility for the control and direction of the investigation in the absence of the SIO;

- the **document reader** who should be a competent investigator with appropriate skills to read all documentation that is to be indexed on messages;

- the **indexer**, who has responsibility to 'index' or record material coming into the investigation, such as nominals, vehicles, telephones, exhibits and other digital evidence, raises actions set by the action allocator and registers any documents associated with the case;

- the role of **Holmes manager** may be carried out either by a member of the MIR or by support staff. The person undertaking this role should be conversant with all aspects of the Holmes system and, where possible, have practical experience of an MIR.

CRITICAL THINKING ACTIVITY 3.1

You are investigating a serious offence, which on its own may justify the implementation of an MIR as there are clear risks associated with a crime of this nature. The potential for further offending may be considered as high; research indicates similar offences have been committed in a different geographical location and while they have not been formally linked there is potential for wider offending to be brought under the umbrella of one investigation and one SIO in the future. This should be factored into your decision making.

Practically speaking, you could implement a full MIR managed through Holmes and this would be the safest option; however, it is resource intensive and slow to start but it would allow you to demonstrate a high degree of integrity in your investigation. Alternatively, you could use local resources with an in-force IMS to record your decisions and rationale; this would be an effective approach if the investigation remained small but perhaps lacks the 'transferability' of investigative-relevant material should the investigation move geographical locations.

Practically speaking either option would provide you with an audit trail of investigative progress but you would need to recognise the balance between resource and short- or long-term efficiency.

REFLECTIVE PRACTICE 3.2

Fast-track actions are those which, if pursued immediately, are likely to establish important facts, preserve evidence or lead to the early resolution of the investigation. In this scenario these may include:

- taking a statement off the victim and any identified witnesses;

- CCTV research at the location and any entry and exit points – the latter may identify modes of transport or direction of travel;

- telephone enquiries with the victim, particularly cell site analysis to establish the location of the telephone;

- crime scene assessment to establish any points of potential forensic transfer;

- financial enquires – the victim may have lost bank cards that if used will generate lines of enquiry;

- intelligence research to identify any other offences in that location;

- house-to-house or shop-to-shop enquiries;

- consideration of a media appeal for witnesses.

Your response to this may prevent any further offences being committed and importantly generate lines of enquiry that may identify the offender.

REFLECTIVE PRACTICE 3.3

As a Crown Prosecutor you would appreciate early engagement for a variety of reasons.

- It means you are aware of the strengths and weaknesses of the investigation from the outset.

- It means you can influence the direction of the investigation.

- It allows you to consider the most appropriate charges.

- It serves to build strong working alliances between the SIO and the Crown Prosecutor.

- It would allow you to start thinking about which counsel you would like to prosecute.

REFLECTIVE PRACTICE 3.4

The Code indicates you are eligible for enhanced rights as a vulnerable victim if:

- *you are under 18 years of age at the time of the offence, or*

- *the quality of your evidence is likely to be affected because you:*

  o   *suffer from mental disorder within the meaning of the Mental Health Act 1983*

  o   *otherwise have a significant impairment of intelligence and social functioning or*

  o   *have a physical disability or are suffering from a physical disorder.*
  (MoJ, 2020a, p 10)

You are also eligible for enhanced rights as an intimidated victim if it is considered that '*the quality of your evidence will be affected because of your fear of distress about testifying in court*' (MoJ, 2020a, p 10).

Victims of the most serious crimes are also eligible for enhanced rights, which also includes '*a close relative bereaved by a criminal offence, a victim of domestic abuse, hate crime, terrorism, sexual offences, human trafficking, modern slavery, attempted murder, kidnap, false imprisonment, arson with intent to endanger life and wounding or causing grievous bodily harm with intent*' (MoJ, 2020a, p 11).

Finally, if someone is persistently targeted then they are eligible for enhanced rights. This refers to a victim having been '*targeted repeatedly as a direct victim of crime over a period of time*', especially if they have been targeted deliberately or if they are '*a victim of a campaign of harassment or stalking*' (MoJ, 2020a, p 11).

CRITICAL THINKING ACTIVITY 3.2

Special measures are designed to allow victims and witnesses the opportunity to deliver their 'best evidence', which in turn should improve conviction rates in this challenging area of policing. Research indicates the use of special measures has the potential to reduce anxiety and improve satisfaction in the criminal justice system (Hamlyn et al, 2004; Kebbell, O'Kelly and Gilchrist, 2007). Clearly, the effective use of special measures can help to improve conviction rates and help build confidence in the CJS; however, the experience of rape victims suggested the use of special measures was inconsistent, and a failure to recognise vulnerability and therefore the availability of special measures means some victims were left unsupported through the CJS (Fairclough, 2020).

CHECK YOUR KNOWLEDGE

1. The major incident room (MIR) is the central hub of a major and serious crime investigation. The MIR is the place where all material gathered during an investigation is collected and stored. Material such as written statements, interview records, information provided by outside enquiry officers and members of the public, reports associated with crime scene examinations, details of exhibits and CCTV images, SIO policy decisions and more are all retained in the MIR.

2. According to ACPO/Centrex (2005, p 51), fast-track actions are investigative actions that when followed immediately are likely to 'establish important facts, preserve evidence or lead to the early resolution of the investigation'.

3. There are a number of advantages to early engagement with the CPS including identifying evidential opportunities, rectifying weaknesses, considering developing a digital strategy, dealing with disclosure issues, developing strategy, considering pre-charge engagement; ensuring the right charge(s) are selected and building robust cases.

4. There are a range of special measures available under the YJCEA (1999), including:

   - screens;

   - live links;

   - evidence given in private;

   - removal of wigs and gowns;

   - pre-recorded evidence in chief;

   - pre-recorded cross-examination/re-examination of a witness;

   - examination by an intermediary;

   - aids to communication;

   - prohibiting a defendant who is charged with a sexual offence from personally cross-examining the complainant;

   - prohibiting an unrepresented defendant from cross-examining child witnesses and complainants;

   - prohibiting the questioning by an unrepresented defendant of certain classes of witnesses;

   - prohibiting the publication of the name of a witness during the lifetime of the witness.

5. There are a number of provisions that are available when dealing with reluctant witnesses, including:

    *   special measures;

    *   Investigation Anonymity Orders;

    *   hearsay provisions under the CJA (2003);

    *   reluctant witness deposition;

    *   witness protection schemes.

6. Barriers associated with the disclosure of mental ill health are the stigma associated with mental ill health and the potential that disclosure will reduce career prospects. For example, disclosure of mental ill health may mean an individual is no longer considered suitable for an important role within an investigative team, such as senior investigating officer or family liaison officer.

CHAPTER 4

REFLECTIVE PRACTICE 4.1

CPS Cymru/Wales	Jenny Hopkins	CPS North West	Martin Goldman
CPS East of England	Frank Ferguson	CPS South East	Kate Brown
CPS East Midlands	Janine McKinney	CPS South West	Victoria Cook
CPS London North	Barry Hughes	CPS Thames and Chiltern	Jaswant Narwal
CPS London South	Lionel Idan	CPS Wessex	Rose Marie Franton
CPS Mersey/Cheshire	Jonathan Storer	CPS West Midlands	Siobhan Blake
CPS North East	Gale Gilchrist	CPS Yorkshire and Humberside	Jan Lamping

REFLECTIVE PRACTICE 4.2

The elements of the Threshold Test which have to be established are:

*   reasonable grounds to suspect that the person to be charged has committed the offence;

*   further evidence can be obtained in a reasonable period to provide a realistic prospect of a conviction;

- the seriousness of the offence justifies an immediate charging decision;

- there are grounds under the Bail Act (1976) to object to bail;

- it is in the public interest to charge the suspect.

CHECK YOUR KNOWLEDGE

1. The CPS was established in 1986 following the Prosecution of Offences Act (1985).

2. There are two stages to the Code for Crown Prosecutors – the evidence stage and then the public interest stage.

3. There are five conditions.

    i.   Reasonable grounds to suspect that the person to be charged has committed the offence.

    ii.   Further evidence can be obtained in a reasonable period to provide a realistic prospect of a conviction.

    iii.   The seriousness of the offence justifies an immediate charging decision.

    iv.   There are grounds under the Bail Act (1976) to object to bail.

    v.   It is in the public interest to charge the suspect.

4. Annex B.

5. *R v Newton* (1982).

6. *R v Goodyear* (2005).

CHAPTER 5

REFLECTIVE PRACTICE 5.1

The results of forensic examinations fall within the definition of material contained in the Code. It is negative information in terms of advancing the prosecution case. However, it clearly has the potential to undermine the case for the prosecution or to assist the case for James Smith and should therefore be disclosed to the defence. It is not necessarily fatal to the prosecution case provided the remaining evidence affords a realistic prosect of a conviction.

REFLECTIVE PRACTICE 5.2

The fact that a CHIS has provided information that Scott Williams was involved in the attack on the victim is clearly relevant information within the Code. It does not advance the prosecution case and it has the potential to undermine the prosecution case or to assist the defence case by suggesting that someone else was involved in the offence. It therefore meets the test for prosecution disclosure.

The fact that the information comes from a CHIS is sensitive and to disclose the identity of a CHIS could place the individual CHIS at risk of serious harm and/or lead to an impact on the willingness of people to come forward to give police information.

Consideration should be given to making a limited form of disclosure by revealing the nature of the information to the defence but protecting the identity of the CHIS.

Turning to the information provided via Crimestoppers, similar considerations may apply. The fact that another man, Michael Jones, has been named has the potential to undermine the case for the prosecution or to assist the case for the defence and the information therefore meets the test for prosecution disclosure.

The fact that the information was given in confidence potentially engages Article 8 ECHR and there is a need to protect the identity of the person who supplied the information. Consideration should be given to making a limited form of disclosure to the defence which protects the underlying sensitivities.

In both cases early dialogue with the CPS will be important to ensure that the disclosure obligations are met.

REFLECTIVE PRACTICE 5.3

The terms are as follows:

- records which are derived from tapes or recordings of telephone messages (for example 999 calls) containing descriptions of an alleged offence or offender;

- any incident logs relating to the allegation;

- contemporaneous records of the incident, such as:

  o   crime reports and crime report forms;

  o   an investigation log;

  o   any record or note made by an investigator (including police notebook entries and other handwritten notes) on which they later make a statement, or which relates to contact with suspects, victims, or witnesses;

o   an account of an incident or information relevant to an incident noted by an investigator in manuscript or electronically;

o   records of actions carried out by officers (such as house-to-house interviews, CCTV, or forensic enquiries) noted by a police officer in manuscript or electronically;

o   CCTV footage, or other imagery, of the incident in action;

- the defendant's custody record or voluntary attendance record;

- any previous accounts made by a complainant or by any other witnesses;

- interview records (written records, or audio or video tapes, of interviews with actual or potential witnesses or suspects);

- any material casting doubt on the reliability of a witness, eg, relevant previous convictions and relevant cautions of any prosecution witnesses and any co-accused.

CHECK YOUR KNOWLEDGE

1. The test for prosecution disclosure is the requirement to disclose to the accused any prosecution material which has not been previously disclosed to the accused and might reasonably considered capable of undermining the case for the prosecution against the accused or of assisting the accused (Sections 3 and 7 of the CPIA).

2. The five main principles which underpin the CPIA are:

i. the duty to pursue all reasonable lines of inquiry;

ii. the duty to record relevant material;

iii. the duty to retain relevant material;

iv. the duty to reveal relevant unused material to the CPS;

v. the duty to review material (continuing obligation).

3. You should:

- include the nature of the defence, and in particular any defences to be relied on;

- indicate the matters of fact on which the defendant takes issue with the prosecution;

- outline why the defence take issue with the prosecution;

- set out the particulars of the matters of fact the defence intend to rely on;

- indicate any points of law (including any point as to the admissibility of evidence) and details of any authority;

- include details of any alibi;

- include details of any witnesses the defence propose to call.

4. Material that the disclosure officer believes would give rise to a real risk of serious prejudice to an important public interest.

5. Type 1: On notice where the prosecution informs the defence of the broad nature of the material.

    Type 2: The prosecution gives notice of an application to the defence but does not tell them the nature of the material.

    Type 3: Secret application.

6. Article 6 is an absolute right.

CHAPTER 6

REFLECTIVE PRACTICE 6.1

Is it a reasonable line of inquiry in the context of the case to seek access to the complainant's mobile phone?

Given that the suspect has confirmed that he was in contact with the complainant by mobile phone on the one occasion on the day of the assault it may be a reasonable line of inquiry to seek access to the complainant's phone for that one day only, given that there is no suggestion at this stage that there has been any earlier contact, and therefore to seek to examine the phone over a longer period would be unjustified at this stage.

REFLECTIVE PRACTICE 6.2

Given the nature of the investigation and the amount of digital material that is likely to be involved, it is important to develop a digital strategy at an early stage. There should be early consultation with the CPS to develop the strategy. Consideration should be given to instructing digital experts.

The case may be suitable for the use of PCE, for example to identify agreed search terms.

The data should be dealt with in accordance with Annex A of the Attorney General's Guidelines (2022).

CHECK YOUR KNOWLEDGE

1. Article 6 ECHR, the right to a fair trial for the suspect, and Article 8 ECHR, the right to respect for a family and private life.

2. Attorney General's Guidelines on Disclosure (2022), Annex A.

3. Article 6 is an absolute right.

4. Police, Crime, Sentencing and Courts Act (2022).

CHAPTER 7

REFLECTIVE PRACTICE 7.1

You are investigating an offence of burglary, during which computers, tablets and other mobile devices were stolen. Section 28(3) of the RIPA (2000) sets out the criteria when directed surveillance may be considered necessary, one of which is for the purpose of preventing and detecting crime. In these circumstances, you are clearly investigating a crime (burglary) and therefore an application for directed surveillance may be justified.

In the same scenario, an application for intrusive surveillance is unlikely to be justified. Section 32(3) of the RIPA (2000) outlines the criteria when intrusive surveillance is necessary, one of which is for the purposes of preventing and detecting serious crime. A burglary during which electrical equipment is stolen is unlikely to fall into the definition of serious crime.

REFLECTIVE PRACTICE 7.2

The Covert Surveillance and Property Interference: Revised Code of Practice (Home Office, 2018b) provides guidance on the concept of proportionality, and asks you to consider three elements which test for proportionality, namely:

- the size and scope of proposed surveillance activity against the gravity of the offences under investigation;

- whether alternative, less intrusive methods of investigation could achieve the same results; and

- what other methods of investigation have been considered but deemed unsuitable.

In this scenario you are investigating an offence which is serious in nature and without intervention the severity of offending is likely to escalate. This means there is a sense of urgency to the investigation. The identity of the victim and offender are unknown, and in the timescales you have, alternative, perhaps less intrusive methods are unlikely to be successful. You may consider making an application for subscriber and/or user details of communication devices as a means of identifying them but this will take time and unnecessarily place the victim at greater risk of harm. Therefore in these circumstances you could justify deployment of directed surveillance as, all things considered, it can be argued as being proportionate to the aims the surveillance seeks to achieve (prevention and detection of crime), and it is the least intrusive option when other, perhaps less intrusive, methods of investigation have been considered but are unlikely to succeed in the timescale available.

CHECK YOUR KNOWLEDGE

1. Primarily a covert investigation is designed to be conducted in a manner which ensures those under investigation are unaware of its existence. In a reactive sense, offenders know only too well that victims and witnesses in the most serious cases can be prevented from providing testimony if they are put in fear of retribution and covert investigation seeks to circumvent this by gathering evidence in an alternative way.

2. The fundamental difference between directed surveillance and intrusive surveillance is the scale of intrusion into the privacy allowed when balanced against the gravity of offences under investigation. RIPA (2000) provides the statutory guidance in this regard; directed surveillance is considered necessary for the prevention and detection of crime, whereas intrusive surveillance is necessary for the prevention and detection of *serious* crime, which means there is much greater latitude in the scale of intrusion permissible because the offences under investigation are much more serious.

3. Part III of the Police Act (1997) and Part 5 of the Investigatory Powers Act (2016) provide the legal framework to lawfully interfere with property belonging to another.

4. Additional guidance indicates participation in criminal conduct is allowed if:

   • the aim could not be achieved in a less intrusive way;

   • the criminal conduct is part of efforts to prevent or detect more serious criminality;

   • the potential harm to the public interest from the criminal conduct is proportionate to the potential benefit;

   • there is no engagement in planning and committing of the crime;

   • the CHIS or UCO only plays a minor role;

   • participation is essential to enable law enforcement to frustrate the principal criminals and arrest them.

5. The aim of the Investigatory Powers Commissioner is to oversee the application and use of investigatory powers, including covert surveillance, the interception of communications, property interference, the acquisition of communications data and the use of covert human intelligence sources. When serious errors are identified the individual concerned may be informed.

6. *R v Loosely* (2001).

CHAPTER 8

REFLECTIVE PRACTICE 8.1

One of the fundamental aims of policing is to be perceived as legitimate in the eyes of victims, witnesses, and suspects. Confidence in the police and wider CJS increases the willingness of victims and witnesses to support prosecutions and means that suspects know they will be treated respectfully, fairly and in a professional manner.

Clearly, when victims, witnesses and suspects are not treated in a respectful, empathetic and professional manner, it will reduce confidence in the justice system and thereby discourage victims and witnesses from supporting prosecutions and create a sense of distrust in the reliability of evidence that is presented in court.

CRITICAL THINKING ACTIVITY 8.1

The effectiveness of the PEACE interview model can mean different things to different people. One measure of effectiveness might be the ability of PEACE to draw out true confessions; another measure of effectiveness may be the propensity for PEACE to reduce the potential for false confessions; and another might be the collective ability of PEACE to draw out accurate and reliable information, which is trusted by the courts, helps convict the guilty and protects the innocent from being wrongly convicted. Equally, the overall measure of effectiveness might be a combination of all.

There is a range of literature and research available to support an argument recognising the value of PEACE. For example, interviews are considered more ethical beyond the introduction of PEACE, which moved away from a focus on obtaining a confession to obtaining a reliable account (Gudjonsson, 2003). PEACE and the approach to investigative interviewing in England and Wales brings greater transparency and accountability, it protects the innocent, yet maintains an ability to extract confessions and at the same time limit the number of false confessions (Meissner et al, 2014) and the use of rapport is considered as the bedrock for an effective interaction and enhances victim and witness recall and builds trust between the interviewer and interviewee (Abbe and Brandon, 2013; Vallano et al, 2015; Macintosh, 2009; Collins, Lincoln and Frank, 2002; Bull and Soukara, 2010).

REFLECTIVE PRACTICE 8.2

You are investigating an allegation of rape, contrary to section 1 of the Sexual Offences Act (2003). The PACE Codes of Practice, Code C (Home Office, 2019) is very clear in that anyone who appears under the age of 18 years shall, in the absence of clear evidence that they are older, be treated as a juvenile. In this case the detained person is a 17-year-old person, which means they will be treated as a juvenile. Furthermore, the Codes of Practice, Code C, para 3.15 mandates a juvenile while in detention will have the support of an AA.

In terms of who may perform the role of AA, again the Codes of Practice, Code C, para 1.7 suggest this could be a parent, guardian or other person over 18 years of age who is responsible for their care or custody, such as a care support worker. Furthermore, the Codes of Practice highlight who cannot perform the role of AA, such as a police officer or someone employed by the police, and you may consider a parent in this situation unsuitable as it may undermine the interview process, but this would need to be carefully considered.

CRITICAL THINKING ACTIVITY 8.2

You are investigating a murder, so high-profile cases with the potential for high-profile mistakes have a big impact on trust and confidence in policing. In terms of the approach to the interview, first, implementing the seven principles of investigative interviewing as defined by the College of Policing (2022) and using them to underpin the PEACE model will help with the acquisition of accurate, reliable and trustworthy material which may support a future prosecution while protecting the suspect if they are innocent of the allegation. In practice this means you will act in a manner which is fair, respects equality and diversity, recognises the HRA (1998) and Article 8 ECHR, and applies an investigative mindset in so much as you will be receptive to alternative explanations, no matter how obscure they may seem.

In preparation for the interview you will consider the interviewee, their needs and characteristics and the interview environment; you will recognise they need the support of an appropriate adult and who that will be. You will recognise the need build a rapport with the suspect through the interview, recognising the 'Engage and explain' element of the PEACE model as important in the process. You will also make decisions in terms of pre-interview disclosure, being clear in what investigative material will be disclosed and when and how you can use the evidence to maximise the potential to expose truth and lies.

Finally you will recognise that an interview which is conducted ethically, is fair and respects the rights of the suspect will not only build confidence in the justice system but also ensure the evidence gathered will be admissible in any future prosecution.

CHECK YOUR KNOWLEDGE

1. Interviews which are conducted with professionalism can:

    *   help direct the investigation, generating lines of enquiry which ultimately may lead to a prosecution or early release of an innocent person;

    *   support the prosecution case, saving time, money and resources;

    *   increase public confidence in the police service.

2. There are seven principles of investigative interviewing.

3. P = Planning and preparation

   E = Engage and explain

   A = Account, clarification and challenge

   C = Closure

   E = Evaluation.

4. A pre-interview briefing is necessary to provide the legal adviser with sufficient information to enable them to understand the nature of the offence(s) under investigation so they can advise their clients in a way which allows them to exercise their rights appropriately.

5. The appropriate adult is someone that acts on behalf of a juvenile, which is a person under the age of 18 or a vulnerable person while they are in police detention or when they are interviewed about a criminal offence. Their role is to protect the rights and welfare and ensure the police act appropriately.

6. There are three types of false confessions.

   i. Voluntary, which are self-induced without external pressure.

   ii. Coerced-compliant, which can be influenced by the custody setting or question types or a means of coping with the demands of the interview.

   iii. Coerced-internalised, which can be influenced by investigators who lead the suspect to believe they have committed the crime even when they have no recollection of it.

CHAPTER 9

CRITICAL THINKING ACTIVITY 9.1

Gang-related criminality often relies on the collective behaviour of a group of individuals who use threats, fear and intimidation to maintain territorial control over a geographical location. As a consequence, criminality flourishes and communities are undermined. The understandable reluctance of some victims and witnesses to provide evidence in support of prosecutions means offending goes unpunished and the benefits of gang membership outweigh the fear of sanction.

The perception of risk of being caught and the collective ability of the group to commit crime needs to change. This is done by removing the burden of responsibility to provide evidence of criminal activity from victims and witnesses and transferring it to the police. This means the likely risks of apprehension and sanction for offending are more certain, much quicker, and in some ways more severe (specific deterrence and rational choice).

At the same time, if association between gang members and their movement can be restricted, and their everyday activities are disrupted, it means their collective ability to commit crime and instil fear in communities is reduced (routine activity and situational crime prevention).

REFLECTIVE PRACTICE 9.1

In this scenario an individual has been convicted of possession of a firearm without a certificate, contrary to section 1 of the Firearms Act (1968). This offence is considered 'serious' according to Schedule 1 of the Serious Crime Act (2007), amended by section 47 of the Serious Crime Act (2015). Furthermore, intelligence indicates broader involvement in drug trafficking and money laundering, which are also offences that may be considered serious under the Act. On this basis, the court may grant a SCPO if satisfied there are reasonable grounds to believe the order would protect the public by preventing, restricting or disrupting involvement by the individual in serious crime throughout England, Wales, Northern Ireland or elsewhere.

In terms of the order, you may consider restrictions on financial affairs, prohibitions on association, movement and travel, and conditions on their modes of communication.

CRITICAL THINKING ACTIVITY 9.2

Stop and search is a valuable tool in the prevention and detection of crime; however, misuse of police powers in this regard has the propensity to create tension in communities and undermine legitimacy in policing. The provision of an automatic right to stop and search under the SVRO aims to provide a balance between acting as a deterrence to repeat offenders and reducing harm in communities that may be disproportionately affected by knife crime. This is, however, a delicate balance and discretion is encouraged when exercising this power to ensure it does not further undermine trust and confidence in policing.

REFLECTIVE PRACTICE 9.2

Investigating offences where cultural differences mean there may be an inherent distrust of the police presents a significant challenge to the prosecution of offenders. As an investigator you have a range of skills, characteristics and professional knowledge that need to be used to encourage victims to pursue criminal prosecutions.

Skills and characteristics such as communication, listening, empathy, diligence, problem solving, drive, determination, resilience, professionalism and a commitment to succeed will collectively build trust and confidence and provide confidence to victims of crime.

Equally, professional knowledge around legislation and the criminal justice system, such as the availability of special measures and facilities offered by civil orders, will help make victims of crime make informed decisions about the options they have available.

CHECK YOUR KNOWLEDGE

1. The three elements required to meet the principles of routine activity theory are:

    i.   a motivated offender;

    ii. a suitable target;

    iii. the lack of a capable guardian.

    When the three elements come together in time and place they create the potential for a criminal event to take place.

2. The criminal standard of proof is set at '*beyond reasonable doubt*'. The civil standard of proof is much lower and is set on the '*balance of probability*', meaning it is more likely than not. Developments in case law associated with civil orders and the civil standard of proof have created an environment where there is an expectation that applications for civil orders should reach a higher threshold than the standard '*balance of probabilities*'.

3. An SCPO is available to police and law enforcement both pre- and post-conviction and is designed to protect the public by preventing, restricting or disrupting involvement by the person in serious crime throughout England, Wales, Northern Ireland or elsewhere.

4. For the purposes of a gang injunction a 'gang' is defined as consisting of at least three people and has one or more characteristics that would allow its members to be identified by others as a group or gang. Gang injunctions aim to disrupt drug dealing or serious violence associated with gang-related criminality and protect the individual from harm.

5. Most female adult victims of homicide are killed in the domestic setting. DVPNs and DVPOs seek to protect victims of domestic violence and abuse from further offending, particularly in cases when there is a reluctance from the victim to prosecute or the evidence fails to reach the threshold for prosecution.

REFERENCES

Abbe, A and Brandon, S E (2013) The Role of Rapport in Investigative Interviewing: A Review. *Journal of Investigative Psychology and Offender Profiling*, 10(3): 237–49.

Albanese, J S (2004) *Organized Crime in Our Times*. Cincinnati, OH: Anderson/Lexis Nexis.

Allen, G and Harding, M (2021) Knife Crime in England and Wales. [online] Available at: https://researchbriefings.files.parliament.uk/documents/SN04304/SN04304.pdf (accessed 22 October 2023).

All Party Parliamentary Group for Children (APPGC) (2014) 'It's All About Trust': Building Good Relationships Between Children and the Police. [online] Available at: www.familylaw.co.uk/docs/pdf-files/appgc_children_and_police_report_-_final.pdf (accessed 22 October 2023).

American Bar Association (ABA) (2021) How Courts Work. [online] Available at: www.americanbar.org/groups/public_education/resources/law_related_education_network/how_courts_work/pleabargaining/ (accessed 22 October 2023).

Anderson, D (2016) Report on the Review of Bulk Powers. [online] Available at: https://terrorismlegislationreviewer.independent.gov.uk/wp-content/uploads/2016/08/Bulk-Powers-Review-final-report.pdf (accessed 22 October 2023).

Association of Chief Police Officers (ACPO/Centrex) (2005) Practice Advice on Core Investigative Doctrine. [online] Available at: www.whatdotheyknow.com/request/387377/response/939365/attach/2/ACPO%202005%20Practice%20Advice%20on%20Core%20Investigative%20Doctrine%20002.pdf?cookie_passthrough=1 (accessed 22 October 2023).

Association of Chief Police Officers (ACPO/Centrex) (2006) Murder Investigation Manual. [online] Available at: https://zakon.co.uk/admin/resources/downloads/murder-investigation-manual-2006-redacted.pdf (accessed 22 October 2023).

Association of Chief Police Officers (ACPO)/National Police Improvement Agency (NPIA) (2009) National Investigative Interviewing Strategy. [online] Available at: https://zakon.co.uk/admin/resources/downloads/bp-nat-investigative-interviewing-strategy-2009.pdf (accessed 22 October 2023).

Attorney General's Office (2022) Attorney General's Guidelines on Disclosure. [online] Available at: www.gov.uk/government/publications/attorney-generals-guidelines-on-disclosure (accessed 22 October 2023).

Bail Act 1976 [online] Available at: www.legislation.gov.uk/ukpga/1976/63#:~:text=An%20Act%20to%20make%20provision,persons%20kept%20in%20custody%20for (accessed 22 October 2023).

Ball, K, Lyon, D, Murakami Wood, D, Norris, C and Raab, C (2006) A Report on the Surveillance Society. [online] Available at: https://ico.org.uk/media/about-the-ico/documents/1042390/surveillance-society-full-report-2006.pdf (accessed 22 October 2023).

Barnes, G, Ahlman, L, Gill, C, Sherman, L W, Kurtz, E and Malvestuto, R (2010) Low Intensity Community Supervision for Low-Risk Offenders: A Randomised Controlled Trial. *Journal of Experimental Criminology*, 6(2): 159–89.

Bates and Others v Post Office Limited Group Litigation (2019) No 6, Horizon issues, EWHC 3408.

Bath, C, Bhardwa, B, Jacobson, J, May, T and Webster, R (2015) There to Help: Ensuring Provision of Appropriate Adults for Mentally Vulnerable Adults Detained or Interviewed by Police. [online] Available at: www.appropriateadult.org.uk/policy/research/there-to-help (accessed 22 October 2023).

Bell, S, Palmer-Conn, S and Kealey, N (2022) 'Swinging the Lead and Working the Head': An Explanation as to Why Mental Illness Stigma Is Prevalent in Policing. *The Police Journal*, 95(1): 4–23.

Bernasco, W, Van Gelder, J L and Elffers, H (1961) *The Oxford Handbook of Offender Decision Making*. New York: Oxford University Press.

Big Brother Watch (2019) Digital Strip Searches: The Police's Data Investigations of Victims. [online] Available at: https://bigbrotherwatch.org.uk/wp-content/uploads/2019/07/Digital-Strip-Searches-Final.pdf (accessed 22 October 2023).

Block, B P and Hostettler, J (2002) *Famous Cases: Nine Trials that Changed the Law*. Winchester: Waterside Press.

Bradley, K (2009) The Bradley Report: Lord Bradley's Review of People with Mental Health or Learning Difficulties in the Criminal Justice System. Department of Health. [online] Available at: https://webarchive.nationalarchives.gov.uk/ukgwa/20130123195930/http:/www.dh.gov.uk/en/Publicationsandstatistics/Publications/PublicationsPolicyAndGuidance/DH_098694#:~:text=The%20review%20has%20kept%20a,services%20needed%20to%20support%20them (accessed 22 October 2023).

Brady v United States (1970) 397 US 742.

Brewin, C R, Miller, J K, Soffia, M, Peart, A and Burchell, B (2022) Posttraumatic Stress Disorder and Complex Posttraumatic Stress Disorder in UK Police Officers. *Psychological Medicine*, 52(7): 1287–95.

Bride, B E and Kintzle, S (2011) Secondary Traumatic Stress, Job Satisfaction, and Occupational Commitment in Substance Abuse Counselors. *Traumatology: An International Journal*, 17(1): 22–8.

Bull, R and Soukara, S (2010) Four Studies of What Really Happens in Police Interviews. In Lassiter, G D and Meissner, C A (eds) *Police Interrogations and False Confessions: Current Research, Practice, and Policy Recommendations*. Washington, DC: American Psychological Association.

Carr, R, Slothower, M and Parkinson, J (2017) Do Gang Injunctions Reduce Violent Crime? Four Tests in Merseyside, UK. *Cambridge Journal of Evidence-Based Policing*, 1: 195–210.

Civil Evidence Act 1995 [online] Available at: www.legislation.gov.uk/ukpga/1995/38#:~:text=An%20Act%20to%20provide%20for,proceedings%3B%20and%20for%20connected%20purposes. (accessed 09 June 2023).

Civil Procedure Rules [online] Available at: www.justice.gov.uk/courts/procedure-rules/civil (accessed 09 June 2023).

Clarke, C, Milne, R and Bull, R (2011) Interviewing Suspects of Crime: The Impact of PEACE Training, Supervision and the Presence of a Legal Advisor. *Journal of Investigative Psychology and Offender Profiling*, 8(2): 149–62.

Clarke, R V (1995) Situational Crime Prevention. *Crime and Justice*, 19: 91–150.

Clarke, R V and Cornish, D B (1985) Modeling Offenders' Decisions: A Framework for Research and Policy. *Crime and Justice*, 6: 147–85.

Cohen, L E and Felson, M (1979) Social Change and Crime Rate Trends: A Routine Activity Approach. *American Sociological Review*, 44(4): 588–608.

College of Policing (2013a) Risk. [online] Available at: www.college.police.uk/app/risk/risk (accessed 22 October 2023).

College of Policing (2013b) National Decision Model. [online] Available at: www.college.police.uk/app/national-decision-model/national-decision-model (accessed 22 October 2023).

College of Policing (2013c) Working with Suspects. [online] Available at: www.college.police.uk/app/investigation/working-suspects#tie-strategy (accessed 22 October 2023).

College of Policing (2014) The Code of Ethics: Reading List. [online] Available at: https://assets.college.police.uk/s3fs-public/2021-02/code_of_ethics_readinglist.pdf (accessed 22 October 2023).

College of Policing (2018) Professionalising Investigations Programme. [online] Available at: https://assets.college.police.uk/s3fs-public/2020-11/Professionalising-Investigations-Progamme.pdf (accessed 22 October 2023).

College of Policing (2021a) Introduction and Types of Critical Incidents. [online] Available at: www.college.police.uk/app/critical-incident-management/introduction-and-types-critical-incidents (accessed 22 October 2023).

College of Policing (2021b) Investigation Process. [online] Available at: www.college.police.uk/app/investigation/investigation-process#initial-investigation (accessed 22 October 2023).

College of Policing (2021c) Undercover Policing. [online] Available at: https://library.college.police.uk/docs/college-of-policing/APP-Undercover-policing-February-2021v2.pdf (accessed 22 October 2023).

College of Policing (2021d) Protective Measures and Civil Orders. [online] Available at: www.college.police.uk/guidance/violence-against-women-and-girls-toolkit/protective-measures-and-civil-orders (accessed 22 October 2023).

College of Policing (2022) Investigative Interviewing. [online] Available at: www.college.police.uk/app/investigation/investigative-interviewing (accessed 22 October 2023).

Collins, R, Lincoln, R and Frank, M G (2002) The Effect of Rapport in Forensic Interviewing. *Psychiatry, Psychology and Law*, 9(1): 69–78.

Cook, T (2019) *Senior Investigating Officers' Handbook*, 5th edition. Oxford: Oxford University Press.

Cook, T, Hibbitt, S and Hill, M (2016) *Crime Investigators' Handbook*, 2nd edition. Oxford: Oxford University Press.

Cordier, R, Chung, D, Wilkes-Gillan, S and Speyer, R (2021) The Effectiveness of Protection Orders in Reducing Recidivism in Domestic Violence: A Systematic Review and Meta-Analysis. *Trauma, Violence, & Abuse*, 22(4): 804–28.

Coroners and Justice Act 2009 [online] Available at: www.legislation.gov.uk/ukpga/2009/25/contents (accessed 22 October 2023).

Covert Human Intelligence Sources (Criminal Conduct) Act 2021 [online] Available at: www.legislation.gov.uk/ukpga/2021/4/contents/enacted (accessed 24 February 2023).

Crime and Disorder Act 1998 [online] Available at: www.legislation.gov.uk/ukpga/1998/37/contents (accessed 14 April 2023).

Crime (International Co-operation) Act 2003 [online] Available at: www.legislation.gov.uk/ukpga/2003/32/contents (accessed 22 October 2023).

Crime and Security Act 2010 [online] Available at: https://www.legislation.gov.uk/ukpga/2010/17/contents (accessed 13 June 2023).

Criminal Appeal Act 1995 [online] Available at: www.legislation.gov.uk/ukpga/1995/35/body/1997-03-31 (accessed 28 September 2023).

Criminal Justice Act 2003 [online] Available at: www.legislation.gov.uk/ukpga/2003/44/contents (accessed 22 October 2023).

Criminal Justice Joint Inspectorates (2021) A Joint Thematic Inspection of the Police and Crown Prosecution Service's Response to Rape. Phase One: From Report to Police or CPS Decision to Take No

Further Action. [online] Available at: https://assets-hmicfrs.justiceinspectorates.gov.uk/uploads/joint-thematic-inspection-of-police-and-cps-response-to-rape-phase-one.pdf (accessed 22 October 2023).

Criminal Procedure and Investigations Act 1996. [online] Available at: www.legislation.gov.uk/ukpga/1996/25/contents (accessed 22 October 2023).

Crown Prosecution Service (2018a) Code for Crown Prosecutors. [online] Available at: www.cps.gov.uk/publication/code-crown-prosecutors (accessed 22 October 2023).

Crown Prosecution Service (2018b) Disclosure: A Guide to 'Reasonable Lines of Enquiry' and Communications Evidence. [online] Available at: www.cps.gov.uk/legal-guidance/disclosure-guide-reasonable-lines-enquiry-and-communications-evidence (accessed 22 October 2023).

Crown Prosecution Service (2018c) The National Disclosure Standards. [online] Available at: www.cps.gov.uk/sites/default/files/documents/legal_guidance/National-Disclosure-Standards-2018.pdf (accessed 22 October 2023).

Crown Prosecution Service (2018d) Disclosure Manual. [online] Available at: www.cps.gov.uk/legal-guidance/disclosure-manual (accessed 22 October 2023).

Crown Prosecution Service (2020a) Charging (The Director's Guidance), 6th edition. [online] Available at: www.cps.gov.uk/legal-guidance/charging-directors-guidance-sixth-edition-december-2020-incorporating-national-file (accessed 22 October 2023).

Crown Prosecution Service (2020b) Victims' Right to Review Scheme. [online] Available at: www.cps.gov.uk/legal-guidance/victims-right-review-scheme (accessed 22 October 2023).

Crown Prosecution Service (2021) Female Genital Mutilation. [online] Available at: www.cps.gov.uk/legal-guidance/female-genital-mutilation (accessed 22 October 2023).

Crown Prosecution Service (2022a) Assisting Offenders (Immunity, Undertakings and Agreements). [online] Available at: www.cps.gov.uk/legal-guidance/assisting-offenders-immunity-undertakings-and-agreements (accessed 22 October 2023).

Crown Prosecution Service (2022b) Offences Against the Person, Incorporating the Charging Standard. [online] Available at: www.cps.gov.uk/legal-guidance/offences-against-person-incorporating-charging-standard (accessed 22 October 2023).

Crown Prosecution Service (2022c) Witness Protection and Anonymity. [online] Available at: www.cps.gov.uk/legal-guidance/witness-protection-and-anonymity#:~:text=Section%2086%20of%20the%20Coroners,in%20connection%20with%20the%20proceedings (accessed 22 October 2023).

Crown Prosecution Service (2022d) Serious Crime Prevention Orders. [online] Available at: www.cps.gov.uk/legal-guidance/serious-crime-prevention-orders (accessed 22 October 2023).

Crown Prosecution Service (2023) Annual Report and Accounts. [online] Available at: www.cps.gov.uk/annual-report-accounts-2022-23 (accessed 22 October 2023).

Dehaghani, R (2016) He's Just Not That Vulnerable: Exploring the Implementation of the Appropriate Adult Safeguard in Police Custody. *The Howard Journal of Crime and Justice*, 55(4): 396–413.

Denley, J and Ariel, B (2019) Whom Should We Target to Prevent? Analysis of Organized Crime in England Using Intelligence Records. *European Journal of Crime, Criminal Law and Criminal Justice*, 27: 13–44.

Department for Business & Trade (2020) Post Office Horizon IT Inquiry 2020: Terms of Reference. [online] Available at: www.gov.uk/government/publications/post-office-horizon-it-inquiry-2020/terms-of-reference (accessed 22 October 2023).

Domestic Abuse Act 2021 [online] Available at: www.legislation.gov.uk/ukpga/2021/17/contents/enacted (accessed 13 June 2023).

Ellison, M (2014) The Stephen Lawrence Independent Review: Possible Corruption and the Role of Undercover Policing in the Stephen Lawrence Case. [online] Available at: https://assets.publishing.service.gov.uk/government/uploads/system/uploads/attachment_data/file/287030/stephen_lawrence_review_summary.pdf (accessed 22 October 2023).

Elliot, R (1998) Vulnerable and Intimidated Witnesses: A Review of the Literature, in Home Office. *Speaking Up for Justice*, 99–207. London: Home Office.

Fairclough, S (2020) Special Measures Literature Review. [online] Available at: https://cloud-platform-e218f50a4812967ba1215eaecede923f.s3.amazonaws.com/uploads/sites/6/2021/12/OVC-Special-Measures-Literature-Review-July-2020.pdf (accessed 22 October 2023).

Family Law Act 1996 [online] Available at: www.legislation.gov.uk/ukpga/1996/27/contents (accessed 13 June 2023).

Farrugia, L and Gabbert, F (2019) The 'Appropriate Adult': What They Do and What They Should Do in Police Interviews with Mentally Disordered Suspects. *Criminal Behaviour and Mental Health*, 29(3): 134–41.

Felson, M, and Eckert, M (2016) *Crime and Everyday Life*. Thousand Oaks, CA: Sage.

Female Genital Mutilation Act 2003 [online] Available at www.legislation.gov.uk/ukpga/2003/31/contents (accessed 15 June 2023).

Finckenauer, J O (2005) Problems of Definition: What Is Organized Crime? *Trends in Organized Crime*, 8(3): 63–83.

Gooch, G and Williams, M (2015) A Dictionary of Law Enforcement, 2nd edition. [online] Available at: www.oxfordreference.com/display/10.1093/acref/9780191758256.001.0001/acref-9780191758256 (accessed 22 October 2023).

Granhag, P A and Hartwig, M (2008) A New Theoretical Perspective on Deception Detection: On the Psychology of Instrumental Mind-Reading. *Psychology, Crime and Law*, 14: 189–200.

Griffiths, A and Milne, B (2013) Will it All End in Tiers? Police Interviews with Suspects in Britain. In Williamson, T (ed) *Investigative Interviewing: Rights, Research and Regulation* (pp 189–211). Devon: Willan Publishing.

Gross, L J (2018) Disclosure – Again. [online] Available at: www.judiciary.uk/wp-content/uploads/2018/06/lj-gross-disclosure-speech-june18-1-1.pdf (accessed 22 October 2023).

Gudjonsson, G H (2003) *The Psychology of Interrogations and Confessions: A Handbook*. Chichester: Wiley & Sons Ltd.

Gudjonsson, G H (2018) *The Psychology of False Confessions: Forty Years of Science and Practice*. Chichester: Wiley & Sons Ltd.

Hagan, F (1983) The Organized Crime Continuum: A Further Specification of a New Conceptual Model. *Criminal Justice Review*, 8: 52–7.

Hagan, F E (2006) 'Organized Crime' and 'Organized Crime': Indeterminate Problems of Definition. *Trends in Organized Crime*, 9(4): 127–37.

Hamilton v Post Office (2021) EWCA Crim 577. [online] Available at: www.judiciary.uk/wp-content/uploads/2021/04/Hamilton-Others-v-Post-Office-judgment-230421.pdf (accessed 22 October 2023).

Hamlyn, B, Phelps, A, Turtle, J and Sattar, G (2004) *Are Special Measures Working? Evidence from Surveys of Vulnerable and Intimidated Witnesses (No. 283)*. London: Home Office.

Hannan, M, Hearnden, I, Grace, K and Burke, T (2010) Deaths in or Following Police Custody: An Examination of the Cases 1998/99–2008/09. Independent Police Complaints Commission. [online] Available at: http://data.parliament.uk/DepositedPapers/Files/DEP2012-1687/Deaths_In_Custody_Report_0811.pdf (accessed 22 October 2023).

Harfield, C and Harfield, K (2018) *Covert Investigation*, 5th edition. Oxford: Oxford University Press.

Hartwig, M, Granhag, P, Stromwall, L A and Kronkvist, O (2006) Strategic Use of Evidence during Police Interviews: When Training to Detect Deception Works. *Law and Human Behavior*, 30(5): 603–20.

Henriques, R (2016) An Independent Review of the Metropolitan Police Service's Handling of Non-Recent Sexual Offence Investigations Alleged Against Persons of Public Prominence. [online] Available

at: www.met.police.uk/SysSiteAssets/foi-media/metropolitan-police/other_information/corporate/
mps-publication-chapters-1---3-sir-richard-henriques-report.pdf (accessed 22 October 2023).

Her Majesty's Crown Prosecution Service Inspectorate (HMCPSI) (2020) 2019 Rape Inspection.
[online] Available at: www.justiceinspectorates.gov.uk/hmcpsi/wp-content/uploads/sites/3/2019/
12/Rape-inspection-2019-1.pdf (accessed 22 October 2023).

Her Majesty's Crown Prosecution Service Inspectorate (HMCPSI) (2020) Disclosure of Unused
Material in the Crown Court. [online] Available at: www.justiceinspectorates.gov.uk/hmcpsi/wp-
content/uploads/sites/3/2021/04/2020-12-03-Disclosure-of-unused-material-in-the-Crown-Court-
accessible.pdf (accessed 22 October 2023).

Her Majesty's (HM) Government (2016) Statutory Guidance Injunctions to Prevent Gang-Related
Violence and Gang-Related Drug Dealing: Revised Guidance. [online] Available at: https://assets.
publishing.service.gov.uk/government/uploads/system/uploads/attachment_data/file/526379/
Statutory_Guidance_-_Injunctions_to_Prevent_Gang-Related_Violence__web_.pdf   (accessed   22
October 2023).

Her Majesty's (HM) Government (2020) Criminal Procedure Rules 2020 and Criminal Practice
Directions 2023. [online] Available at: www.gov.uk/guidance/rules-and-practice-directions-2020
(accessed 22 October 2023).

Her Majesty's (HM) Government and Philips, C (1981) Royal Commission on Criminal Procedure.
[online] Available at: www.ucpi.org.uk/wp-content/uploads/2022/09/royal_commission_on_criminal_
procedure-report.pdf (accessed 22 October 2023).

Her Majesty's Inspector of Constabulary (HMIC) (2009) Major Challenge: The Thematic Inspection of
Major Crime. [online] Available at: https://assets-hmicfrs.justiceinspectorates.gov.uk/uploads/major-
challenge-20090630.pdf (accessed 22 October 2023).

Her Majesty's Inspector of Constabulary (HMIC) (2012) A Review of National Police Units Which
Provide Intelligence on Criminality Associated with Protest. [online] Available at: https://s3-eu-west-
2.amazonaws.com/assets-hmicfrs.justiceinspectorates.gov.uk/uploads/review-of-national-police-
units-which-provide-intelligence-on-criminality-associated-with-protest-20120202.pdf   (accessed   22
October 2023).

Her Majesty's Inspector of Constabulary (HMIC) (2014) Crime-Recording: Making the Victim Count.
[online] Available at: https://assets-hmicfrs.justiceinspectorates.gov.uk/uploads/crime-recording-
making-the-victim-count.pdf (accessed 22 October 2023).

Her Majesty's Inspector of Constabulary (HMIC) (2015) The Welfare of Vulnerable People in Police
Custody. [online] Available at: https://assets-hmicfrs.justiceinspectorates.gov.uk/uploads/the-welfare-
of-vulnerable-people-in-police-custody.pdf (accessed 22 October 2023).

Her Majesty's Inspector of Probation (HMI Probation), Her Majesty's Inspector of Constabulary, Her Majesty's Inspector of Prisons and Care Quality Commission (2014) A Joint Inspection of the Treatment of Offenders with Learning Disabilities Within the Criminal Justice System: Phase 1 from Arrest to Sentence. [online] Available at: https://webarchive.nationalarchives.gov.uk/ukgwa/2013012 8112038/http://www.justice.gov.uk/downloads/publications/inspectorate-reports/hmiprobation/ learning-disabilities-thematic-report.pdf (accessed 22 October 2023).

Her Majesty's Inspector of Constabulary and Fire & Rescue Service (HMICFRS) (2021) A Joint Thematic Inspection of the Police and Crown Prosecution Service's Response to Rape. Phase One: From Report to Police or CPS Decision to Take No Further Action. [online] Available at: https://hmicfrs.justicein spectorates.gov.uk/publication-html/a-joint-thematic-inspection-of-the-police-and-crown-prosecution- services-response-to-rape-phase-one/ (accessed 22 October 2023).

His Majesty's Inspector of Constabulary and Fire & Rescue Service (HMICFRS) (2022) The Police Response to Burglary, Robbery and Other Acquisitive Crime: Finding Time for Crime. [online] Available at: https://hmicfrs.justiceinspectorates.gov.uk/publication-html/police-response-to-burglary-robbery- and-other-acquisitive-crime/#:~:text=The%20police%20response%20to%20burglary%2C% 20robbery%20and%20other,and%20theft%20of%20and%20from%20a%20motor%20vehicle (accessed 22 October 2023).

Hogarth, R M (2001) *Educating Intuition*. Chicago: University of Chicago Press.

Home Office (1981) The Yorkshire Ripper Case: A Review of the Police Investigation of the case by Lawrence Byford, Esq., CBE., QPM., Her Majesty's Inspector of Constabulary. [online] Available at: https://assets.publishing.service.gov.uk/media/5a7b2010e5274a319e77d319/1941-Byford_ part_1_.pdf (accessed 6 January 2023).

Home Office (2011) Contest: The United Kingdom's Strategy for Countering Terrorism. [online] Available at: https://assets.publishing.service.gov.uk/government/uploads/system/uploads/attachment_data/ file/97995/strategy-contest.pdf (accessed 22 October 2023).

Home Office (2014) Intercept as Evidence Review. [online] Available at: https://assets.publishing. service.gov.uk/government/uploads/system/uploads/attachment_data/file/388111/InterceptAsE vidence.pdf (accessed 22 October 2023).

Home Office (2015) Serious Crime Act 2015. Fact Sheet: Improvements to Serious Crime Prevention Orders. [online] Available at: https://assets.publishing.service.gov.uk/government/uploads/system/ uploads/attachment_data/file/415969/Fact_sheet_-_SCPOs_-_Act.pdf (accessed 22 October 2023).

Home Office (2017a) A Practitioner Toolkit: Working with Young People to Prevent Involvement in Serious and Organised Crime. [online] Available at: https://assets.publishing.service.gov.uk/government/ uploads/system/uploads/attachment_data/file/958840/6.7152_HO_Updates-SOC-Prevent- intervention-toolkit_v5_2_.pdf (accessed 22 October 2023).

Home Office (2017b) Guidance on Slavery and Trafficking Prevention Orders and Slavery and Trafficking Risk Orders under Part 2 of the Modern Slavery Act 2015. [online] Available at: https://assets.publishing. service.gov.uk/government/uploads/system/uploads/attachment_data/file/610015/110417_-_ statutory_guidance_part_2_-_GLAA_updates-_Final.pdf (accessed 22 October 2023).

Home Office (2018a) Serious and Organised Crime Strategy. [online] Available at: www.gov.uk/ government/publications/serious-and-organised-crime-strategy-2018/serious-and-organised-crime-strategy-accessible-version (accessed 22 October 2023).

Home Office (2018b) Covert Surveillance and Property Interference: Revised Code of Practice. [online] Available at: https://assets.publishing.service.gov.uk/government/uploads/system/uploads/ attachment_data/file/742041/201800802_CSPI_code.pdf (accessed 22 October 2023).

Home Office (2018c) Communications Data: Code of Practice. [online] Available at: https://assets. publishing.service.gov.uk/government/uploads/system/uploads/attachment_data/file/822817/ Communications_Data_Code_of_Practice.pdf (accessed 22 October 2023).

Home Office (2019) Revised Code of Practice for the Detection, Treatment and Questioning of Persons by Police Officers. [online] Available at: https://assets.publishing.service.gov.uk/government/ uploads/system/uploads/attachment_data/file/903473/pace-code-c-2019.pdf (accessed 22 October 2023).

Home Office (2020) Crime Outcomes in England and Wales, Year to September 2020: Data Tables. [online] Available at: www.gov.uk/government/statistics/crime-outcomes-in-england-and-wales-year-to-september-2020-data-tables (accessed 22 October 2023).

Home Office (2021) Beating Crime Plan. [online] Available at: www.gov.uk/government/publications/ beating-crime-plan/beating-crime-plan (accessed 22 October 2023).

Home Office (2022a) Crime Outcomes in England and Wales 2021 to 2022. [online] Available at: www.gov.uk/government/statistics/crime-outcomes-in-england-and-wales-2021-to-2022/crime-outcomes-in-england-and-wales-2021-to-2022 (accessed 23 October 2023).

Home Office (2022b) Extraction of Information from Electronic Devices: Code of Practice. [online] Available at: https://assets.publishing.service.gov.uk/government/uploads/system/uploads/ attachment_data/file/1110883/E02802691_Electronic_Devices_Code_of_Practice_WEB.pdf (accessed 22 October 2023).

Home Office (2022c) Covert Human Intelligence Sources: Revised Code of Practice. [online] Available at: https://assets.publishing.service.gov.uk/government/uploads/system/uploads/attachment_data/ file/1123687/Revised_CHIS_Code_of_Practice_December_2022_FINAL.pdf (accessed 22 October 2023).

Home Office (2022d) Interception of Communications: Code of Practice. [online] Available at: www. gov.uk/government/publications/interception-of-communications-code-of-practice-2022 (accessed 22 October 2023).

Home Office (2022e) Serious Violence Reduction Orders: Draft Statutory Guidance. [online] Available at: www.gov.uk/government/publications/serious-violence-reduction-orders (accessed 22 October 2023).

Home Office (2022f) Domestic Violence Protection Notices (DVPNs) and Domestic Violence Protection Orders (DVPOs) Guidance. [online] Available at: www.gov.uk/government/publications/domestic-violence-protection-orders/domestic-violence-protection-notices-dvpns-and-domestic-violence-protection-orders-dvpos-guidance-sections-24-33-crime-and-security-act-2010 (accessed 22 October 2023).

Home Office (2023a) Guidance on Part 2 of the Sexual Offences Act 2003. [online] Available at: www.gov.uk/government/publications/guidance-on-part-2-of-the-sexual-offences-act-2003 (accessed 22 October 2023).

Home Office (2023b) Impact Assessment (IA), the Home Office: Proposals to Strengthen and Improve the Functioning of Serious Crime Prevention Orders (SCPOs). [online] Available at: www.gov.uk/government/consultations/strengthening-the-law-enforcement-response-to-serious-and-organised-crime/impact-assessment-accessible#d------options-considered-and-implementation (accessed 22 October 2023).

House of Commons (2022) Investigation and Prosecution of Rape. [online] Available at: https://committees.parliament.uk/publications/9600/documents/166175/default/ (accessed 22 October 2023).

House of Commons Justice Committee (2018) Review of the Efficiency and Effectiveness of Disclosure in the Criminal Justice System. [online] Available at: https://publications.parliament.uk/pa/cm201719/cmselect/cmjust/859/859.pdf (accessed 22 October 2023).

House of Lords (2002) Judgments – *Clingham (formerly C (a Minor) v Royal Borough of Kensington and Chelsea* (on Appeal from a Divisional Court of the Queen's Bench Division); *Regina v Crown Court at Manchester Ex p McCann (FC) and Others (FC)*. [online] Available at: https://publications.parliament.uk/pa/ld200102/ldjudgmt/jd021017/cling-1.htm (accessed 22 October 2023).

Human Rights Act 1998 [online] Available at: www.legislation.gov.uk/ukpga/1998/42/contents (accessed 23 February 2023).

Independent Police Complaints Commission (IPCC) (2011) Ratcliffe-on-Soar Power Station (Operation Aeroscope) Disclosure, Nottingham Police. [online] Available at: www.statewatch.org/media/documents/news/2012/apr/uk-ippc-final-operation-aeroscope-report-march-12.pdf (accessed 22 October 2023).

Information Commissioner's Office (2022a) Investigation Report: Mobile Phone Data Extraction by Police Forces in England and Wales. [online] Available at: https://ico.org.uk/about-the-ico/what-we-do/mobile-phone-data-extraction-by-police-forces-in-england-and-wales/ (accessed 22 October 2023).

Information Commissioner's Office (2022b) Who's Under Investigation? The Processing of Victims' Personal Data in Rape and Serious Sexual Offence Investigations. [online] Available at: https://ico.org.uk/media/4020539/commissioners-opinion-whos-under-investigation-20220531.pdf (accessed 22 October 2023).

Innes, M (2003) *Investigating Murder: Detective Work and the Police Response to Criminal Homicide.* Oxford: Oxford University Press.

Investigatory Powers Act 2016 [online] Available at: www.legislation.gov.uk/ukpga/2016/25/contents/enacted (accessed 22 October 2023).

Jones v Birmingham City Council (2018) EWCA Civ 1189. [online] Available at: www.bailii.org/ew/cases/EWCA/2018/1189.html (accessed 22 October 2023).

Kassin, S M and Gudjonsson, G H (2004) The Psychology of Confessions: A Review of the Literature and Issues. *Psychological Science in the Public Interest*, 5(2): 33–67.

Kassin, S M and Kiechel, K L (1996) The Social Psychology of False Confessions: Compliance, Internalization, and Confabulation. *Psychological Science*, 7(3): 125–8.

Kebbell, M, O'Kelly, C and Gilchrist, E (2007) Rape Victims' Experiences of Giving Evidence in English Courts: A Survey. *Psychiatry, Psychology and Law*, 14(1): 111–19.

Kelly, L, Adler, J R, Horvath, M A H, Lovett, J, Coulson, M, Kernohan, D, Gray, M, Hillier, J and Nicholas, S (2013) Evaluation of the Pilot of Domestic Violence Protection Orders. Home Office. [online] Available at:https://assets.publishing.service.gov.uk/government/uploads/system/uploads/attachment_data/file/260897/horr76.pdf (accessed 22 October 2023).

Léonard, M J, Saumier, D and Brunet, A (2020) When the Lawyer Becomes Traumatized: A Scoping Review. *SAGE Open*, 10(3).

Léonard, M J, Vasiliadis, H M, Leclerc, M È and Brunet, A (2021) Traumatic Stress in Canadian Lawyers: A Longitudinal Study. *Psychological Trauma: Theory, Research, Practice, and Policy*, 15(S2): S259–67.

MacEachern, A D, Dennis, A A, Jackson, S and Jindal-Snape, D (2019) Secondary Traumatic Stress: Prevalence and Symptomology amongst Detective Officers Investigating Child Protection Cases. *Journal of Police and Criminal Psychology*, 34: 165–74.

Macintosh, G (2009) The Role of Rapport in Professional Services: Antecedents and Outcomes. *Journal of Services Marketing*, 23(2): 70–8.

Magistrates' Courts Act 1980 [online] Available at: www.legislation.gov.uk/ukpga/1980/43/contents (accessed 22 October 2023).

Malkinson v R (2023) EWCA Crim 954.

Marx, G T (1988) *Undercover Police Surveillance in America.* Berkley, CA: University of California Press.

Marx, G T (2015) Surveillance Studies. *International Encyclopedia of the Social & Behavioral Sciences*, 23(2): 733–41.

McKay, S (2015) *Covert Policing Law and Practice*. Oxford: Oxford University Press.

McKinnon, I G and Grubin, D (2013) Health Screening of People in Police Custody: Evaluation of Current Police Screening Procedures in London, UK. *The European Journal of Public Health*, 23(3): 399–405.

McKinnon, I, Srivastava, S, Kaler, G and Grubin, D (2013) Screening for Psychiatric Morbidity in Police Custody: Results from the HELP-PC Project. *The Psychiatrist*, 37(12): 389–94.

Medford, S, Gudjonsson, G H and Pearse, J (2003) The Efficacy of the Appropriate Adult Safeguard During Police Interviewing. *Legal and Criminological Psychology*, 8(2): 253–66.

Meissner, C A, Redlich, A D, Michael, S W, Evans, J R, Camilletti, C R, Bhatt, S and Brandon, S (2014) Accusatorial and Information-Gathering Interrogation Methods and their Effects on True and False Confessions: A Meta-Analytic Review. *Journal of Experimental Criminology*, 10(4): 459–86.

Metropolitan Police Service and Crown Prosecution Service (2018) A Joint Review of the Disclosure Process in the Case of *R v Allan*. [online] Available at: www.cps.gov.uk/sites/default/files/documents/publications/joint-review-disclosure-Allan.pdf (accessed 16 July 2023).

Miceli, T, Segerson, K and Earnhart, D (2022) The Role of Experience in Deterring Crime: A Theory of Specific Versus General Deterrence. *Economic Inquiry*, 60(4): 1833–53.

Ministry of Justice (MoJ) (2013) The Witness Charter Standards of Care for Witnesses in the Criminal Justice System. [online] Available at: https://assets.publishing.service.gov.uk/media/5a7c6c4340f0b62aff6c190c/witness-charter-nov13.pdf (accessed 15 January 2023).

Ministry of Justice (MoJ) (2015) Criminal Procedure and Investigations Act 1996 (Section 23(1)) Code of Practice. [online] Available at: https://assets.publishing.service.gov.uk/government/uploads/system/uploads/attachment_data/file/447967/code-of-practice-approved.pdf (accessed 22 October 2023).

Ministry of Justice (MoJ) (2020a) Code of Practice for Victims of Crime in England and Wales. [online] Available at: https://assets.publishing.service.gov.uk/government/uploads/system/uploads/attachment_data/file/936239/victims-code-2020.pdf (accessed 22 October 2023).

Ministry of Justice (MoJ) (2020b) Criminal Procedure and Investigations Act 1996 (Section 23(1)) Code of Practice Revised in Accordance with Section 25(4) of the Criminal Procedure and Investigations Act 1996 and Presented to Parliament Pursuant to Section 25(2) of the Act. [online] Available at: https://assets.publishing.service.gov.uk/government/uploads/system/uploads/attachment_data/file/931173/Criminal-procedure-and-investigations-act-1996.pdf (accessed 22 October 2023).

Ministry of Justice (MoJ) (2021a) The End-to-End Rape Review Report on Findings and Actions. [online] Available at: www.gov.uk/government/publications/end-to-end-rape-review-report-on-findings-and-actions (accessed 22 October 2023).

Ministry of Justice (MoJ) (2021b) Review of the Criminal Courts in England and Wales (2001). [online] Available at: www.criminal-courts-review.org.uk/auldconts.htm (accessed 22 October 2023).

Ministry of Justice (MoJ) (2023) Knife and Offensive Weapon Sentencing Statistics: July to September 2022. [online] Available at: www.gov.uk/government/statistics/knife-and-offensive-weapon-sentencing-statistics-july-to-september-2022#offhistory (accessed 22 October 2023).

Misuse of Drugs Act 1971 [online] Available at: www.legislation.gov.uk/ukpga/1971/38/contents (accessed 23 February 2023).

Modern Slavery Act 2015 [online] Available at: www.legislation.gov.uk/ukpga/2015/30/contents/enacted (accessed 22 October 2023).

National Centre for Policing Excellence (2005) Practice Advice on Core Investigative Doctrine. [online] Available at: https://library.college.police.uk/docs/acpo/Core-Investigative-Doctrine.pdf (accessed 22 October 2023).

National Crime Agency (2020) National Strategic Assessment of Serious and Organised Crime. [online] Available at: www.nationalcrimeagency.gov.uk/who-we-are/publications/437-national-strategic-assessment-of-serious-and-organised-crime-2020/file (accessed 22 October 2023).

National Crime Agency (2021) National Strategic Assessment of Serious and Organised Crime. [online] Available at: www.nationalcrimeagency.gov.uk/who-we-are/publications/533-national-strategic-assessment-of-serious-and-organised-crime-2021/file (accessed 22 October 2023).

National Police Chiefs' Council (NPCC) (2021a) Major Crime Investigation Manual (MCIM 2021). [online] Available at: https://library.college.police.uk/docs/NPCC/Major-Crime-Investigation-Manual-Nov-2021.pdf (accessed 22 October 2023).

National Police Chiefs' Council (NPCC) (2021b) Major Incident Room Standardised Administrative Procedures (MIRSAP 2021). [online] Available at: https://library.college.police.uk/docs/NPCC/MIRSAP_V1_Nov_2021.pdf (accessed 22 October 2023).

Newburn, T (2007) *Criminology*. Devon: Willan Publishing.

Newburn, T, Williamson, T and Wright, A (2007) *Handbook of Criminal Investigation*. Devon: Willan Publishing.

Nicol, C, Innes, M, Gee, D and Feist, A (2004) Reviewing Murder Investigations: An Analysis of Progress Reviews from Six Police Forces. [online] Available at: https://library.college.police.uk/docs/hordsolr/rdsolr2504.pdf (accessed 22 October 2023).

OCGM Manual (2010) *Organised Crime Group Mapping Manual*. London: National Coordinators Office.

Office for National Statistics (ONS) (2022a) Homicide in England and Wales: Year Ending March 2021. [online] Available at: www.ons.gov.uk/peoplepopulationandcommunity/crimeandjustice/articles/homicideinenglandandwales/yearendingmarch2021 (accessed 22 October 2023).

Office for National Statistics (ONS) (2022b) Offences Involving the Use of Weapons: Data Tables. [online] Available at: www.ons.gov.uk/peoplepopulationandcommunity/crimeandjustice/datasets/offencesinvolvingtheuseofweaponsdatatables (accessed 22 October 2023).

Paternoster, R and Piquero, A (1995) Reconceptualizing Deterrence: An Empirical Test of Personal and Vicarious Experiences. *Journal of Research in Crime and Delinquency*, 32(2): 251–86.

Police Act 1997 [online] Available at: www.legislation.gov.uk/ukpga/1997/50/contents (accessed 22 October 2023).

Police and Criminal Evidence Act 1984 [online] Available at: www.legislation.gov.uk/ukpga/1984/60/contents (accessed 22 October 2023).

Police, Crime, Sentencing and Courts Act 2022 [online] Available at: www.legislation.gov.uk/ukpga/2022/32/contents/enacted (accessed 22 October 2023).

Proceeds of Crime Act 2002 [online] Available at: www.legislation.gov.uk/ukpga/2002/29/contents (accessed 22 October 2023).

Policing and Crime Act 2009 [online] Available at: www.legislation.gov.uk/ukpga/2009/26/contents (accessed 10 June 2023).

Prosecution of Offences Act 1985 [online] Available at: www.legislation.gov.uk/ukpga/1985/23 (accessed 22 October 2023).

R v Ali (2019) EWCA Crim 1527.

R v Donovan and Kafunda (2012) EWCA Crim 2749.

R v Goodyear (2005) EWCA Crim 888.

R v GS and Others (2005) EWCA Crim 887.

R v H & C (2004) UKHL 4.

R v Hancox and Duffy (2010) EWCA Crim 102.

R v Loosely (2001) UKHL 53. [online] Available at: https://publications.parliament.uk/pa/ld200102/ldjudgmt/jd011025/loose-1.htm (accessed 22 October 2023).

R v Mason (1988) 86 Cr App R 349.

R v Mayers and Others (2008) EWCA Crim 2989.

R v Mealey (1974) Cr App R 59.

R v Newton (1982) 77 Cr. App R 13.

R v Nottle (2004) EWCA Crim 599.

R v Olu and Others (2010) EWCA Crim 2975.

R v R and Others (2015) EWCA Crim 1941.

R v Riat (2012) EWCA Crim 1509.

Redmayne, M (1999) Standards of Proof in Civil Litigation. *The Modern Law Review*, 62: 167–95.

Regulation of Investigatory Powers Act 2000 [online] Available at: www.legislation.gov.uk/ukpga/2000/23/pdfs/ukpga_20000023_en.pdf (accessed 22 October 2023).

Rose, C (2011) Ratcliffe-on-Soar Power Station Protest Inquiry into Disclosure. [online] Available at: http://specialbranchfiles.uk/operation-aeroscope-reexamination-reviews-reports/ (accessed 22 October 2023).

Royal Commission on Criminal Procedure (1981) Report of the Royal Commission on Criminal Justice. [online] Available at: www.gov.uk/government/publications/report-of-the-royal-commission-on-criminal-justice (accessed 22 October 2023).

Runciman, W G (1993) Royal Commission on Criminal Justice. [online] Available at: https://assets.publishing.service.gov.uk/government/uploads/system/uploads/attachment_data/file/271971/2263.pdf (accessed 22 October 2023).

Sanders, B (2019) *Oxford Dictionary of Gangs*. Oxford: Oxford University Press.

Sentencing Act 2020 [online] Available at: www.legislation.gov.uk/ukpga/2020/17/contents (accessed 22 October 2023).

Serious Crime Act 2015 [online] Available at: www.legislation.gov.uk/ukpga/2015/9/contents/enacted (accessed 10 June 2023).

Serious Organised Crime and Police Act 2005 [online] Available at: www.legislation.gov.uk/ukpga/2005/15/contents (accessed 22 October 2023).

Sexual Offences Act 2003 [online] Available at: www.legislation.gov.uk/ukpga/2003/42/contents (accessed 13 June 2023).

Shepherd, E (2007) *Investigative Interviewing: The Conversation Management Model*. Oxford: Oxford University Press.

Shillibier v R (2006) EWCA Crim 793. [online] Available at: www.casemine.com/judgement/uk/5a8ff7b360d03e7f57eb1556 (accessed 22 October 2023).

Sloan, F A, Platt, A C, Chepke, L M and Blevins, C E (2013) Deterring Domestic Violence: Do Criminal Sanctions Reduce Repeat Offenses? *Journal of Risk and Uncertainty*, 46(1): 51–80.

Snook, B, Eastwood, J and Barron, W T (2014) The Next Stage in the Evolution of Interrogations: The PEACE Model. *Canadian Criminal Law Review*, 18(2): 219–39.

Spurrell, E (2023) Merseyside PCC Supports New Pilot to Further Tackle Knife Crime and Serious Violence. [online] Available at: www.merseysidepcc.info/news-and-events/news/merseyside-pcc-supports-new-pilot-to-further-tackle-knife-crime-and-serious-violence/ (accessed 22 October 2023).

Stelfox, P (2009) *Criminal Investigation: An Introduction to Principles and Practice*. Devon: Willan Publishing.

Stern, W (1939) The Psychology of Testimony. *Journal of Abnormal and Social Psychology*, 12: 287–96.

Teixeira de Castro v Portugal (1999) 28 ECHR 101.

Vallano, J P, Evans, J R, Schreiber Compo, N and Kieckhaefer, J M (2015) Rapport-Building During Witness and Suspect Interviews: A Survey of Law Enforcement. *Applied Cognitive Psychology*, 29(3): 369–80.

Velazquez, E and Hernandez, M (2019) Effects of Police Officer Exposure to Traumatic Experiences and Recognizing the Stigma Associated with Police Officer Mental Health: A State-of-the-Art Review. *Policing: An International Journal*, 42(4): 711–24.

Victims' Commissioner's Office (2020) Rape Survivors and the Criminal Justice System. [online] Available at: https://cloud-platform-e218f50a4812967ba1215eaecede923f.s3.amazonaws.com/uploads/sites/6/2021/12/Rape-Survivors-and-the-CJS_FINAL-v2.pdf (accessed 22 October 2023).

Victims' Commissioner's Office (2021) Victims' Commissioner Briefing on the Data Extraction Power Clauses in Part 2 Chapter 3 of the Police, Crime, Sentencing and Courts Bill. [online] Available at: https://bills.parliament.uk/publications/41921/documents/412 (accessed 22 October 2023).

Vrij, A, Granhag, P A and Verschuere, B (2015) *Detecting Deception: Current Challenges and Cognitive Approaches*. Hoboken: John Wiley & Sons.

Walsh, D W and Milne, R (2008) Keeping the PEACE? A Study of Investigative Interviewing Practices in the Public Sector. *Legal and Criminological Psychology*, 13(1): 39–57.

Wikström, P O H, Ceccato, V, Hardie, B and Treiber, K (2010) Activity Fields and the Dynamics of Crime: Advancing Knowledge About the Role of the Environment in Crime Causation. *Journal of Quantitative Criminology*, 26(1): 55–87.

Williamson, T, Milne, B and Savage, S (2013) *International Developments in Investigative Interviewing*. London: Routledge.

Wilson v Commissioner of Police of the Metropolis and National Police Chiefs' Council (2021) No. IPT/ 11/167/H.

Woolmington v DPP (1935) AC462.

Wright, M (2013) Homicide Detectives' Intuition. *Journal of Investigative Psychology and Offender Profiling*, 10(2): 182–99.

Youth Justice and Criminal Evidence Act 1999 [online] Available at: www.legislation.gov.uk/ukpga/ 1999/23/contents (accessed 22 October 2023).

INDEX

Note: Page numbers in **bold** denote tables.